The old
BOLD
PILOT

A PILOT'S JOURNEY

E. HAMILTON LEE ONCE FAMOUSLY SAID,
"SON, THERE ARE OLD PILOTS AND THERE ARE BOLD PILOTS
BUT THERE ARE NO OLD BOLD PILOTS"

CAPT. SHAKTI LUMBA
CAPT. PRIYANKA ARORA

INDIA · SINGAPORE · MALAYSIA

Notion Press Media Pvt Ltd

No. 50, Chettiyar Agaram Main Road,
Vanagaram, Chennai, Tamil Nadu – 600 095

First Published by Notion Press 2021
Copyright © Capt. Shakti Lumba 2021
All Rights Reserved.

ISBN 978-1-68563-389-9

DEDICATION

This book is for my beloved Mother,
the late Mrs. Lakshmi Lumba
To whom I owe everything.
She told me a story. A story that awakened
the passion to fly which made me
the person I am today.
Thank You Ma

CONTENTS

ACKNOWLEDGEMENT

This book is in your hands because of five people. If not coaxed, goaded and bullied by my wife Ila, my two children, Pallavi and Shiv, my fellow pilot and friend, Subir Hari Singh, IAS and TCA Srinivas Raghavan, I would have simply sat back in my garden and enjoyed my memories alone.

Special mention for Renu Rao, my sister-in-law, my friend Capt. Anirudh Tyagi, husband to my niece, Anita and dear friend, Priti Mishra Issar. Their suggestions, ruthless but eminently helpful, hopefully has saved me from possible charges of sexism and libel.

Tito, or Debadatta Das, gave me the journalistic perspective and value of the account of my flying days, thus finally enthusing me enough to start this journey.

I also like to proudly acknowledge Mr Brijesh Kumar, IAS (Retd), Mr Probir Sen IAS (Retd), Mr Anil Baijal IAS (Retd) – all CMDs of Indian Airlines, along with, Air Marshal Denzil Keelor (Retd) PVSM, KC, AVSM, VrC., Mr Kiran Rao (Ex Airbus), Mr AK Chopra Jt DGCA (Retd), Mr Rakesh Gangwal and Rahul Bhatia of IndiGo, who along with the dearly departed Capt. Karminder Singh (Ralph) and former CMDs of Indian Airlines,Capt AM Kapur (Cap), Capt. Kamni Chadha, Mr. R. Prasad along with Capt. SL Bagchi my ICPA Guru. They steered my career and were are part of my journey.

My editor and ex-journalist, Rina Sen Goel, who read and polished the manuscript. She has ensured that the arcane language of aviators was transformed to be suitable for a wider audience keen about the exciting world of aviation. I wish to acknowledge her efforts and professionalism.

Last but not least, I am grateful to the lovely *Peeya,* Priyanka Arora, my co-author, for her understanding, support and encouragement.

FOREWORD

I first met Capt. Shakti Lumba in late 1990, during an interaction with pilots of Indian Airlines on invitation by Air Marshall SS Ramdas, the CMD. At that time, I was The Inspector General of the Indian Air Force, sent on secondment to the Ministry of Civil Aviation, to set up a Flight Inspection Directorate in the DGCA.

Capt. Lumba stood out in this group. He was forthright with his opinions, knowledgeable, passionate about aviation and flight safety. I immediately requested the CMD to second him to me to assist in my assignment. Capt. Lumba was largely instrumental in setting up the Flight Inspection Directorate, and initially running it.

Indian Airlines very sensibly inducted him into Management. Here we both were in various committees on pilot shortages and turn around strategies for the Airline. He contributed hugely to both these crucial issues with Indian Airlines. But it was with the success of Alliance Air, his brainchild, that he shone, an airline he started and managed against all odds, by sheer force of will and extraordinary leadership.

I found Capt. Lumba's confidence and his courage of conviction a rare and sterling quality. I have rarely seen such leadership and upstanding bearing in Indian Civil Aviation.

I am honored to be asked to write the FOREWORD to his book which I am very much looking forward to reading.

Air Marshal Denzil Keelor (Retd.) PVSM, KC, AVSM, VC

Gurgaon, Haryana

AUTHOR'S NOTE

"A pilot must have a memory developed to absolute perfection.
But there are two higher qualities which he also must have.
He must have good and quick judgment and decision,
and a cool, calm courage that no peril can shake"
– Anon

This book has taken over five years to write and is a reality only due to the constant prodding of my family and friends, who felt that my decades of aviation experience was unique and needed to be told. The nuts and bolts of keying it in, was painstakingly done, with one finger, in 'NOTES' on my Apple 6, 8 and the XR, **one letter at a time**!

In 2009, I decided to retire from the rat race. I was convinced there was more to life than killing oneself for "The Corporate". I am sure there are many who secretly wish that they could just step off and retire. They hold back due to financial constraints or family obligations, but mainly due to a fear of the unknown. I have never regretted my decision, nor has my family.

I had planned for such a day well in advance, and bought some land in Mangar village, between Gurgaon and Faridabad, nestled in a picturesque valley in the Aravali ridge, to settle down. On it, a rudimentary farm was set up, while I was still in service. On leaving IndiGo in 2009, I decided to move to the farm and start construction of our dream home.

Living on-site in a tiny porta cabin, while we supervised the construction, it was an adventure of a different kind. Thankfully, most of our belongings were in storage. The Commonwealth Games of 2010 had gobbled up most of the construction material and more importantly, all the skilled and unskilled construction workers. As a result, our house took two long years to build. We got very well acquainted with our porta-cabin!

This was the time when tragedy struck: all my precious books, documents including my flying logbooks and my personal diary, which were in storage, were totally ruined by termites. Nothing could be retrieved and I lost them all. Perforce this book has had to be written largely from memory and that is why there are few or no dates specified, only periods.

I had till now taken from society. Now that I had retired, my long-held dream to give back to society took shape. This we did by setting up two NGOs – one was a Women's Self Help group and the other an Education Society – these gave me the immense joy of giving back. The latter works closely with rural Government Schools in 5 villages around my farm, now called Laksh Farms.

I wish to emphasize that this is a memoir of MY aviation journey as I remember and perceived it. Many who may have been a part of this journey may have a different perception. They are fully entitled to their perception, as I am to mine.

Capt Shakti Lumba

Laksh Farms Mangar,

Faridabad (Haryana)

COAUTHOR'S NOTE

"Deftly they opened the brain of a child,
and it was full of flying dreams.''
– Stanley Kunitz

"There are old pilots and there are bold pilots. However, there are no old, bold pilots" This is told to almost every student pilot on the first day of training. I believed in it like it was Gospel.

Until I met Capt. Shakti Lumba, the original "badass" of Indian Aviation.

This book is a left seat view of his 'flying life". The journey of how he got his wings, figuratively and literally. From his early years when he nursed a dream to commune with the skies and his unbridled passion to fulfil that ambition, Capt. Lumba had done it all boldly.

The book is a vivid recollection of his experiences as he cruised through making memories and history together.

Capt. Lumba's fascinating journey in aviation as a pilot and Airline Executive parallels the evolution of modern Indian Aviation – from the 1970s to 2009. Not merely did he have a ringside view of the seminal moments of that period, more often than not he was one of the major protagonists within that very ring. In sharing his personal journey as a pilot, richly peppered with incidents, vignettes and behind-the-scene developments, he chronicles the story of contemporary Indian aviation.

So, dear readers, this is your Co Pilot and Co Author Capt. Priyanka Arora. Welcome aboard. I'll take you through my Captain's exciting journey.

The book takes you on a flight, as you stand at the shoulder of Capt Lumba's swivel seat, while he commands the aircraft and I get the honor and privilege of being his first officer.

Having a ringside view of Shakti's career, I am intimately aware of the truth of the events that he describes here. Others may disagree. There will be those who may not agree with Shakti's point of view, or who may have a different perception of events described herein. Names of individuals have thus been changed to protect their personal privacy and professional lives.

Those who know Capt. Lumba, know well that he is not one to bear a grudge or grind an axe. For those who don't, it is important to know this about Him so as to have an objective outlook upon all that's written in this book.

Dear Readers, we are ready to take off. Please fasten your seat belts, sit back relax and enjoy the read!

Capt. Priyanka Arora

Goa, India

THE FIRSTWORD

"If you want to grow old as a pilot,
you've got to know when to push it, and when to back off."
– Chuck Yeager

Shakti and I had just a nodding acquaintance while at St Stephens. We got to know each other over our shared passion for aviation later, which laid the foundations for a lifelong friendship.

In an era when flying was taken up by kids who thought it was a glamorous way to stop studying, the two of us stood out from the crowd as avid readers of anything aviation related. Shunning 'guide' books, we reveled in going down and accessing the basic references to get a grip of the theory of flight, aircraft and engines, navigation, meteorology, aeromedicine, etc. We haunted 'English Book Depot' in Connaught Place (now Rajiv Chowk) which had the best collection of aviation related material in town.

Over the years we built up a shared library that was the envy of the flying clubs. Not only did we have the latest available books but also some hard- to- get restricted air force publications like AP129, AP1234, etc. which we cajoled out of long-lost uncles!

The result of all this reading was that we were the only two trainees who passed all the theory papers, the first time, that too at one sitting. The usual mode was to sit for one or two papers at a time over the period of the flying training. Our training progressed in parallel and once we got our Private Pilot's License and were legally permitted to take a non-fare paying passenger on flights, we regularly flew together, one as the Pilot-in-Command and the other as an observer with a critical eye on flying skills or as the safety pilot when flying on instruments. This was the time for fine tuning our flying skills.

Our paths diverged after qualifying our respective CPLs. But we stayed in close touch with my re-living the flying experience vicariously through Shakti's career in the north-east – through innumerable letters and later when he had overnight layovers in Bangalore. His home has always been, and continues to be my address when in Delhi, where the conversation continues.

The job of being just a throttle jockey would not occupy Shakti's mental faculties for long. Observing the incompetence around it was inevitable that he would drift into union activities. His behind-the-scenes strategic direction to ICPA, born out of his earlier informal internship with their former General Secretary, contributed to emphasizing safety aspects and well-being of the community.

Shakti has always taken full advantage of the opportunities that came his way whether in UCPA or Huns or ICPA to deepen his domain knowledge. His natural curiosity, sharp intelligence, analytical mind and his ability to interact with peers and mine their experience gave him an in-depth knowledge of aviation as a whole. This placed him in a unique position to conceptualize and kick-start Alliance Air and later set-up the operational side of Indigo. It is to the credit of successive MDs of Indian Airlines that they recognized his abilities and gave him the freedom that enabled him to show a different way forward. After his achievements at Alliance, it was a no brainer to be selected for another serious start up.

I have always been an admirer of Shakti's ruthless honesty and courage that never prevented him from speaking truth to the powers that be. This honesty he extended to himself as well. He understood his limitations which is evident from his refusal to accept the post of CEO in Alliance Air when offered. He saw his role as an analyzer of issues for greater gain. It never was for personal advantage. His rare virtue of accepting full responsibility and supporting the people working with him when mistakes occurred has ensured their undying loyalty through thick and thin. This is reflected by their willingness to follow him whenever called upon and give an early warning at critical times.

Readers will find this book more than just a memoir. There are valuable lessons of personal behavior and integrity that are invaluable to ruminate about. In addition, the historically accurate perspectives of starting an airline and running an airline provide valuable tips for students studying aviation management or even for executives operating in that space today.

Subir Hari Singh, IAS (Retd)

Bangalore (India)

1. ONCE UPONs A TIME

"Somewhere over the rainbow way up high,
there's a land that I heard of once in a lullaby,
somewhere over the rainbow skies are blue,
and the dreams that you dare to dream really come true"
– The Wizard of Oz

My story begins with a story. A story that my mother told me.

I was born in 1950 in Rampur, Uttar Pradesh, India. The Nawab of Rampur, a progressive man, was one of the first to accede to the Indian Union. He oversaw a mini-industrial boom in Rampur around India's Independence. Home to several sugar plantations, a textile mill, modern sugar mills with an associated distillery, Rampur had its own dedicated thermal power plant.

My father, Har Swarup Lumba, migrated to the city in 1940, while India was still under British rule, with a dream of building a life in a bustling new industrial region.

His dream was short lived! At only 44, he passed away, leaving my mother a young widow, with her eldest child just 12 years old and her youngest, Shakti, me, merely two.

My young mind could not comprehend the sudden disappearance of my father. It was confusing that someone who was here one minute, was not there the next. I had a lot of questions.

To protect me from the dreadful reality and the pain of understanding such a loss, my mother told me an old folk tale that my father was now living in the stars.

In that instant, my tender mind decided that I was one day going to fly into the skies and bring my father back to us!

In later years, I learnt that we belonged to the village "*HookiChitti*" in Nakodar, District Jullundur, Punjab. Ours was a wealthy *zamindar* family and one of my ancestors was apparently not a good man. According to local folklore, he was cursed by a religious, god-fearing woman, whose family he had harmed. The curse was that for the next seven generations, no male Lumba child would live beyond the age of 45. In successive generations, male Lumba members did indeed die before 45. My father and his brothers didn't survive to see 46 years. Nor did their fathers and grandfathers.

The curse was the reason why the family abandoned the village and their lands and no Lumba has ever returned to HookiChitti.

In 1992, when I went to do "*Pind Daan*" for my mother's soul, the specific family pandit in Kurukshetra, who maintains a complete family tree genealogy that runs into many generations, told me about the dreadful family curse! My elder brother Mohan, I and my cousin Om were members of the 8th generation! The fact that I'm telling this story means the curse has run its course. Believe it or not!

As was the wont of many kids in Rampur, Nainital was the 'school' destination. Nainital was only about eighty miles from Rampur and famous for its boarding schools. I followed my older brother Mohan to St Joseph's College (SJC), popularly called SEM. Short for SEMINARY. In those good old days formal education didn't start until the age of five! We had not heard of day schools or play schools for children. All psychologists and pediatricians were of the opinion that only at the age of five was a child able to emotionally and socially handle more than 20-25 people.

So, at the ripe age of five, I started my formal education. SEM was earlier a seminary until it was taken over 1892-93 by Edmond Ignatius Rice's Irish Christian Brotherhood that ran many of India's premier schools, of which St Columbus in Delhi is one.

My sisters studied at St Mary's Convent the sister school, fondly called SONN (School of Nutty Nuns) which was run by German nuns. So we were SEM boys and they were SONN girls.

It is said that you enter a boarding school a boy and leave a man. This happens to most who live away from family and the emotional dynamics of dealing with relatives is limited. Understanding of emotions is restricted to what you experience, mostly in isolation. Connections with people back home are thin. Maybe there were various other reasons, but this was my truth. Boarding school laid the foundation of my journey.

While being alone was never an issue for me, I had the fortunate company of authors like Nevil Shute, Ernest Gann, Antoine de Saint-Exupéry and Richard Bach. They kept the fire for flying burning. But I had no idea where and how to begin. The only information I had was of Air Force pilots, which did not help me beyond helping me to figure out I needed to choose Science as my stream of education if I wanted to understand aviation concepts better. And so, I did.

I was the kind of student the teachers constantly remarked as a "can do better". Honestly, I admit I could have done better, but my level of application helped me to handsomely scrape through to the next class.

Most of my effort went into reading. Learning comprehension and the nuances of the English language from the books of authors like Charles Dickens. My favorites were Leslie Charteris novel "The Saint" and Capt. W.E. Johns' series on "Biggles" the perfect inspiration for someone who was sure he wanted to become a pilot.

In my senior year in school, a graphologist called Piloo Patel was called, curiously enough, by the St Joseph's administration to guide the children in their career path. The graphologist would analyze the students' handwriting to understand personality traits and recommend future career paths.

I hated cursive writing — there's really no real reason why, I just did. This did not impress the graphologist at all, and he suggested I take up a career as a salesman!

He gave the same advice to my friend, David Ezekiel. David's dad Capt. Joe Ezekiel was a legendary pilot with the Indian Airlines. Obviously, this advice did not sit well with either of us! We were adamant that we wanted to fly, so the career recommendation went flying out of the window. Of course, we proved the graphologist wrong when both David and I became airline pilots.

By this time, I had gone one step higher, and wanted to become a Naval Aviator.

Why naval pilot, you ask? It had a lot to do with the dashing white uniform, the golden wings and the effect the outfit had on girls!

Aviation was a small part of the Indian Navy in the 1960s. Interested candidates would apply and meet the Naval Commander who would then evaluate and decide. However, one needed to have an intermediate level of education to apply. Hence a graduate degree was essential.

So, it was *"Chalo Dilli"* for me after my ISC when I found my way to St Stephen's College, Delhi University.

The 60's was a glorious decade for students. It was a a time when getting admission into the renowned St. Stephen's College, was not a duel to death and did not require the sacrifice of your first born.

It was a simple process of submitting your application and documents and going through an interview.

The first person I met at college was the famous Robert Sahab, head clerk at Stephen's to whom I submitted my application. The easily likeable man provided me an interview slot a week later with the college Principal, Mr. Sircar and the Dean, Mr Rajpal.

What I remember clearly about that interview was how we spoke about everything except academics. We discussed my hobbies, football, my aims and ambitions, but nothing about science. Before I knew it, I was admitted into the Bachelor of Science course at St Stephen's College! The cherry on the cake was that I was eligible for a hostel room at "The Residence, as it was called, only after 6 months. The Residence consisted of six blocks; Allnutt North and South, Rudra North and South and Mukerji East and West.

I was finally allotted a room in Rudra North in December 1967. Till then I stayed with my cousin Om Lumba, who was in Senior Management of Indian Airlines. My nieces and nephews, Anil, Pavan, Kiran and Neera introduced me, the country bumpkin, to urban Delhi.

The College Residence became for me, the hub where life unfolded, unabashed and glorious. We Stephenians were snobs and those in residence considered themselves a notch above the day scholars.

The "Scholars in Residence" enrolled in various college societies and clubs. I quickly became a member of the Wodehouse Society, The Hiking Club, and The Shakespeare Society. Through these societies, my social life expanded, allowing for interactions with students from diverse backgrounds. All this would hold me in good stead in the years to come.

There is very seldom a direct link between one's career and what one studied in college. It is the experience of going through three years of residential college that makes a boy into a man.

Living in Residence had its restrictions, too. Curfew was set to 10 p.m. – no exceptions. The "gyp" or the room boy would bring about the night register called "The Reg" for attendance soon after curfew. A night off campus needed prior approval of the Dean. But it was not all bad. Inviting students from other colleges and getting invited to dinner on Guest Nights to their colleges was commonplace.

On a warm autumn day in 1969, accepting one such invite, I found myself at the hostel of Hans Raj College as a guest of Deepak Stokes. Deepak's grandfather, Samuel Evans Stokes, a Quaker from Philadelphia, had come as a Christian missionary to India from the United States in January 1904 and is credited for starting apple cultivation in Himachal Pradesh's picturesque Kotgarh valley. As the story goes, he became disenchanted with Christianity and converted to Hinduism, changing his name to Satyanand.

During a visit to Kotgarh, as a guest of another friend, Sushil Bhalak ("Thotu"), I also met the Stokes family. Thotu who was studying in Sri Ram College of Commerce had introduced me to Deepak.

Serendipitously, Deepak was a NCC Air Wing Cadet and loved flying. He was totally smitten. So was I. What was the best way to get started, I asked him?

"Gliding" he said.

2. THE BEGINNING

"The fascination of flight can't be expressed with words.
But it really lies beyond the capabilities of human endeavour.
Once you've experienced it, you'll never be able to forget it."
— Friedrich Oblessor

Gliding occupied all my waking hours thereafter! So, over the following weekend, I decided to visit the only place I knew that had something to do with it—The Safdarjung Airport.

Safdarjung was the main airport for New Delhi till a new airport was commissioned at Palam in 1962. It was also home to the Delhi Gliding Club, a poor cousin to the more glamorous Delhi Flying Club. The gliding club operated from a large hangar and used the grass strip adjacent to the main and only runway.

Safdarjung Airport, earlier known as Willingdon Airfield, came up in 1928 and the home base of the Indian National Airways (INA). It was nationalized and merged along with a number of other airlines into Indian Airlines Corporation (IAC) in 1953. Safdarjung Airport was the INA's main base and housed the legendary DC-3, better known as the Dakota, which had proven itself as the mainstay transport aircraft for the Allies during World War II.

A staff housing complex next to the airport came to be known as INA Colony. In typical entrepreneurial fashion, a market had sprung up to meet the daily needs of INA Colony's residents and became popular as The INA market.

So, there I was at the Club early in the morning. Little knowing that gliding took place only in the afternoon. Enquiring around, I was told that Captain Wason, Chief Gliding Instructor, would be available in the afternoon. To kill time, I decided to visit my maternal uncle, A.K. Seth, formerly a mechanic with the Indian National Airways and now an engineer with Indian Airlines. He lived close by in the INA colony.

Over lunch, I shared the purpose of my visit to the club. To my good fortune my uncle knew Capt. Wason personally and promptly offered to introduce me. It took just one cup of tea and not much persuading for Capt. Wason to take me for my first up-in-the-air experience.

Gliding is a total experience of which pushing the glider back to take off point between launches is an integral part. That afternoon I helped some other aspiring pilots push the Rohini, a dual, open cockpit glider out of the hangar. We rolled her out to what I was told was the eastern end of the grass strip. I was asked to sit on the left seat and was helped to get strapped in.

"Take this bag," one of the students said with a smug smile.

"It's called the air sickness bag," another told me "If you get airsick, do not throw up over the side of the glider, because the slip stream will deposit it all onto your face." I had been given my first face-saving instruction.

Captain Wason sat on the right seat. The winch steel rope was hooked to the bottom front of the glider, while two students held the wing tips.

I held on to the side as instructed, the stick on my side was removed. The winch rev up could be heard and then I felt the tug as the glider started to move. At first slowly, but then it picked up speed and rumbled down fast on the grass strip. In the next moment, there was total silence. We had taken off! Soared off into the air!

The flight lasted a few minutes, but each moment flying was exhilarating. In each of those moments, I felt an unbridled joy such as I had never conceived possible.

Time stood still for me as the wind rushed past my face and through my hair in astounding juxtaposition with the peaceful quiet.

To this day, I cannot find superlatives to adequately describe the bliss of that moment. I was in love. Hook, line and sinker. Soon, I was a regular at the gliding club notching up dual launches at only ₹2 per launch.

In the following months, I found my way to the Delhi Flying Club at every opportunity, chasing my dream.

The Delhi Flying Club was established in 1928 to popularize and evangelize the spirit of aviation in the youth of India. Once the new airport was operational at Palam, Prime Minister Jawaharlal Nehru bequeathed Safdarjung Airport to the Delhi Flying Club, giving it grandfather rights.

Unfortunately, under the National Airport Authority Act (which was superseded by the Airport Authority Act), all airports in India became the property of Airport Authority of India.

The Delhi Flying Club stood with all its legends for nearly a century till its very recent eviction. The land it was on has more commercial value than the club itself.

After the nationalization of airlines in 1953, domestic aviation went through a sea-change. From over 20 private airlines with several score aircrafts, the industry now became restricted to just Indian Airlines (IA) and Air India (AI), both Corporations.

Both airlines were given the mandate under the Air Corporation Act to provide safe, efficient, regular, economic air transport services for the nation, domestically by IA and internationally by AI.

The air route network also got drastically reduced. Very few large cities, apart from the top four metros, were connected by air.

What I had not thought through while love of flying coursed through my veins, was of course, job opportunities. There were very few jobs. Air India only recruited from the Indian Air Force. Therefore, there was only one employer of civil pilots—the Indian Airlines.

It was time for some homework.

The rates of flying an aircraft for training is paid on an hourly basis. In the 1960s, it was ₹10/hr, which was increased incrementally by the time I started flying in late 1969, to ₹25/hr. To get a pilot's license I needed to fly 250 hours which meant that I needed to spend only ₹7000, which at that time carried quite a lot of weight! There were pretty much no barriers to becoming a pilot. The flying training was subsidized by the government to attract people to aviation. To give you a perspective, today the amount spent in learning to fly is over ₹ 40,00,000.

For someone training to be a pilot, the government subsidy quota was only for 50 hours of flying a year. If flying purely at subsidized rates, it would take 5 years to accumulate the required 250 hours flying experience to obtain a Commercial Pilot Licence (CPL). Those in a hurry could do this more quickly by paying the non-subsidized rate of Rs121/hr. The requirement for initial flying was basic: an ICAO class II Medical Examination from a DGCA (Director General of Civil Aviation) approved General Practitioner and an oral technical exam on the aircraft that training was to be imparted.

The first step towards becoming a professional pilot was to obtain a Student Pilot License (SPL). So, one September day in 1969, I walked across to the Delhi Flying Club. That is where I met two of the Club's legendary icons: the head flight clerk Atal Sahab or *"Dada"* and the head waiter *"Mama"*. *Dada* was the first point of contact for anyone starting to fly. He explained to me that I first had to become a flying member of the Club.

I was sold a booklet on basic aviation terminology and principles of flight, sagely titled "Learn to Fly" for ₹20. Along with that I was given a medical form to be filled by a DGCA approved doctor in Sarojini Nagar, just a hop across the railway line to the south of the club.

I was to study from the book for my oral exam and get my medical examination done, then come back and meet *Dada*. Simple instructions, which I followed.

He gave me a date for my SPL oral exams, which was two weeks later.

Capt. Jamwal, the Chief Flying Instructor (CFI) of the club at that time conducted my oral exam. I breezed through the test. I had to; I had been studying for two weeks!

The DGCA would take about a fortnight to issue a Student Pilot's Licence and Capt. Jamwal advised me to undergo a powered flight air experience. My limited gliding experience was no substitute. He told me to request any Private Pilot License holder to give me the air experience joy ride. A private pilot was authorized to carry non-paying passengers.

Most aspiring pilots were required to undergo an air experience just to see whether they got air sick or realized they had a fear of flying once they got up in the air.

The Delhi Flying Club used to be a watering hole for budding pilots, "Gas Bags" telling tall tales about flying and their other exploits in the air, over endless cups of tea with a never-ending supply of pakoras and bread-omelette. *Mama* and his team were as good at maintaining their high-flying clientele as they were at chasing them to recover money owed.

This is the place my friendships were forged. A lifetime of them. I made my longest lasting friendships at the club, Subir Hari Singh and Harinder Singh, *Dirty Harry* are two names that became an integral part of my life, thanks to the club.

I also became friends with Rajinder Pushkarna, "Pushy". He was then a holder of a Private Pilot's Licence. Which meant he was allowed to carry a passenger on flight. I requested and he agreed to take me on a round trip flight from Delhi to Rohtak and back.

The Pushpak MK2 was the standard side by side trainer aircraft. It was manufactured by HAL (Hindustan Aeronautics Limited). It was similar to the Aeronca, constructed on a metal frame covered with fabric powered by a 90 hp Continental piston engine with a wooden propeller. It was designed for side-by-side dual instruction. The control wheels and rudders on each side were interlinked.

The instrument panel consisted of a magnetic compass, airspeed indicator, altimeter and turn indicator — a far cry from today's advanced trainer aircraft with fancy avionics and GPS.

Navigation was done with the aid of a compass. The pilots flew a predetermined course with the help of check points on the ground— this was called Map Reading. Course correction of heading for wind effect had to be done so as to maintain the track on the ground. This is known as Dead Reckoning Navigation. Basically, if you reckoned wrong, you could end up dead!

And so, one day in October, two barely striped pilots took off from New Delhi for Rohtak, Haryana. We were on a VFR (Visual Flight rules) flight plan which was restricted to 2000 ft' above sea level. Which means we could not fly above that height.

Turns out we didn't need to. I could see a full view of the grand Himalayan range from right where we were. On that beautiful CAVOK (Ceiling and Visibility OK) day, it was just us and empty blue skies.

The flight to Rohtak was amazing. I was wonderstruck by the power flight experience, the speed, the sense of freedom and the aerial view.

Pushy demonstrated the effect of controls. A slight left turn on the wheel brought the left wing down while the right went up and the airplane gently turned left. Exactly the opposite for a right turn.

A light push forward made the nose go down and the aircraft descended; a slight pull back and it climbed. Adding power made the nose go up and reducing made the nose drop. Pushy let me gingerly handle the controls explaining that only gentle pressure was required not force.

"It's like making love to your beloved," he said. "Learn how she needs to be touched and caressed; never force yourself upon her." I was thrilled at the ease of the analogy!

We turned around over Rohtak and set course for New Delhi. The air had now gotten bumpy, and the ride became 'choppy'. My first experience with turbulence was a relief as I did not feel air sick. It felt like riding on a rough road at high speed.

When we were about ten miles from New Delhi, we heard a loud thud and the aircraft vibrated as the nose went up.

Pushy pulled the throttle back slightly to reduce the vibration. I saw that he was pushing the stick forward with both hands and trying to set the elevator trimmer to nose down. He was sweating and asked me to help him control the aircraft which appeared to have developed a mind of its own. After a few minutes of fighting with the controls, we finally saw the Safdarjung runway.

The traffic pattern was clear, and we headed for a straight in approach for Runway 12. Once the throttle was pulled back further to start the glide for the landing, the vibrations seemed to reduce.

The landing was literally arriving with a bang! My first heavy landing experience. Pushy was unnerved and said that it was the most difficult landing he had ever made. Blissfully ignorant of the danger we had survived, I remember being ecstatic, pulsing with excitement with all the adrenaline rushing inside me.

We parked on the tarmac and did the post flight walk around. To our horror, we found a small vulture had made a hole in the left horizontal stabilizer and was still stuck in it. Two of the three bolts holding the stabilizer had sheared, leaving the stabilizer hanging on just one bolt.

The chief engineer was aghast. "It was sheer luck that you both survived the flight," he exclaimed after seeing the gaping hole in the machine. "You could have fallen from the skies like a rock, if you hadn't throttled back, the elevator would have detached," he added.

Fate was not the Hunter that day. We were just thankful to the Universe for watching out for us.

I had gotten my first air experience, topped with my first brush with turbulence and my first heavy landing and bird hit —which happened to be the deadliest bird hit I would see in my whole career.

Yet, and yet, I was not scared just but excited. I had No Fear of Flying.

Fate, The Hunter did find one of us on another day, fifteen years later.

Capt. Rajinder Pushkarna, dear Pushy, was killed in a crash after take-off from Kathmandu. He had joined Royal Nepal Airlines flying the single engine Pilatus Porter. It was mostly used as a single pilot aircraft commercially. It could be used also as a dual trainer. The unfortunate accident however, was not attributable to pilot proficiency or pilot error but to negligent load and balance. The 2nd pilot "Stick" had been removed to carry a passenger and a bag. It was this unsecured bag that moved aft after take-off, jamming the stick 'stub' with it the elevator causing the aircraft to stall after take-off. Poor 'Pushy' would have been unable to push the nose down to try and recover from the stall. The fatal crash was inevitable... Pushy's number had come up.

Back at the Delhi Flying Club, things were picking up for me. I had gotten my SPL and was allotted Capt. Betala as my flight instructor. Under him I was to undergo dual flying instruction. Capt. Betala was an accomplished artist and sculptor in his free time, and a very conservative pilot.

I quickly learnt that flying training was conducted under Visual Flight Rules (VFR). This meant the visibility requirement was 5 nautical miles and the pilot had to maintain a distance of 1000 feet in three dimensions – from a cloud and the ground.

Flying was also with reference to the horizon. Entering clouds was illegal mainly as it could lead to a fatal loss of control arising out of lack of visual clues and false sensory perceptions caused by the human ear.

To fly blind one needed special instrumentation and training under Instrument Flight Rules (IFR). Capt. Betala was not instrument rated, so most flying days were scrubbed for being non-VFR. Frustrating, but life-saving.

While every take off is optional, every single landing is mandatory. Hence, one of the biggest challenges of learning to fly is learning to land.

The Pushpak was a tail dragger, which made learning to land more challenging. You needed a perfect 3-point touchdown or you were destined to bounce and waltz along the runway, a huge embarrassment with dangerous consequences and a tight rap on the knuckles from the instructor!

The art was to gradually round off the glide and flare the plane to check the descent at the right height. Raise the nose up just right to get all three wheels touching down at the same time.

Sounds like rocket science? Well… it almost was!

As the legend goes: "True pilots flew tail draggers, sissy ones flew the tricycle gear aircraft."

I had to demonstrate that I was consistently capable of executing a safe take-off, straight and level flight and a normal landing (without crashing and killing myself), before I could be deemed capable of my First Solo.

It took over 6 months, many a clip behind the ears, raps on the head, and colorful language from my redoubtable instructor, describing my abilities or appalling lack of. It took me 10 hrs of circuit and bumps before I was ready for Solo. Finally, on the 10th of March 1970, after a routine sortie and uneventful landing, Capt. Betala unhooked his seat belt, opened his door, got out while I was still at the controls.

"You can go solo. Do everything I taught you. Do one circuit. I'll see you in the Club house after you land". He nonchalantly threw the magic words at me as he walked away, never looking back.

Going Solo was a big deal and is still considered one of the best days in any pilot's life. As I taxied back to the beginning of the runway the rest of the club was lined up waving. "Happy Landings" was the cheer in the air.

I was very excited and equally nervous. Praying, and mentally going through the maneuvers as I had been taught.

"Always remain ahead of the airplane. Fly with your mind and then use your hands and feet. To use your hands and feet first and then apply the mind later usually results in broken airplanes and dead pilots". Capt. Betala's words echoed in my head.

Since there was no Radio Telephony (RT) Equipment fitted on the Pushpak, air traffic was controlled by a series of lights flashed from the Control Tower.

Red meant Stop, which meant Hold Position for aircraft on ground or go around for aircraft in the air. Flashing White meant return to bay or keep circling depending on whether you were on land or in air. Green meant clear to enter runway and take off or clear to land, as appropriate.

I finally got the 'Green Light' from the Tower, took a deep breath and taxied onto the runway centre line, and slowly opened power applying right rudder pressure to counter propeller rotation spin. The tail came up. Slight rudder to correct for the yaw and then a slight back pressure on the control, on achieving 60 knots and we were airborne! I was elated and indescribably happy. I can safely say I felt as free as a bird.

Approaching 1000 feet I turned left to join the standard rectangle circuit pattern that I had practiced for 10 hours over the last six months. Taking off from runway 30 and turning downwind, one headed towards the All-India Institute over which one turned base leg and started the glide to the runway ensuring that the air speed indicator remained at the gliding speed of 60 knots, while constantly monitoring it came nowhere near the Redline at 40 knot which was the stalling speed below which the aircraft stops flying and succumbs to the force of gravity, basically making the aircraft fall to earth like a rock. My final turn brought me in line with the runway aiming point inside the threshold.

The ground came up slowly and then rapidly, slight flare, nose up and I had landed. A perfect 3 pointer!

The sense of accomplishment that a pilot feels on his first Solo landing can never be upstaged by any other achievement in his lifetime. A pilot never forgets his first solo.

After I taxied in, shut the engine and climbed out, all the other trainees mobbed around while 'congratulations' flew thick in the air!

Elated, I entered the club and threw the customary First Solo party. There was a new swagger to my walk. And why not?

I was a PILOT.

3. UP IN THE AIR

"Those Magnificent men in their flying machines
They go up-tiddly-up-up
They go down-tiddly-down-down
They enchant all the ladies
And steal all the scenes
Up, down flying around"
– John McCarthy

By the end of 1970, I was juggling classes in college and clocking flying hours at the Delhi Flying Club. Flying was a slow and frustrating process. Both Subir and I had earned our PPL (Private Pilot License) and cleared all the CPL (Commercial Pilot License) written exams including Morse Code (sending and receiving) and Radiotelephony (RT), in the first attempt. No mean feat for a student who scraped through school exams

Flying was slow as the student to aircraft ratio at the Delhi Flying Club was almost 30 to 1 for the six operational aircraft the club had. Besides, cost of flying had seen a steep rise to ₹121 per hour. I had an important decision to make. The twin impediments now to obtaining a Commercial Pilot License were only money and aircraft availability. It was then that Subir suggested that we check out the Patiala Aviation Club.

The CFI there was the legendary "*Ralph*" (Capt. Karminder Singh), who fully lived up to his regal antecedents of the royal family of Patiala. The Club came highly recommended by D.P. Singh, (Manu) who was a friend of Subir— both their fathers were from the Indian Forest Service. Manu had already got his flying stripes from Patiala, after which he had joined St. Stephen's in the first year.

We decided to check out Patiala Aviation Club. Sure enough, early one morning we set off for Patiala on my "Bobby" motorcycle.

Pilots are notoriously bad navigators on the ground and as the magic of Google Maps was not at hand in those days, we finally arrived at the Patiala Aviation Club at around 4 p.m., after losing and finding our way several times. Directed to the CFIs office, we knocked and entered.

Capt. *Ralph*, was a handsome Sikh resplendent in a pink turban and the ubiquitous Ray Ban Aviator sun glasses. He sat leaning back in a chair precariously balanced on two legs, neatly polished shoes resting on the table in front of him. He was reading a copy of "Flying Magazine". Ralph enjoyed a colorful reputation, but he was bigger than life in person, and one of the most stylish aviators I had met.

His eyes twinkled when he saw two young "*chikoos*". We introduced ourselves and mentioned that Capt DP Singh had sent us to him with a glowing recommendation that Patiala was the best place to complete our flying hours.

He immediately launched into a cautionary lecture about the amount of hard work and study involved in obtaining firstly, a Private Pilot License, and then the backbreaking task of obtaining the coveted Commercial License. Also, a student's flying progress was dependent on how many CPL papers he could pass.

Patiala was the only club that had a dedicated Ground School, headed by Ralph's brother George. Yet despite this facility, most flyers in Patiala were stuck at the 150-200 hour stage. Since they couldn't pass the CPL License examinations despite numerous attempts.

We patiently waited for our turn to speak…and show off! We proudly informed *Ralph* that we both held PPLs and also that we both had cleared all CPL issue requirements including Morse & RT. We only need to pile up the required hours.

In a flash, his feet were off the table and we had his complete attention.

"Lakhi, machine nikaal, asli pilot aaye hain!" He bellowed to the Club's Chief Engineer, Lakhbir Singh. ("*Lakhi* get out the machine, real pilots have come!")

Two mechanics wheeled out a Pushpak and *Ralph* give us a quick check ride. Just one circuit each. He seemed satisfied that we could fly. Another Pushpak was wheeled out and he bid us to go and shoot some circuits and landings but to land well before sun set.

After our sorties, we trooped into Ralph's office where we met the flight clerk, U.C. Pandey. Pandey was a student pilot of 5 years with 250 hours but had no CPL because he was unable to clear the all-important air navigation paper. He sized us up, obviously fretting that we had flown without any club membership or depositing any money. As he was filling in an invoice for two hours of flying each, Ralph walked in and said, "*No Charge, ENCO Hai*" he scowled at Pandey as he wrote "ENCO" in bold letter across the authorization log.

Ralph, in that instant, became our hero! ENCO stood for *Exercise Not Carried Out*.

ENCO, as a process and its practice, peculiar only to Patiala Aviation Club had an interesting history. The Government provided flying at subsidized rates in the form of a fuel quota every year. Every flying club always had quota fuel left over because of over logging by pilots. This fuel could not be used officially again. However, the fuel had to be used up before each yearly fuel audit. The fuel used and flight time logged had to be equitable.

Patiala had the ENCO as a novel way to use up this fuel by letting serious students fly free of cost in the evening with the stipulation that the flying not be logged. ENCO flying was popular among those of us who loved flying as it didn't cost a penny. The downside was that since aircraft hours were not logged, each aircraft actually flew more hours between checks than it was supposed to.

Another downside of over-logging was it produced 'unemployable' pilots. Such pilots had obtained a qualification but lacked the requisite skill and knowledge. They collectively lacked both passion and motivation, both extremely important to be a professional pilot. This issue has plagued the industry in the '60/70s and does even today. It remains one of the causes for the swelling ranks of '*unemployable*' pilots.

Besides our countless unlogged hours, the Patiala Aviation Club provided the opportunity to remain up in the air officially as opposed to being ground bound at the Delhi Flying Club. At Patiala Aviation Club, the aircraft to student pilot ratio was well below 10.

With our uppity Anglicized education, Subir and I were treated like outsiders by the Club's aspiring pilots, mostly strapping Punjabi and Haryanvi men. We simply let our skills in the cockpit do the talking. It was not long before we were part of the inner circle of Patiala Aviation Club.

A pilot's vanity lies in his desire to being addressed as 'Captain' much like students in medical school like to be addressed as 'Doctor'. The Major Domo of the club hostel where we stayed was "*Khemi*" (Khem Chand), a Nepali who exploited this weakness to the fullest.

A veritable shower of "CAPTAIN!!!" would drip from Khemi's mouth when he was collecting tips for his daily booze fix! But a stingy response would elicit a shower of Nepali curses! His favorite was – "Pick up any stone and you see hundreds of unemployed pilots like you underneath – like little ants!"

When we weren't flying, we were driving to the hills. We would borrow a friend's Chevrolet Impala, fill it with club's excess 80 octane aviation fuel for only ₹1 per bucket, sold on the quiet by the enterprising mechanics at *Ralph's*. We would zoom off to Dhali, in the Shivalik Hills (enroute to Shimla,) a favorite pit stop for beer and pickled meat, mostly wild boar and deer eaten with fresh baked bread.

Being in Patiala was a lot of fun, but by the time we had logged 150 hours each, money to pay for the flying was running near empty. Subir and I decided to take a break to arrange for funds.

I went back to my hometown Rampur to scrounge for money for my flying. My brother-in-law, a Colonel in the Indian Army, suggested I try for the Air Force since flying there would be free and also provide me an assured career. I hated the thought of being confined in the regimented 'Yes Sir, No Sir, and three bags full, Sir" perception I had of the Defense Services.

I wanted to choose a career which came with freedom. Freedom to tell your boss "To go to Hell" or "I Quit." Without having to undergo a court- martial for it. In hindsight, I am glad that 'freedom' was the moot point. I ended up using said "freedom" more than once in my aviation career!

At that time, I just needed the money to go back to Patiala.

Meanwhile, there was a Shakespearean drama being played out at home! I pulled out all the tricks available at my disposal -emotional blackmail, tantrums, even a tactical attack of tears – with my Mother. After a long month of persistent cajoling and persuasion, my poor Mother gave in, and sold off an acre of my inherited land to provide for my flying. Mission success.

I raced back to The Patiala Aviation Club and so did Subir. Probably impressed by our dedication, Ralph decided to help us out. He arranged for us to fly a private De Havilland DH-82, popularly known as The Tiger Moth. Which was owned by a former student pilot, Diljeet Singh, now a resident of Canada.

The Tiger Moth was a legend. Before the 2nd World War, it was the standard fully aerobatic trainer aircraft in most Air Force academies.

It was an open cockpit, tandem biplane, two wings stacked one on top the other on either side of the fuselage. Struts and the load bearing flying wires ran between the top and bottom wings and were reputed to sing in the wind. The airplane was made of wooden spars and ribs covered with fabric and dope. One look at it and we were hooked!

Esso, the petroleum company, had run a very successful campaign which I had come across in an old issue of FLYING magazine with a Tiger refueling a Tiger Moth from an Esso fuel truck with the caption "Put a TIGER in your Tiger Moth". Frankly, Subir and I felt like tigers at that stage.

An hourly rate of ₹70 per hour agreed to between Ralph and us. This still ₹51 cheaper than the unsubsidized rate and a huge saving in training cost.

What excited us most was that the Tiger Moth's C of A (Certificate of Airworthiness) listed it in the aerobatic and night category. Ralph had cautioned us that even he would not do aerobatics on it, since the spars were 1935 vintage and he was not confidence of its past maintenance and prohibited us from even attempting loops.

He taught us how to stall the aircraft, put it in a spin and recover. These were lifesaving basic maneuvers which were prohibited on the Pushpak.

To be able to fly The Tiger, we had to obtain a rating on it. Which meant passing its specific Airframe and Engine exam.

We were handed just a few typed leaflets about the Tiger's Engine, limitations etc. That was the sum total of information made available to us! That slim sheaf of leaflets was bolstered with hours of study at the Aeronautical Society of India library in New Delhi. Armed with data from that handsome library, we had enough technical information to brave the exam. Both of us passed.

We were made a peculiar request by the DGCA Examination Branch. They requested us for all the notes we had compiled on the Tiger. Secretly chuffed, we agreed.

Little did we know that even DGCA had little or no material available on the Tiger and that they had reset an earlier 1956 test set, the only set they had on the aircraft type.

Raring to go now, we rushed to Agra where we found Hori Lal and Sons, then India's biggest buyer of airplanes and aviation scrap. We were looking for air force surplus flying suits, leather jackets and helmets. We found two sets in reasonably good condition, but there were no boots and gloves.

After a wide search, we finally found suitable boots and gloves at the Yashwant Place Market near Chanakya Cinema in New Delhi.

Back in Patiala, decked in our new gear, we had to do a couple of dual sorties under Ralph's instruction.

I now realized I had a problem. I was not able to land the plane with any finesse. Landing the Tiger was different from landing the Pushpak. On the former you had to look, straight ahead in the front, judge the height above the ground and then at the right time flared the airplane to land. The Tigers nose high attitude resulted in a high cut off angle, limiting forward visibility. The pilot flying sat on the rear seat and could not see the ground straight ahead. As a result, one had to look on either side to judge one's height. I found it difficult judging change in perspective to judge the landing flare. I was mishandling almost every landing I attempted. Thankfully Subir was doing better than I was.

Uncomfortable with myself, I sought Ralph's advice. "How do I judge the height to check my glide to flare the aircraft?" I asked. In typical Ralph-speak, he replied: "*Jab Gand Phatte check de do*" (when your arse twitches give a check). -Golden Words.

This tip worked for me on the Tiger Moth and every aircraft type I flew subsequently.

Then he taught us 'wheelers', where you fly or rather roll the aircraft with power on to the turf smoothly on the main wheels with the tail in the air.

As our confidence is flying the Tiger Moth increased, Ralph gave us free rein over the plane. Flying the Tiger from Patiala was fun, exciting, demanding, adventurous and very glamorous. We were two young pilot jocks in leather jackets, leather helmets and long white scarves around the neck, similar to Hollywood heroes. It made us into instant celebrities wherever we landed, simply because the aircraft embodied the entire romance of flying.

We weren't complaining. But it wasn't all fun and games.

Through those months, Ralph imparted some of the most valuable flying lessons. As our flying hours increased, he insisted that we master the art of low flying on both the Tiger and Pushpak, the latter which we flew ENCO. Low flying is literally below 100 ft' just above the treetops. His logic was "you guys will anyway try it, so that you don't kill yourselves it is better I teach you."

Actually, low flying was totally illegal. If caught, it meant a 3-month license suspension. When flying below 100 feet, the effect of wind on the airplane is dramatically different from that at 1,000 feet above the ground. There was also ground effect to keep in mind.

Ralph started to take us out on low flying sorties on both the Tiger and Pushpak. He showed us the effect of wind on turns at low altitudes, the need for constant look out for trees, high tension wires and birds. I realized what a serious business it was to know the correct techniques involved in Low Flying – a combination of skill, vigilance and immense concentration, awareness of illusions and changes in perception with speed relative to the ground.

Buzzing houses, control towers and girls hostels was strictly forbidden.

These pointers made us much better pilots and helped us in challenging flying moments in years to come.

The low flying experience stood me in great stead when later I was flying the F27 in the Assam valley along the Brahmaputra River. During the monsoon the cloud base there would normally go below 200 feet.

Flying cross country in poor visibility from Patiala to New Delhi, when the whole northern belt was fog bound was a piece of cake for us. This was because we were taught well. By one of the best around —Ralph. All we had to do was to pick up the Patiala – Rajpura road and from Rajpura pick up the railway line and follow it low and slow all the way to New Delhi. We were supposed to be flying under Visual Flight Rules (VFR) but we considered ourselves IFR (I Follow Road/Rails) pilots!

Ralph also had an ulterior reason for teaching us low flying. As winter approached, the bird migration to the subcontinent started and the birds settled down on the numerous "*jheels*" (water bodies) all over Punjab. Ralph's favorite sport was duck hunting – from the air! He would ask one of us to be ready by 5 a.m. near the hangar.

A Pushpak with its left doors removed would be ready. For this sortie the pilot flying would sit on the right and Ralph on the left with his shotgun. We would take off at first light and obviously, flying low. He knew where the ducks would be nesting. One low pass would get them in the air and on the second pass he would shoot.

The challenge of the sport was not killing sitting ducks but those flying, when you too were flying faster than them. Our flyingchallenge was not to fly into them but keep to their right so that Ralph could shoot from the left. He never shot more than four-five birds, and that too only for the table. Old faithful *Khemi* was there to retrieve the birds and in return got a handsome tip.

Another exercise we had to do was timed circuits. No turning base over a landmark like we used to over the AIIMS in Delhi. When Ralph found out that students were using a particular large tree as a landmark, he had it chopped. Patiala had 2 ALGs (additional landing grounds) within 10 nautical miles of the Airfield to practice actual force landing. We spent many an hour practicing force landings with simulated engine failure.

Flying cross country in an open cockpit airplane would get awkward if one was solo but having another person in front to act as navigator would be a real asset. Subir and I alternated flight legs as pilot flying and the pilot not flying. The pilot who was navigator would be sitting in front, and the one actually flying would be behind. Instead of communicating via the ancient speaking tubes (no radio, no intercom) we preferred hand signals. To bellow into a speaking tube, over all the noise, while also checking the ground, trees and sky, and more importantly, inquisitive birds, was just too much of a hassle.

We had learnt more than just flying with Ralph. He was a veritable encyclopedia of practical aviation tips and how to use signs of Nature to guide us. For example: Judging the surface wind by watching the birds take off because they always took off into wind. A herd of cows mostly graze with their back to the wind. In India, all mosques face west, towards Mecca.

Another important aspect where his advice was invaluable was in the matter of what to do if you desperately wanted to pee. The standing instructions were "Take a Pee before getting into the cockpit". A practice I followed throughout my flying career.

Ralph being Ralph, he also gave us a Plan B. Which was to carry a couple of condoms in case of an emergency. He would emphasize: "Do Not Force Land in case your bladder acts up. Just pee into the condom, tie a knot and toss it over the side when you are over an isolated stretch."

Did we? We may or may not have!

What we did do though, was to manage to accumulate our flying hours much quicker than we would have in any other scenario.

Every time we took off from Patiala, we had 36 hours to fly and be back before the DI (daily inspection) expired.

Our routine was flying to Delhi for a layover, staying at the Safdarjung Airport guest rooms attached to the airport restaurant, where the per night tariff was a princely sum of ₹2.

We weren't princes, but we assumed we were likable, and thus proceeded to convince the manager *Lala* to extend credit for our overnight stays. His son Sandeep later became a pilot too and joined Indian Airlines. He too was called Lala.

During the day, there were always pretty girls dying for joy rides, and a romp later. We would wake up early next morning to take the Tiger Moth for another quick spin before coming back to Delhi for a final stopover on way back to Patiala. All this before the 36-hour deadline was over.

Flying the Tiger besides demanding attention and concentration was also very mentally and physically tiring. The engine, propeller and slip stream noise was our constant companion, the red ribbon tied to the strut our stall indicator.

And, we were always cold, bloody cold.

Starting the Tiger each morning away from main base was a challenge. The pilot not flying was responsible for starting, which was mainly swinging the propeller which was an art.

First the aircraft had to be turned by lifting the tail so that it faced into wind. Wheels 'chocked' and the prop turned counter-clockwise a few turns while ignition was switched off, to loosen any congealed oil and drain extra fuel from the carburetor. When ready to start the pilot would announce "Ignition On" and then "Contact". With a quick clockwise flick of the prop, the engine was expected to crackle and start purring. It seldom did. It usually required a number of attempts. Subir and I would usually flip a coin to see who got the first leg and the loser the first start.

Like any beautiful woman, our Tiger had its pet quirks. At times the engine could (and would) just die on us due to fouled spark plugs. Thankfully, this never happened in the air! Our Tiger never left us high and dry!

Once on a quick trip to Jaipur, we were asked to hurry our turn around as they were expecting the scheduled Indian Airlines B737 flight from Bombay.

We quickly refueled, swung the prop and were taxiing to back track when the engine died. We were bang on the runway.

I got out, cool as a cucumber, and took the spark plug spanner out of the toolbox. I could see the ATC jeep rushing towards us, flashing its headlights. I unhurriedly unplugged the spark plugs, filled them with fuel, went to the side of the runway, struck a match to burn the fuel in order to clean out the plugs, refitted them, checked for tightness, capped them and yelled "Ignition on" followed by "Contact" and swung the prop.

The engine purred alive. The ATC officer, who had reached us by now, was staring at us with his mouth hanging open. He couldn't believe his eyes.

We quickly departed Jaipur much to the relief of ATC. The footnote worth remembering is that we never got permission to land in Jaipur in the Tiger Moth again!

By 1972, we were ready for our CPL Skill test.

The skill tests had to be completed at a controlled airfield, as the Directorate General of Civil Aviation would only accept flight test reports duly verified and stamped by the Air Traffic Controller. The test required a barograph machine to be carried to record the test. The read out from the machine was to be certified too.

The airfield of our choice to conduct the tests was Delhi. Skills test for a CPL along with a 100 nautical mile cross country was required, as well as CA40 day and night tests of at least 45 minutes. (CA40 was the form required for certifying the test. They ended up being referred to as CA40 tests.)

For the night cross country, the instructor would sit in the aircraft to monitor the test. For this, one also needed to have had accumulated 10 hours of night flying.

For an aircraft to be night rated, all it needed was a battery to power the landing and wing tip lights. Also, the aircraft needed an artificial horizon (attitude indicator). Unfortunately, the Tiger Moth did not have an artificial horizon but an inclinometer.

Since we were type rated on both the Pushpak and the Tiger, we clocked most of the night hours on the Pushpak. However, both the day and night test (CA40) for license issue had to be done on the same aircraft. Ralph decided to do both tests on the Tiger.

We had completed the day test by 3pm and had to wait till half an hour after sunset for the night test. Sunset was at 1730 hrs and our tests were slotted for 1800 that day.

The owner of the Tiger Moth, Daljit was in town and had arranged with Ralph to fly his aircraft for about an hour. He took off at 1600 hrs with his lady friend and was to land back by 1700. We were waiting on the Delhi Flying Club lawns which extended almost up to the runway.

Daljit landed on time, returned and parked the plane in the dispersal a short distance from the hangars.

The Tiger Moth did not have brakes and needed to be stopped by cutting the engine. The metal tail skid acted like the brakes on aircraft movement, using friction to stop.

Usually, the grass strip next to the runway is used for take-off and landing so that the tail skid did not damage the runway surface.

We could see Daljit climb out of the aircraft. The prop was still turning and wheels were not chocked.

The gallant (but stupid) man then helped his lady friend out of the front seat and both of them started walking away from the aircraft. We immediately realized what was likely to happen and started running towards the aircraft, yelling at Daljit to turn back. The aircraft had started moving.

Daljit could not hear us over the engine noise but saw us running and gesticulating. He turned around to see his beloved aircraft taxi into the metal wall of the hangar. Still running and breathless, we saw the prop shatter and the starboard wing break, right in front of our eyes. And along with the Tiger our CPL hopes crashed too.

Our beloved Tiger died in front of our eyes and was written off. It was damaged beyond repair. If there is a thing of actually feeling one's heart break, that was the first time.

Though wounded deeply, we knew we had to move on. So, it was back to the good old reliable and sedate Pushpak for our skill tests.

In those days, there were only two-night rated Pushpak aircraft in North India. One in Karnal and the other one in Patiala.

As bad luck would have it, the night flying Pushpak of Patiala had to undergo a Certificate of Airworthiness renewal, which meant it was grounded for some time. So was the one in Karnal.

Our night flying Pilot Instructor, JS Mann, (Mann Sahab) took a liking to Subir and me, as he considered us serious flyers. He made concerted efforts to locate a night rated Pushpak for our night check at Flying Clubs all over India, but none was airworthy.

Later in life, Mann Sahab joined Indian Airlines and flew as my co-pilot. Our first flight was a little strange, both addressing each other as Sir, me since he had been my Instructor and he, as I was his Captain. We soon overcame this and I made every effort to share my knowledge and experience with him, as he had with me when I was his student.

Finally, after a 30-day wait, the Pushpak in Patiala was brought back on line after much prodding by Ralph and thanks to the brilliant Lakhi. In anticipation of the night rated aircraft being made available, we had carried out our CA40B day check on a Pushpak and awaited our night check.

But as if the fates were against us, another hurdle cropped up. Dense winter fog had set in across Punjab. Flying cross country from Punjab was a long-drawn task at the best of times. In winter it was a game of patience.

With several Air Force bases in the vicinity, flying cross country from Patiala required an Air Defense Clearance (ADC No) besides the Civil Flight Information Clearance (FIC No). To obtain the ADC No., one had to make a 'lightening trunk call' to the Adampur Air Force Station. Often, when the weather was good enough to fly, the ADC No. could not be easily obtained (usually lines were down), and by the time it was, the weather would have deteriorated.

Subir and I were in Delhi waiting for Ralph, but no aircraft was able to come from Patiala due to bad weather. Another urgent factor was Ralph's medical was shortly due—and hence his license —was to expire. He also had an eye infection that had been troubling him and we knew he would not clear his medical assessment the next day.

On that fateful day it was foggy in Delhi. Fingers crossed, we waited at Safdarjung Control Tower. We kept checking if any flight plan from Patiala had been filed.

The answer was always negative.

Finally, at 3 p.m., the deep hum of an aircraft was heard overhead. Ralph had reached Delhi!

"You buggers! I flew at 50 feet just to reach you all, and that, too, without an ADC or FIC No." he roared.

He had flown in gross violation of all rules! But everyone knew and respected Ralph too much to ever consider filing a violation against him. Ralph was the King of Flying in North India! A legend.

It finally seemed like luck was on our side, and even the visibility had improved to VFR minimum. We successfully completed our Night Check.

The next day, Ralph visited the Air Force Central Medical Establishment, AFCME, and as expected, got grounded for the next six months.

Luckily for us, the long wait to complete all the CPL requirements was over. We filed our papers with DGCA forthwith, and I was issued with the coveted Commercial Pilot's License in October 1973. I was now a professionally qualified pilot and could prefix Captain before my name.

I was now Captain Shakti Lumba, a Commercial Pilot. I had a Pilot in Command rating for a two-seater single engine (land) airplane. My entry into the professional pilot world.

Patiala and Ralph had essentially helped complete my boyhood dream. All the hours at the Patiala Aviation Club shaped me into the professional I was becoming…

On 3 June 1993, a Bharat Swati prototype, a two-seat trainer designed by the Technical Centre of Directorate General of Civil Aviation and built by Bharat Heavy Electricals Limited, was being test flown at Haridwar. The aircraft crashed when its starboard wing broke off after coming out of a loop, killing the pilot, *Ralph* (Capt. Karminder Singh).

Ralph died with his shoes on, up in the skies, in an airplane, the only way he would have liked to go. His death was the end of a golden chapter in Indian Aviation – a larger-than-life legend, a mentor loved and missed by all the pilots he had taught and influenced.

4. EMPTY BLUESKIES

"If you have flown, perhaps you can understand the love a pilot develops for flight. It is much the same emotion a man feels for a woman, or a wife for her husband.'
– Louise Thaden

The dream of being a pilot was now a reality. Now I had to making a living off the dream. After obtaining the CPL, a pilot in those days had three options.

Get a job as a pilot, or obtain an Assistant Flight Instructor's Rating (AFIR) to start piling flying experience, and lastly find any kind of work anywhere.

The first option was closed at that time. The only employer that hired pilots with a CPL and 250 hours experience, was Indian Airlines. But industrial unrest and infamous "Lock Out" ordered by Prime Minister Indira Gandhi, had brought the workforce to its knees. The lockout was implemented by Air Marshal P.C Lal, retired Chief of Air Staff, IA's then Chairman and Managing Director. Not only was there a hiring freeze in effect, those pilots who were selected immediately prior the lock-out were also benched.

The second option was to pay for the additional experience to obtain an Assistant Flight Instructor's Rating (AFIR). That meant spending more money and not earning any. Assistant flights instructors flew for gratis just to pile up flying experience. My mother was in no position to spend more money on my flying training. Thus, option two was also closed.

Option three had a catch of its own. While a college degree was not required for a pilot, all other jobs, reasonably asked for a graduate degree. Most of us aspiring pilots were not graduates. I was compelled to toy with the fanciful idea of completing my B.Sc. by finally sitting for the two Advanced Math final year papers that I had dropped. I could not however ignore my total lack of mathematical ability or interest in the subject.

The bottom line was that although I spent three rousingly happy years at St Stephens, I was not a graduate. I was a "drop-out" and was not ashamed —later in life I got to know about many successful "drop-out" billionaires. To name a few; Michael Dell, Steve Jobs, Mark Zuckerberg and Bill Gates! I was in great company!

So, I joined the ranks of the unemployed pilots.

I chose to stay in New Delhi, instead of returning to Rampur. My monthly allowance of ₹100 stretched fairly well, mainly because I was hosted by family and friends. Living was cheap, and credit was easy. Being a pilot – albeit an unemployed one— lent and undeniable patina to my personality!

Life was still good!

Initially, I stayed with my elder sister Jyoti and her husband Maj. Satish Malhotra, in their house at the Defense Services Officers Enclave in Dhaula Kuan, (DK1). The DSOI Club was located here too.

There I became a part of the DK gang of "dependent" girls and boys. We played hard, partied harder, and loved and lost our hearts. In our defense, we would have probably worked hard too, had an employment avenue been open to us!

Every morning I was picked up by one of my fellow pilots and we went to Safdarjung Airport to see aircraft land, listen to rumors about potential work, clown around and try to steal a joy ride. Our favorite haunt was Lala's restaurant at the airport.

Subir, more practical than I, started preparing for the Civil Services Exam with Rau's Study Circle. He was selected for the Indian Police Service, IPS in the 1975 batch, but unsurprisingly, it disappointed him enough to reappear for the exam next year. He sailed through with better ranking and joined the Indian Administrative Service, IAS in 1976.

While training for the Civil Services, he met the lovely and talented Jija Madhavan, who he had the good sense to marry later.

The year I entered the job market was marked with high inflation. Despite the government's best efforts as claimed by Finance Minister, Y B Chavan, in his Union Budget speech of 1974, prices and unemployment continued to rise. Pilots like me, were utterly frustrated. There were just no flying jobs on the horizon and little alternate employment options.

It was an era when leftist ideas ran strong in the country and unions and associations were seen as the only means to get one's demands accepted by Government. One day in late 1974 I decided that I had had enough, and proposed to my fellow unemployed friends that we form an association to bring our plight to the attention of the Government. Thus, the Unemployed Pilot's Association, UCPA, was born.

We knew nothing about registering a union or any modalities thereof, so we just declared ourselves a union. We gathered small donations of ₹10, 15 and 20 from the members which we used to print letterheads. The letterhead proudly said:

unemployed commercial pilots association,

office: the airport restaurant,

safdarjung airport. new Delhi.

Unfazed, with the letterheads ready, we started shooting off letters to everyone, from the Prime Minister to the President. Our main argument was that while the Government had subsidized flying to encourage aviation, many young people had trained to be pilots, but the government was doing nothing to generate jobs. Fortunately for us, Rajiv Gandhi, the Prime Minister's elder son, was a pilot with Indian Airlines and through his good offices, selected pilot batches, on hold since the 'lock out', were inducted by IA. This move reduced the pressure on the UCPA, but only marginally, as the number of unemployed pilots kept increasing in the association. We had reached a desperate situation.

Merely writing letters to the government seeking jobs for pilots was getting us nowhere. We had no '*locus standi*' with any of the aviation bodies, we were completely ignored. Like we didn't exist.

An emergency meeting of the union was called and we voted for 'direct action.' Direct action meant hunger strikes, and '*Dharnas*' (a sit in) to bring our plight to the attention of the public and the government.

We gathered at the strategic Sardar Patel Bhavan roundabout, just outside the Ministry of Civil Aviation and Communications and the Airlines House, the IA Headquarters. We had planned to lobby with members of Parliament and make the rounds of ministers' bungalows.

It was a different world in the 1970s and, unlike today, access to Union Ministers was easier. Security personnel were scarce. All each Minister had was a personal bodyguard,'The Shadow' who accompanied the minister wherever he went. They were friendly, non-aggressive, and even helpful at times.

Slowly, the Press started reporting about our action and finally, the Minister of Civil Aviation, Mr. Raj Bahadur granted us an audience one day. We had a 'white paper' listing problems and solutions ready for discussion.

Our main demand was that we needed alternate employment till pilot posts opened up. Job opportunities were available in various departments under the Ministry but since most pilots were not graduates, they were not eligible even to apply. We explained how much study and time obtaining a CPL entailed and requested that the Government should deem the CPL as being equivalent to a graduate degree, at least for all civil aviation jobs.

Our other demand was that all hiring at Indian Airlines be done on the basis of merit, instead of unfair nepotism. We also requested for pre-employment written tests, group discussions, followed by a personal interview.

The Minister listened attentively, was sympathetic and promised to look into our demands and suggestions. He requested we call off our agitation in good faith.

This we did.

True to his word, the Ministry came out with a notification stipulating that the CPL will also be the minimum qualification for all Civil Aviation jobs under the purview of the Ministry of Civil Aviation and Departments.

This covered the DGCA, Air India, Indian Airlines and International Airport Authority, then responsible only for the Land side activity for Delhi, Bombay, Calcutta, and Madras International Airports.

Rapidly, pilots started getting recruited in DGCA as Air Traffic Controllers, and in the Flight Safety departments of Air India and Indian Airlines, and in ground jobs as well.

UCPA was given the first right of refusal for the contract porter baggage service at the International Airports and City to Airport bus link. Lacking the financial resources, we had no objection to ex-servicemen operating the bus link. Only two pilots took up the porter service contract in Calcutta as partners. The trade union bug had bitten me!

Meanwhile, my living arrangements were in for an upheaval. My brother-in-law was posted out of Delhi. I moved in with Subir, living out of two small rooms over a garage in Vasant Vihar, New Delhi.

Tarun Manilal came back into my life again when I met him at Modern Bazar which had started in the basement of a flat in 'C' block Vasant Vihar. Tarun had started flying same time as me and then pushed off to the US to complete his flying and now had joined the ranks of 'Unemployed' pilots. He came from a family involved in aviation: Tarun's father, Capt. Lalit Manilal, had retired from the Indian Airlines in the early 1960s and after spending many years with Esso Aviation Services, took up the Cessna agency for India. His mother Leela, was a journalist with the Hindustan Times of which George Verghese was the Editor.

Leela Manilal gave me the opportunity to write freelance for Hindustan Times, and my first in-depth, full page article was on what the future of aviation should be, titled "Empty Blue Skies". Establishing the premise that aviation was of paramount importance for the mobility of the economy, I proposed that essential for the country's growth was the denationalization of aviation, permitting private airlines to operate, introduction of air taxi operators and charter operators. In short total deregulation of government controlled Civil Aviation.

Unfortunately, my thinking was way before its time, and my article was probably dismissed as pipe dreams! However, twenty years later, Air Taxi operations became a reality in 1992, and the Air Corporations Act was repealed in 1994, permitting air operations by private airlines.

But the upside of the article was that the Hindustan Times had paid me a princely sum of ₹600 for my effort! I now moved to Defense Colony and was now living as a PG (Paying Guest). After clearing the IAS exam and interview, Subir got a suitable rank and pushed off to the IAS academy in Mussoorie.

Through Tarun I met his fiancé, Anumeha Rai, daughter of Indra and Shauket Rai. Her cousin, Lakshman Rai, Tipu, was a Dosco (alumni of the Doon School) working in the captive Power Generation business with his father, Ranjit Rai. Those were days of massive power shortages and their Company, Rai & Sons, supplied and maintained large industrial diesel generators.

Tipu and I became good friends. I was fond of his father Ranjit Rai, (Shakuat Rai's brother) whom I called Roger, his mother Amma and her brother, Ajay Malik, known as Charlie to the world. Tipu and Charlie were not only family but later became business partners, also dealing in large diesel generator sets. One of the companies they represented was Skoda.

We were tight, close knit friends at about the time Tarun and Anu got married. Tipu and his family invited me to move into their huge house at 3, Prithvi Raj Road in Lutyen's Delhi. By then, I was spending most of my time with them anyway. Roger was a true foodie and a great cook. Amma loved playing cards. She taught me how to play Flush (Teen Patti) and Rummy (with its variations Papplu and Tapplu).

Charlie used to take a cricket team aptly named "Malik's Eleven" to the Lawrence School, Sanawar, where his children studied. Tipu and I were a part of this team. Those trips are a cherished memory, replete with matches won and lost and the warm hospitality extended by the then headmaster, Shomi Das.

On one of my multiple visits to Charlie and Tipu I met their chartered accountant of firm Sharp&Tannon. He mentioned that he was handling the account of a new airline. I was very intrigued. The airline, Huns Air was a non- scheduled airline. It was promoted by industrialist, Suresh Kilachand, son of Tulsidas Kilachand. They were also the makers of Fiat cars, sugar, distilled alcohol, synthetic rubber and chemicals. Charlie's dear friend, the chartered accountant, offered to speak to Mr. Kilachand for me. And boy, did he come through. I met Suresh Kilachand shortly after for a brief meeting and landed the job as a trainee pilot at ₹600 a month.

Huns Air had purchased a Vickers Viscount from Indian Airlines, which was phasing them out to be replaced by the new Boeing 737s. Huns had obtained a Non-Scheduled Operators Permit and was contracted to do Air India sub charters to Sharjah in the UAE. A second Viscount was expected later in the year.

On the Sharjah run, Huns flew fresh meat charters each morning from Mumbai, a five-hour flight on the Viscount.

It was a financially viable contract. Each flight carried 5 tons of fresh meat at ₹8/kg and the return flight brought back 40 deportees at ₹1000 each. The outbound leg met the operating cost and the return was net profit. Doing 3 flights a week was lucrative business.

Till the second aircraft was acquired, I was to work in the Delhi office and also pass the DGCA Technical Exam on the Viscount. Only after that, would I be taken up for conversion training.

And so, I started my first real job in Aviation in early 1976.

This job laid the foundation for my future career and provided me with invaluable experience and knowledge of all aspects of an Airline's operation, except flying.

I never did get a chance to go to Bombay for flying training because I was soon running the Delhi office, under supervision of a Director. I reported to RS Bahadur and Mr. PJ Lalwani, both retired directors of Indian Airlines, hired for the influence they could wield in smoothening the relations between Huns Air and Indian Airlines, on whom Huns was totally dependent for its existence.

My job entailed three roles. I was wearing three different hats at any given time, depending on who I was meeting and what I was getting done that day. The three roles were Operations Manager, Engineering Manager and Commercial Manager.

With the Indian Airlines, I had to coordinate with various departments – Engineering, Stores, Finance and Operations. The Director Operations at that time was Captain A.M. Kapur, Capt. Kapur or just *Cap* to a few.

He was a veteran pilot of Indian National Airways and a legend. *Cap* later became the combined Chairman of Indian Airlines, Air India and International Airports Authority – the only person in Indian Aviation to hold all three senior positions concurrently and competently.

I would coordinate with him for pilot recurrent training and the loan of Instructor/Examiners to carry out bi-annual route checks, and to do odd flights when one of our Captains was unavailable. With time, he grew quite fond of me and referred to me as "*Badmaash*'. This was fortuitously a nickname bestowed with affection, as *Cap* was later instrumental in giving me the chance to work for Indian Airlines later.

My role included meeting Directors of Engineering, Stores, Production Planning and Control for scheduling component removal and overhauls, procuring consumable spares and shipping them to and from Bombay as AOG, Cargo. I also quickly learnt that nothing moved without the approval of the Director of Finance! With Air India I worked with the office of Manager, Northern India for sub charter authorization and planning. This multi-headed on the job training held me in good stead in later years.

With the DGCA, my duties were slightly different, but crucial. I dealt with the Director, Aeronautical Inspection for Dart Engine life development and extension of component life, and the Director of Transport, who authorized all non-scheduled flights and overflight permissions. Non Scheduled International Flights required overflight authorization from Civil Aviation Authorities of all countries whose territory they would fly over, under The First of the Five Freedoms of the Air Governing International Aviation.

This clearance was issued vide a YA number, once the file was cleared by the Director The YA number was transmitted via a AFTN network to all FIRs (Flight Information Regions) and the respective Civil Aviation Authorities. YA was the code for Aviation authority followed by 2 letters identifying the authority. This number was entered in the remarks column of the Flight plan filed with Air Traffic Control before Departure. No YA number, No flight. The YA clearance is now no longer required.

During my days at the Patiala Aviation Club, the ADC number was the prize, and now it was the YA number. But obtaining this wondrous number was only half the battle unless it was transmitted, to be called a job well done.

Being officially employed gave me the tenuous stability I was looking for. I rented my own '*barsati*' in Defence Colony, and more importantly hired my Man Friday, Xavier. My biggest joy however, was being able to afford a second-hand two door Triumph Herald!

Suresh Kilachand or Sethji as he was called, had a two-acre farm in Village Bijwasan on the Najafgarh road called Huns Farms, right next to the very opulent Oberoi Farms. It had a rather nice three-bed room country home with a pool and a cute outhouse consisting of a one-bedroom cottage.

Once Sethji got to know of my family's 'farming' background, he asked me to move into the cottage and also help with the farm's upkeep. His plan was to start using the farm for weekend entertainment – which meant scotch, cards and dinner. I took him up on the offer and moved into the farm with my man Friday

The garden soon had plants, flowers and vegetables. The pool was cleaned regularly and the main house maintained in a livable condition.

And before I knew it, Huns farms became the Saturday night haunt of the Who's Who of Aviation. Every dignitary from the Ministry to DGCA to Air India and Indian Airlines visited. We had all the bright stars gathered on the lawns of Huns Farms..

Sethji was a shrewd businessman. He had learnt that to survive   in aviation he needed good Public Relations. One way of doing it   was wining and dining officials, who could later be approached for a "favorable consideration" and speedy disposal of his polite requests.

Sethji was the perfect host. Scotch was rare in those days, just as good wines, cigars, cognacs and cheese were. We at Huns were able to keep a good supply of duty free stuff – all sourced on the return 'deportee' flights from Sharjah. We added another dimension of inducement –that of a cards session of 'teen patti' or Flush with moderate stakes.

Sethji would never play. There was a simple house rule. The host never won at cards. Thus, I was designated to play cards using Sethji's money to lose. This was an excellent business investment. Huns airlines stayed in the good books of all who mattered.

Here, allow me to let you in on a quirky secret. The winner at a private card game carries a sort of 'winner's guilt'. This is useful to ask them for favors! I used this knowledge carefully, but well. All that 'winner's guilt' led to royal treatment when I visited their offices. As a Stephenian, I was already considered 'upper crust', so I was able to bypass the lower level of bureaucracy to have one-on-one meetings with the senior officers and Directors, with whom I had lost at 'cards' the previous weekend. I was smart enough to know that my work was appreciated. But it had nothing to do with me being a pilot. I wasn't flying at all. Because I was doing so well in New Delhi, they kept delaying my transfer to Bombay.

Without a doubt, my training and exposure at Huns laid the foundation of my future career in Airline Management. I learnt about an airline holistically, gaining comprehensive understanding of all departments crucial for the overall success of an airline – namely, Operations, Commercial, Engineering, Regulatory and Public Relations issues.

Rather unexpectedly, and soon, Sethji started having issues with clearing his Indian Airline dues. His cheques would bounce. The airline stopped accepting cheques from him.

The Director of Finance instructed Indian Airlines to demand payment in advance by bank drafts. No business was to happen until an advance payment was made. This needed quick resolution.

In working with so many departments, I had made friends across the spectrum. R. Prasad, the IA regional finance manager, was one of them. He offered a very simple solution. "There is a restriction of cheques signed by Suresh Kilachand, not Shakti Lumba." His solution worked.

An account in my name was promptly opened in a bank at Golf Links. Sethji would deposit cash into my account on a Friday and I would issue the cheques on Monday. These cheques would be honored. This worked out very well for all of us.

My credibility with Indian Airlines was solid by this time. In fact, IA accepted me as a guarantor for a Dart engine that Huns took on lease. This engine was never returned since the airline closed down.

It became R. Prasad's favorite riposte to me years later when he was CMD and I was giving him a hard time from the ICPA.

With operations running relatively smoothly, Huns wanted to expand. Indian Airlines had two serviceable Viscounts in Kolkata flying the Kolkata-Rangoon-Port Blair route.

The Port Blair runway Load Classification Number (LCN) was lower than that stipulated for the Boeing 737. Boeing had a 737 version with low pressure tyres to cater for low LCN runways. These were wider balloon type tires that spread the load out over a larger area and were ideal for Port Blair. They also burnt more fuel due to increased drag since after retracted the wheel jutted out below the aircraft belly.

There was clearly an opportunity here. A few rousing weekend parties later, IA was persuaded to go for the LP tyre version of the B737. Huns got to buy the two Viscounts at book value.

I was on a roll at work. I had travelled miles from my unemployment days, and worked my way up gradually. I had developed what I thought was well earned self-confidence, but which was frequently blurring into arrogant brashness.

One regular work day in late 1977, I walked into my office to find a very pretty girl sitting at my desk. "My name is Ila Jugran" she said looking at the question mark on my face "I have been asked to work here." She was smiling.

"You are more than welcome to work here, Miss. But the first thing you need to work on is moving your ass out of my chair and find a place to sit, which isn't here."

I had served the worst possible concoction of arrogance, brashness and topped it with the cherry of being an insufferable prick. All of it in just one sentence. Her smile was gone and so was she.

I eventually got to know that, Ila had recently moved back from the USA. Her father had been in the Foreign Service and had served as the Consul General in West Africa. He had unfortunately died of a heart attack. Her mother, Manju Jugran, was the niece of the then Minister of Chemicals and Fertilisers, H. N. Bahuguna. He was a prominent and popular politician. Since a lot of Kilachand's empire was in chemicals, Ila had ended up with a job in one of their companies, Huns Agencies.

I took little notice of Ila in the early days even while working in the same office. I have a feeling she did not care either. After the brilliant first impression, it couldn't have been much else.

One day a good friend of mine, Raza Bilgrami, was visiting me at work. He started an unusual conversation.

"There is a drop dead gorgeous chick working in your office and yet you find the time to chase skirts around town. What a waste of effort."

"Who?" I asked, "aaaHer." He was pointing right at Ila.

"Come off it, man." I commented and ignored him and the pretty girl… again! For the time being, at least.

Raza's statements had made me introspect a little! I recognized I was too brash. I had not only been rude to Ila, but had also brushed off her impact on me! She was indeed gorgeous and I was an idiot. The situation needed to be rectified. I started by being nice. She was angry and cold. I did not blame her. She had every right to be standoffish. It took a while, but we began to warm up to each other. We got to talking and had long conversations. There was a connection like you have with old friends. Both of us felt it. It was either my charm or the blazing effect of my dimples, that the lovely Ila was as attracted to me as I was to her.

I would get to office early just to spend more time with her. She was there early, too. We would talk and catch up about our lives before the madness of work began. It was a glorious morning routine.

One morning, early as usual, I was waiting on the terrace for her to reach office. I saw her walking looking up at me and then "Wham" – she walked straight into a tree. I was both concerned and amused. This incident was an 'A-ha' moment for me.

Later that day, when we were alone in office, I walked up to her and 'smooched' her on her lips and said. "I stake my claim,", and walked away, leaving her flustered and speechless. I was just being me!

In the first week of April 1978, Ila's Uncle Vijay Bahuguna and his sister Rita Bahuguna casually dropped in, ostensibly to say "hello" to their niece. But their real objective was obvious. They were here to check me out!

They must have approved, and reported back to the matriarch of their family. Being influential politicians, the Bahuguna family did a reference background check on my family in Rampur. Within two days, I was invited for lunch to 5, Sunheri Bagh Road, the Minister's official residence.

Mrs Kamala Bahuguna did not even wait for the dessert. "What are your intentions with Ila, our niece? We don't believe in this dating and courtship business", she sternly announced.

Taken aback, I managed to reply that my intentions were pure and honorable. Which meant marriage of course, but I said I was not even settled and I needed to get a proper job before considering it.

"That's all rubbish," was the retort. " When I married Bahuguna ji, he barely had ₹2 in his pocket. He also didn't have a job so all this talk of getting settled is rubbish. Call your mother to Delhi. We wish to discuss further with her". An order was delivered.

I now had to call home and explain the situation. My sisters and mother were thrilled. My mother had been after me for a long time to get married. She had said in as many words that she would be more than happy with anyone I got home as her daughter-in-law.

Ila, who was "Guddi" to her family, was a Garhwali Brahmin. Her parents were from Pauri Garhwal. My mother had no regrets or reservation at my choice of bride. She considered Guddi as a Lakshmi, proudly announcing to everyone *"Lakshmi Ghar ayegi mere bete ki Kismat khul jayegi."*(When Lakshmi comes into our family she will bring good fortune to my son)

My family met Ila's mother and the Bahuguna family within a week of the momentous lunch. On 17th April 1978. We were engaged and married a little more than a month later on 22 May 1978. A day before I turned 28. The universe was rooting for me!

My personal life was in prime shape, but my professional life looked up magnificently. A week before we were married, Indian Airlines finally advertised for pilot vacancies after 6 years and stipulated that selection would be merit based and also based on pre-employment written tests covering aviation subjects, psychometrics, and group discussions and followed by a personal interview.

Civil Aviation Minister Raj Bahadur had delivered again.

There was a mad scramble to renew expired license, which required two 30-minute flight tests, one by day and one by night. In North India there was only one night flying serviceable Pushpak, in Karnal, and a very large number of licenses needed to be renewed.

The UCPA stepped in: all of the ATC officers at Safdarjung Airport were old friends who had been helped by the UCPA. They too were also keen to renew their licenses.

Capt. Cheema was the instructor in charge of Karnal Flying club. He flew the Pushpak in to Delhi. A list of expired licenses was made, money collected and the Pushpak flew day and night, only landing every half hour to "show" pilot change or to refuel.

What the Pushpak was doing was giving joy rides, and god bless them, the ATC was religiously showing these joyrides as flying tests as per the list given to them. Check forms were being filled and counter signed. In a few days, all expired licenses were sent to DGCA for renewal.

Subir was in Mussoorie, but his flying tests were done and his license renewed since his medical was valid.

As far as I know, this perhaps was the only case in aviation of mass fudging done anywhere in the world; that too with the tacit knowledge of the authorities. Aviation had just got a boost and no one, even the DGCA, was willing to play spoilsport and deny pilots at least an opportunity after years of agonizing wait.

Having gotten my license renewed, I bought IQ books and dug out my aviation notes in order to prepare for the Indian Airlines pre-employment tests, while on my honeymoon with Guddi in Garhwal.

After we got back, we took up a one bedroom set at E3/3 Vasant Vihar, bang opposite E1/18 where Subir used to live.

Elsewhere, at Huns, Sushila Sukumaran, Suresh Kilachand's companion, who oversaw Huns Agencies, had started giving Guddi a hard time. Why this change had come about, was a mystery. I would find Guddi in tears sometimes when I returned to office after a day out on the field. We decided we had had enough. We submitted a joint resignation and walked out.

Shortly after that, IA pilot entrance test was held at the Union Public Service Commission. The airline had 50 vacancies and nearly 2,000 pilots appeared for the test. Only 150 had passed.

I was one of them. The next hurdle was the interview in July.

Subir had come down from Mussourie for moral support. His own application – 'through the proper channel' – was rejected by the Academy Director, who was unable to comprehend how anyone could consider leaving the IAS for something as frivolous as flying. If anyone was born to fly and loved aviation it was Subir, but fate had other plans for him.

On the day of the interview, I woke up with a fever. My interview slot was for 3pm. I decided to go to Airlines House in the morning to get a revised interview date. Subir and Guddi accompanied me to Airlines House. On the way we crossed not one but two elephants, a sign of good luck.

The Flight Manager, Ram Bhavnani, was a friend. I requested him for an interview change, citing my fever. He suggested I send in a note to *Cap* explaining the situation. *Cap* decided to call me in immediately! I walked into the Board Room and to my surprise almost every person in the room was either familiar, or someone I had dealt with almost on a regular basis and on weekends at Huns Farm.

Except for two gentlemen — Air Marshal Bhalla who was then the ACS Ops at Air Headquarters. His son Gopal later joined Indian Airlines and we became good friends. The other was the Indian Airlines Director of Training, Capt. Napoleon Pereira, who, everyone called *Nap*. So did I, something I was going to regret in the days to come.

Except for *Cap*, everyone was surprised to see me. They had no idea that I was a pilot; for them I had worn different hats. *Cap* broke the ice and asked for chai- samosa and a Disprin for me. Over chai, we chatted. I used to smoke a pipe and with *Cap's* permission, I lit up. *Nap* was all daggers, but I was among friends.

By the time we were done with tea, *Cap* stated, "Guys, we have all worked with this *Badmaash* for over two years and know more about him and his abilities that any interview could establish. I have no questions." Nor did Gopal Kapoor of Air India or V.N. Kapoor from DGCA. Three Kapoor's in the same interview board was like divine intervention.

Air Marshal Bhalla quizzed me about my family background and a little about what I had done since I got my license. He was impressed that I had flown the Tiger Moth, an aircraft he never got to fly. Only *Nap* tried to play hard ball, but the board stopped him short.

After the Indian Airlines interview, I got an interview call from Royal Nepal Airlines, RNAC. A Capt. Bobby Rana interviewed me. My having studied in St Joseph's College, Nainital, SEM, was enough qualification for landing the job. Apparently, several of Bobby Rana's cousins had studied at the same school.

Even though I cleared the interview and made the select 50 list, Indian Airlines decided to induct the selectees in three batches.

This is when the pull-push pressure came in and I got to know from Ram Bhavnani that my name had been removed from the first batch to accommodate Jay Prakash Narayan's recommendations from Bihar.

I was now placed in the second batch. The first batch was slated to report for training but there was no news of the second batch. Many trips later, Ram informed me that the list was bring controlled by the MD's office and I had slipped to the third batch.

Guddi and I dropped by to meet her mother and told her what had happened. Both of us were decidedly upset about the shenanigans unfolding. My mother in law promptly told Guddi's cousin, Vijay Bahuguna, and he his father. Minister Bahuguna was now Mamaji.

He called me and showered his amazing words in true Indian soap opera style: "*Ullu ke patthe, poori duniya ka kaam karta hoon aur apne jamai ka nahi kar sakta? Apne aap ko kya samajhta hai, itna ghamand hai?*" (I do so much for the whole world and you're too proud to ask me for help?")

I explained that I did not think of it this way. I had genuinely felt things were working out in my favor, in the normal course.

He asked his PA to connect him to the office of Morarji Desai, then Prime Minister of India. He spoke to the PM's PS, V. Shankar, a senior IAS officer who had earlier served as IA General Manager.

The situation was explained as to how pressures were affecting his son in law's future. V. Shankar immediately got cracking

By the time we reached home, an Indian Airlines car was parked outside with a letter of appointment as Apprentice pilot on a stipend of ₹700 per month. I was to report for training on 4th Dec 1978.

In the 1970s, (and perhaps even today) India was a different beast. The bureaucracy was so vast and strong, that without such influence, one would just not get anywhere.

As luck would have it, couple of days later, a letter of appointment arrived from RNAC as co-pilot on a salary of Nepalese Rupees 3500 with a reporting date of 30th Nov 1978.

I was now in a quandary — which job should I accept, IA or RNAC? I had had no flying job for six years and now had two job offers. Guddi was bringing me the luck of Lakshmi that my mother had predicted.

I sought counsel from Manu (Capt. D.P. Singh) and a distant relative, Capt. Kamni Chadha who was a Dy. Operations Manager in Indian Airlines at CTE (Central Training Establishment), Hyderabad. Both advised me to take the IA offer since it was a career.

My decision was made.

All of us selected for training from North India were booked by train, leaving New Delhi railway station at 7am on the 3rd of December.

Guddi and I did the rounds, visiting friends and relatives to say my good byes. All of them promised to be at the station to wish me farewell.

The night before, we set the alarm for 5 a.m. It did not go off. I got up in a panic at 6 a.m. and rushed to the station, just in time to see the train pull out. All those who had come to see me off, gaped at me, incredulous. I had missed the train to the flying job that I had always wanted. Irony was laughing out loud. Guddi, however had a sneaky suspicion I did it on purpose as I hated train travel.

Early that winter morning, we passed the hat around to collect the ₹400 airfare. Next morning, I flew to Hyderabad on the Indian Airlines Caravelle.

My first journey on a jet aircraft and the beginning of a life-long love affair.

5. THE AIRLINE PILOT

"If you don't think you're the best pilot in the business,
maybe you're in the wrong business. If you think you could never
make a mistake, you are really in the wrong business."
– Randy Sohn

No one is fond of sticky situations in life and the same is true of me. But it didn't take long for me to become the marked man.

After landing in Hyderabad, I reported to the Old Central Training Establishment (CTE), located on the city side of Begumpet airport. The Old CTE was in the Ronald Ross building which housed the Trainee Pilot Hostel, poor cousin of the elite Pilot Hostel in the new CTE, with its fancy air-conditioned rooms, modern kitchen, dining hall and obliging waiters to fetch and carry.

We were the 23rd course of apprentice pilots, and shared the hostel with the 22nd course, in twin sharing rooms. It was a grand reunion of old friends and colleagues, separated by the fortunes of the selection process.

However, my jubilation was short lived. A jolt of some magnitude awaited me. I walked up to the room allotment list posted outside the dining hall. This list differed from the one that the Director of Training, yes, the very same *Nap* Pereira, held in his hand. His list did not have one name. You guessed right; it was Shakti Lumba. To my acute embarrassment, the man missing from the rooming list had also reported for training, as instructed by the Director. The hapless fellow, who I had knocked off the rolls, had been working as an Air India steward and was close to Nap's daughter!

I was now a marked man. Our classes were to be held in the new CTE which was on the Air Force side of the airport across the runway in Ferozguda. We all hired bicycles so cycled across the runway, my ubiquitous pipe in my mouth every day.

Our batch consisted of real 'characters'. My roommate was Sanjay Khot (Khattia), a Bombay boy, who drove a yellow & black cab when unemployed. There was I.M. Hussain, a tailor and master cutter, who enjoyed introducing himself with, "I Am I.M. Hussain". There was G.S. Ganesan (Gunns), aerodrome officer from the Airport Authority Fire Fighting and Safety Services; Murli Bhat (Burly Mutt), blue eyed boy of Tata Aviation, Jamshedpur; Sanjay Sen (Shanghai), the crop duster; 'Gusty' Nariman (Gus), the mad Parsi; Mervin Sequeira, (Merv) aka Pope Pius; Deepak Edwards (Dum Dum); Masterji, Subodh Sinha (BL); Rajiv Arora (Lauda), Rastogi (Rusty), Mehboob Bhat (Boobs), and last but not least Shamsundar, who was sadly lost to us during training. He was supernumerary with his brother-in-law, Capt. Golikeri, on a flight that crashed, killing all on board... a double tragedy for the family.

We had to make our own mess arrangements. To avoid extra effort, we quickly joined the 22nd batch, which already had a system of pooling for food, and had hired a cook and helper. Most days, however, we ate at the airport restaurant on the first floor of the airport terminal, which had a good view of the whole runway.

I owned a copy of Richard Bach's Jonathan Livingston Seagull that Sanjay Sen decided he simply had to have. I drove a hard bargain and traded it for a complete set of Air Force sectional maps (restricted) covering all of India and neighboring countries. It was a veritable goldmine. I can never forget the look on Sanjay Sen's face just days later, when we passed the airport book shop and saw, prominently displayed in the window: Jonathan Livingstone Seagull. I promptly bought it.

On our first day at CTE, we assembled in the navigation classroom to meet the faculty. They trooped in, and after the usual welcomes, work hard advice and other homilies, we were asked to introduce ourselves. Upon hearing my name, *Nap* pointed towards me and snapped, "You go to my office, right now"! The entire batch and faculty were stunned into hushed silence and I felt like I had been punched in the solar plexus.

With an eerie sense of having been teleported back to school, I waited outside his office. *Nap* arrived shortly and barked at me: "I remember you from the interview. Who the fuck do you think you are by calling everyone by their first name? You will call me 'Sir'. You may call me a bastard but you will prefix that with a 'Sir'."

He wasn't done. He pointed to a line of contrasting tiles on the floor, comparing it to the proverbial line of discipline, "You cross that line and I will sack you. I don't like smart asses, I don't like smart alecks and frankly, I don't like you."

Chastened and red-eared, I came out and bumped into Capt. Kamni Chadha. I narrated the incident to him and he calmed me down and said in Punjabi. "*Chhadd de, who paji hai. Do din liye aayahai, udde baad to mainu hi centre chalana hai*" (Forget it, he's an ass. He has come for two days, after that I only will have to run the Centre"). It was a mighty consolation!

Pilot Training was serious and hard work. It included 6-8 weeks of general aviation studies that covered navigation, plotting, flight planning, maps, en-route and approach charts (Jeppesen) radio aids, weather, air regulation. A minimum score of 70% was required to pass every module.

Then, there was a rigorous six week course on aircraft technical and performance studies, covering every aspect of the aircraft, followed by two DGCA exams, failure in any of which meant being scrubbed from training. Only after successful completion of ground school would the actual flying training start.

For the second part of the training, we had to decide upon the aircraft we wanted to be type rated on, and this was to be done on the very first day. There were two choices: the Hawker Siddeley HS 748, "Avro", manufactured by Hindustan Aeronautics Limited (HAL) under license, and the Dutch made Fokker Friendship F27. The Avro's were operating out from bases like Mumbai, Chennai, Hyderabad and Delhi while the FokkerFriendship F27 flew out of Calcutta only.

One day, midway through our course, we were at the airport restaurant, idly watching Boeing departures, when we saw the Hyderabad Delhi flight take off. The take-off did not seem right and before our horrified eyes, the aircraft came down and crashed at the end of the runway. In command was Capt. Joseph, an old timer and RD of Southern Region. We ran …Murli, Sanjay Sen, Khot, Gunns and I.

Frozen in panic, the safety services stood confounded, unable to even fix the hoses to the trucks. Gunns was the hero of the hour, taking over the firefighting as he had been trained to do in his previous professional avatar. Luckily, there were no fatalities, only some injuries, some heavily bruised egos and one burnt airplane.

Before our technical ground classes were to start, we were all assembled and told that a problem had presented itself. Everyone had opted for the Avro, and at least four were required for the Fokker. There was silence. Indian Airlines then asked for four volunteers. More silence. I had a brainwave and cheerfully suggested that we have a lucky draw of names. Chits and a box appeared, and Capt. Chadha did the honors.

Reaching in, he pulled out the first chit, opened it… and called out my name! I was too dumbstruck to hear him thereafter! The other three names were Deepak Edwards, Subodh Sinha and Murli Bhat. Subodh and Murli didn't mind but Deepak and I were devastated. Deepak turned to me with a reproachful "LUCKY draw, you said? Thanks a lot, pal"!

However, what seemed to be a punishment posting soon turned out to be the envy of our batch. The four of us went on regular hangar visits to Calcutta to familiarize ourselves with the Fokker, and for this we got an additional ₹75 as dearness allowance. Every other week wecame back to regale the other trainees of our batch with tales of Park Street, Blue Fox, Flury, Nizam's Kathi, Chowringee, New Market, Free School Street and the good life that Calcutta generally had to offer.

I managed to stay ahead of the pack during our training, by buckling down and concentrating on work. After all, we were told that the performance in the CTE would determine our seniority. For a pilot, seniority is everything.

Three S's govern a pilot's life: Seniority, Salary and Sex. In that order. Seniority determines where you are posted, it determines when you will be upgraded, the aircraft you fly and your pay and allowances. Seniority, therefore, is therefore, the Holy Grail.

Soon we were sent to Delhi for our flying training which entailed twenty hours of actual airplane training. 10 hours by Day and 10hrs by night. A Fokker flight, IC-412, would fly into Delhi from Calcutta at about 1300 hrs (1 pm) every day and leave the next morning.

The Fokker did not have a simulator and the company had to pay for the fuel for the flying hours. The instructors were stingy with the amount of time we could fly, and were far more demanding. But the flip side for us was that they could not make our life the living hell that was the norm with the Avro simulator that the rest of our fellow trainees worked on.

Since seniority would be determined on the basis of our performance in the CTE, Indian Airlines was soon faced with a conundrum. There were two different kinds of aircraft, one had a simulator and one did not. The playing field was not level, so how could they compare everyone equally and fairly?

Nap Pereira came up with the diabolical idea of a consolidated exam? It was referred to as the *'The Napssens'*. This exam had aviation general questions, aircraft type specific technical questions, a complete flight plan, a flight plot, interpretation of standard instrument Departure and Arrival procedures for a complete flight between two major airports, including ATC reports on appropriate radio frequencies and so on. In all fairness, it was an exam well designed to test a pilot's total knowledge and understanding of the basics.

This exam carried 80 per cent weightage towards seniority along with the technical and general aviation tests, the remaining 20 per cent being at the discretion of the Director of Training.

Obviously, *Nap* acted on his grudge against me, and gave me a zero. This did little to affect my overall result as all he achieved was to peg me down from the top of the pile to second. In subsequent batches, the discretion of the Director of Training was diluted as airlines were stepping in to the jet age, and seniority was critical as well.

By late 1979, my training was complete and I got my first posting orders to Calcutta. Ila joined me there. Initially, we were a little overwhelmed by the sheer hordes of people in the city, but as we got used to it, we got over our initial demo phobia, and came to realize that Calcutta was a city with character, history, and culture. A city with a true soul. It is a city in which the richest as well as the poorest could survive, indeed, for the princely sum of one rupee, you could get excellent chai and toast on the pavement.

Initially, Ila and I stayed with the parents of an old friend of mine, Deepak Sahai, from my Huns Air days. His parents stayed in an apartment complex on Wood Street, and generously agreed to put us up while I looked for a suitable place. An added advantage of living here was that on one of the upper floors of that apartment complex lived Capt. Robin Williams, the Regional Director of Indian Airlines. Even though I did not interact with him socially, a certain unspoken comradeship developed, as we crossed each other in our similar uniforms… the epaulettes on my shoulder with one and a half stripes while his blazed with four beautiful ones. The question of even striking up a conversation did not arise – his pedestal was too lofty – but a pleasant recognition had been established, which would help me in the not too distant future.

Soon, I started looking for a house in earnest. My salary had now become ₹1,200 per month, and there would be allowances when I flew. Pilots got ₹125 for any flight during lunch time and the same amount if the aircraft landed after 1930 hrs (7:30 pm). We also got ₹50 for tea. These were tax free meal allowances which were given twice a month, and over a period of time they made up about 50 per cent of a pilot's wages. But all this was still not enough to get acceptable accommodation in the elite part of Calcutta.

The only option left to us was Salt Lake City, then known as Bidhan Nagar, an area that was just coming up, and for ₹300 a month, Ila and I found a nice place there. Notwithstanding the good things about Calcutta like its culture and its soul, the city was a civic mess. For a young professional, 1979-81 was a terrible time to live and work in that city. With 18-hour power cuts being the norm, living conditions were terrible. The metro was under construction, roads were being dug up and commuting was a long and tedious nightmare.

We had chosen Salt Lake because it was near the airport. The short cut into town was by crossing a bridge over a *nalah* to *Ulta Danga*. You booked a cab for the day, ran all your chores and dovetailed this with social commitments and entertainment. In our case, this meant shopping in New Market, doctor visits (Ila was pregnant!) and a movie.

On 30th of January 1980 we were blessed with Pallavi, my daughter. It was also Subir's birthday. He thanked us for the birthday present.

Winter was fog season in Calcutta, and this naturally delayed all flights. Robin Williams would often sit on the Briefing Desk and tell us stories of the good old DC3 days 'when pilots were pilots.' My pipe-smoking habit, which I thought was a very fitting vice for a pilot, nonetheless was disliked by some, and I faced some bullying.

One fine winter morning, Williams addressed the pilots and to my surprise, said, "I hear some of the Captains are giving "British Airways" a hard time because he smokes a pipe." There was pin drop silence. He pointed to me and said, "Young man, you smoke a pipe anywhere you want to, any time you want to, and if anyone gets on your case for it, he will have to answer to me."

That nodding acquaintance, waiting for the elevator at the Wood Street high rise, had paid off! After that, Williams continued to refer to me as 'British Airways' owing to my thin physique, fair, rosy cheeked look.

I soon realized that pipe smoking was actually a bit bothersome in the cockpit as there was nowhere to place the damn thing. Also, Calcutta had many more pilots from Bihar, and they loved their Paan. To win their favor, we co-pilots would get them paan: it soon became the deciding factor for co-pilots to fly a good sector from the left or right seat. If one ate paan, a right seat sector was assured. But there was one more trump card: *paan* with Baba Zarda 120 (flavored chewing tobacco). If you were a man of such calibre as to be able to eat *paan* with Baba Zarda, the left seat was yours. I was such a man and having got a taste of the left seat, one wanted to occupy it permanently.

A pilot then required a Senior Commercial Pilots License (SCPL) to be the Pilot-In-Command for any aircraft below 21,000 kg and above 5700kg. The pilot's association was quite strong and had laid down a rule that in 3 years 2 months' time, a pilot should be taken up for command as long as he attained the requisite qualification. If not, then the person would get the captain's scale of pay and would upgrade to 3 striped epaulette. A co-pilot with a CPL wore one and a half stripes, on obtaining an SCPL he graduated to two and a half stripes. On becoming a Captain Three stripes. Fifty percent of Captains in the Captains grade were placed in the Commanders grade and wore four stripes.

Meanwhile, miserable in Calcutta, I had requested Captain Kamni

Chadha several times to transfer me to Delhi. He fobbed me off, asking me to get the SCPL first. He assured he would sort things out then. I felt he thought I would not pass the exams for the next three years. To prepare for the SCPL exam, you either did self-study or took tuition. Several navigators, rendered redundant since they had been replaced by superior technology, had become navigation and performance instructors in CTE or posted as Base Flight Managers. These instructors gave tuitions.

In Calcutta, the flight manager was Mr. Easwaran, Eash to all. He held classes on SCPL and ATPL subjects in the evening. Teaching meteorology, navigation, radio aids and other such subjects, except, the technical stuff. The problem was that he charged a stiff ₹300 per subject with a guaranteed pass stipulation. If you didn't pass, he promised to give the money back, but in reality, he would just not charge the person till the candidate cleared the exam. No money changed hands or was returned!

This didn't make sense to me. I got three others from the 23rd batch and we formed a study circle. We would go it on our own. We invested in the famous kerosene 'Vizag Lamps', really bright buggers that burnt for over eight hours on one tank full, as Kolkata's power situation continued to be dismal.

So, there we were, a bunch of earnest hopefuls, sitting around a large dining table, brightly illuminated by the Vizag lamp, earnestly studying from Ground Studies for Pilots – an excellent book on aviation basics. As luck and providence (and hard work) would have it, all four of us in the study circle cleared all the SCPL papers in the first shot. *Eash* had a success rate of only 30 per cent. His ego was hurt and he felt slighted by the cheek of a young co-pilot. I was once again a marked man and I ended up with the most miserable low allowance flights.

After the written tests, there was an oral exam conducted by 'Aviation's Terror', the Director of Air Crew Standards, Mr. B.S. Rao, who had been the navigator on Air India's Kashmir Princess, a Lockheed L-749A Constellation plane that crashed due to a bomb explosion into the South China Sea in 1955. He was the only survivor. Mr. Rao was a highly respected man in aviation. He was also the main examiner for the Shipping Master Certificate.

On the fateful day of interview, although nine of us had qualified, seven did not turn up. Basically, it was known that all the numerical that one had attempted in the written exam were expected to be solved again in front of him. All those who 'cogged' the numerical, just vamoosed, fearing Rao's wrath.

I went in and Mr. Rao, noting that I had passed all papers in the first attempt, asked, "Who did you study with?"

I replied, "I studied on my own."

He gave me a sharp look, and started asking me questions on navigation. I told him that the books I studied with, did not cover certain parts of navigation called "Meridional" parts, where you mathematically calculated your flight tracks. This was used in the World War II era and was not in the syllabus anywhere in the world, apart from India. He then spent the rest of the interview teaching me Meridional navigation. "I like people like you. You are passed," he said, and let me go.

In less than two and half years into my career in Indian Airlines, a rank 'junior' frankly, I had received the SCPL. It was 1981, and Captain Kamni Chadha had become the Operation Manager in the Airline Headquarters. True to his word, he spoke to the Director of Operations and a month later my transfer orders to Delhi were notified. As they could not single out a junior for a lone transfer, everybody senior to me in Calcutta awaiting a transfer were also transferred!

Work from Delhi was now different. In Delhi there was only one flight. All of a sudden, from an average of 50 hours in a month, flying was reduced to 30 hrs a month, as there was only one F27 flight out of Delhi. The flights to J&K had been shifted on to the Avro.

As some of the Fokker pilots were upgraded to Boeings, a few Captain vacancies opened up and all of a sudden it was decided that we were to be taken up for command training. This we completed with relative ease, and I started flying as a Captain. There we were, flying as the captain of an airliner with two and a half stripes on our shoulder. Often the co-pilot beside us had four stripes. These pilots were in the Commanders grade but had failed their F27 Command upgrade even after three attempts. They had however been Captains on the DC-3.

The age gradient was also very steep. There was also a financial downside. I was flying as a Captain on Co- pilot pay and allowances, since the Captain's grade was only admissible on completing 3 years and 2 month service. We objected to this financial disparity as being discriminatory. We were flying as captains on co-pilot's scale of pay and on co-pilot allowances. We turned to the Union, and after receiving

several representations, Indian Airlines fixed the aberration and gave us back pay.

A PILOT's WIFE

Fatigue, Stress, Jet lag and pressure are heard oft in a pilot's life

but have you ever thought how apt they were to describe the state of a flier's wife

Every morn, after seeing the bread earner take-off she sighs and starts her everyday chores

housework, homework, tantrums, PTA and much more

for whether it is the daily menu or academics of Pinki and Pappu

bad marks show neglect on Ma's part! Straight A's, my! Aren't Papa's kids smart!!

The transport is at the gate 'sahab aaj nahin aayenge'—

oh shit, what a drag the aircraft must have had another snag.

his favorite roast goes back on the shelf

I'll have to take the dogs to the vet myself

Sorry kids, no movie tonight alone at the wedding, I'll try to look bright

Just when life takes a turn towards a more settled trend

less parties are cancelled, more functions to attend

Just when she starts to feel like an ordinary gal

comes that horrible, unavoidable 10 days posting to Cal

but mother hen that she is, warm and snug, she keeps her nest within her budget, she does her best

for overspending, Papa's lid will flip we need the dollars for the America trip!

funnily enough, this the neighbors do confirm suddenly she is beautiful, radiant, glowing and warm

you can be sure; you don't have to check on the phone

her world is complete; her Captain is home!!

Ila Lumba

Soon the airline withdrew the Delhi-Calcutta Fokker service and now we started going to Calcutta on 'postings'. This was the best time of my career. During 'postings', one spent 10 days at a time twice a month at The Grand Hotel, now called The Oberoi Grand. It was the best address in town. I loved it, but Guddi hated it, and expressed her feelings well in a poem.

The Calcutta-Agartala flight was the most popular flight for the airline ground staff. Before departure, the crew were overwhelmed with requests to bring back pineapples, oranges or the Bengali's favorite fish the 'Hilsa' (Elish Mach) from the Padma river – to be procured from across the airport fence which separated India and Bangladesh. Hilsa in Bangladesh cost a quarter of what it did in Calcutta. The requests were on paper to which was attached the required money. The slips with the money was handed over to the airport manager at Agartala, who arranged the requirements as per the slips. This was precious cargo and took priority over passenger baggage and cargo! Once the aircraft returned to Calcutta, it was mobbed by the staff. Each staff's name was called out and their precious cargo handed over.

On one such flight, I had my first serious flying incident. It was the worst time of year for flying in that area which was February to May. This was peak 'Norwester' *Kalbaisakh* season. Norwester's were vicious and violent thunderstorms caused by the mixing of three air masses: Moist Warm from the Bay, Hot Dry from the Gangetic plains and Cold Dry from the Himalayas. The thunderstorms formed in a hammerhead shape, and in less than 60 minutes, they could go up to 60,000 ft' and moved like hurricanes.

One had to respect these *motherfuckers* and stay as far away from them as possible, for if you wandered into one, the windshear forces could break an airplane. All the Fokker flights were often affected by them as they all flew over Bangladesh, and crossed the Brahmaputra to enter the Assam valley, as this was the connectivity being provided. Afternoon flights were particularly precarious, as the thunderstorms would sweep past Calcutta by four to six in the evening.

On this occasion, we took off from Agartala at about 2 p.m. in the afternoon, I saw this huge thunderstorm developing south west, but way beyond Dhaka. Our flight route was from Agartala to Comilla, overhead Jessore, to Calcutta. Giving the disturbance a wide berth of more than

60-80 miles, I set course from Comilla towards Chittagong, planning to then come around from the Bay into Calcutta. The problem that I did not foresee was that these thunderstorms regenerate over water, and following the path of the river, they move at breath taking speeds. I was halfway on my flight path when all of a sudden it became dark and the Fokker shuddered from a massive jolt. After that initial jolt, the plane became nearly uncontrollable.

Normally on that sector we flew at 12,000 ft' but in this instance, we kept getting thrashed by the windshear, causing up and down drafts. We were sucked up to 20,000 ft' and thrown down to 8,000 ft' in a matter of minutes, before suddenly coming into a lull. I knew that the passengers would be in bad shape.

In the Fokker, behind the cockpit was the galley and then the cabin. In a part of the galley, the baggage was kept netted. It was a 40-seater aircraft but only 39 seats were sold, one being kept for the forward cabin crew. Usually, Commercial begged for the seat, which was given with the permission of the cabin crew, of course. In this case, the cabin crew would either sit in the cockpit jump seat or on the dry store's trunk in the galley. On this flight, she chose to sit in the galley and due to extreme turbulence, the baggage netting gave way and the baggage collapsed on top of the forward cabin attendant. She was trapped below the baggage. The rear cabin attendant's seat was adjacent to the rear baggage hold. Its netting also gave way and she too got trapped below the baggage.

Repeated cabin calls elicited no response from our incapacitated crew. I asked my co-pilot 'Ravan" to see if he could go check out the cabin and let me know about the state of the passengers and our crew.

The Fokker cockpit door was a folding door and so could be folded open. He crawled over the baggage and went to the cabin door which had a window and came back and told me, "Sab mar gaye" (All are dead).

Horror gripped me and the first thing that came to my mind was that this was end of my command and career. This thought was strangely liberating, and I now flew uninhibited. We had reached calmer skies, though it was still dark and we were somewhere over the Bay of Bengal near the coast. We took our bearings and set course direct for Calcutta. We got caught in another disturbance, getting thrashed but with less

severity, and finally found ourselves over Calcutta Airport. I had already transmitted a Distress "Pan Pan Pan" call and advised of injuries and possible fatalities on board.

We got priority landing and just like in the movies – the fire trucks and ambulances were alongside chasing the aircraft down the runway.

After we landed, I shut down the engines and completed the after-landing checklist. Then took off my 3 stripe epaulettes and my wings and placed them on the console and lit a cigarette to calm myself down. Both Ravan and I sat there quietly without speaking, knowing that someone would come. The cabin door was opened from outside and passengers started deplaning from the rear. By the time we came into the cabin after retrieving our front cabin attendant who had a broken arm, all forty passengers had deplaned. They had severe head injuries, some were profusely bleeding, but to my immense relief, there were no deaths.

Meanwhile, the operations manager from Indian Airlines came and even while I was briefing him, the DGCA's air safety inspector, A.K. Chopra, turned up. He declared the aircraft sealed and directed the crew to accompany him for recording of statements. I picked up my wings and stripes and handed them to him. He put them in his pocket. We all went to his office and were kept segregated in separate rooms as we gave our statements of what happened. The dreaded inquiry had just begun.

I explained everything in detail, the weather brief at Agartala, the altitude and speed flown, the use of Fasten Seatbelt signs, announcements, etc. I described the scenario and my use of the weather radar and how I tried to avoid the thunderstorm but that it had caught up with me. I did tell him that the Fokker had been just on the periphery of the storm for had we entered it, the aircraft would have been torn apart.

Chopra went to the aircraft to examine the seat belts. The seat belts in the Fokker in those days were not positive lock type belts, like the ones in modern day aircraft but were friction lap straps, similar to the ones found in earlier cars.

He tested every seat belt and found that each one failed as it opened on being pulled. Chopra determined seat belt failure was the cause of the injuries to the passengers when they were literally weightless due negative "g" and their heads struck the overhead reading lights and air nozzles.

The problem for Indian Airlines now was to avoid passenger hospitalization, since, if in an aircraft related injury hospitalization is for more than 24 hours, it gets categorized as an "Accident". Thus, all of Indian Airlines got busy in ensuring that the passengers got out of hospital as soon as possible. Passengers were given money, reparation and anything possible to leave the hospital.

The next bombshell was a call to me from the Managing Director's office. I had to explain the entire incident, as the DGCA had grounded the entire Fokker fleet till further notice. I was instructed to return to base FAS (First Available Service).

However, as technically the matter was in the purview of the DGCA, their permission was sought for my return. Chopra wanted to meet me before I left. The airline transport took me and Ravan to the Regional DGCA Safety office where Chopra handed me my wings and stripes and told me that I had been cleared to fly.

No Blame! "Prima Facie nothing could be established to determine that crew proficiency was in any way the cause of the incident. He told us he had checked our radar plot from Dacca ATC and the FDR (flight data recorder) read outs were pretty much as we had said. The F27 in those days did not have a CVR (cockpit voice recorder)

He added: "You sustained more than the stipulated limit of +2.5G and -2G, young man. You experienced extreme turbulence. You are lucky you were in an F-27 and not an Avro."

I asked him why the Fokker Fleet was grounded, and he told me this will only be till the fleet got positive lock seat-belts as the existing seat-belts were unsafe.

I then flew back to Delhi by the evening flight, relieved and happy that both my professional integrity and Command were intact.

It took Indian Airlines a fortnight or so to procure the seat-belts on an AOG (Aircraft-On-Ground) basis. Once the seat-belts had been changed and inspected by the DGCA, the aircraft C of A was restored and the Fokker fleet started flying again.

A.K. Chopra and I became very close friends after this incident, out of sheer mutual respect. In subsequent years, our arguments on safety

and operational issues were always intense and frequently heated. I won some, lost some. A.K. Chopra became the foremost aircraft accident investigator in the country, and handled the really sensitive cases like the B737 Ahmedabad crash in 1988 and the Charkhi-Dadri mid-air collision between a Saudi Boeing 747 and a Kazakhstan Airlines Ilyushin IL-76 in 1996. We both advanced in our careers in aviation and when he was the Joint Director General of Civil Aviation in the DGCA, I was Chief of Operations with the fledgling low cost carrier (LCC) IndiGo.

I am glad I got to return to flying the Fokker from Calcutta, as this was perhaps the only time that the skills I had acquired in learning how to fly were utilized to the fullest. The Fokker connected the entire North East consisting of Assam, Arunachal, Manipur, Mizoram, Meghalaya, Nagaland and Tripura. It was the region's lifeline. Flight IC-211 was the most important, as it connected the region from Calcutta via Guwahati, to Tezpur, Jorhat, Lilabari, Dibrugarh and Tezu, zig zagging across the mighty Brahmaputra river, in stage lengths lasting 8 to 14 minutes. There were no radio aids on this route except ancient Non Directional Beacons (NDBs) that were of little use in adverse weather. Only Guwahati had a VOR and CAT1 ILS. The Air Force provided a GCA (Ground Controlled radar approach) at Tezpur and Chabua which were Fighter bases. Chabua airfield served both Dibrugarh, and Tinsukia.

The NDB was totally useless as a navigational aid as the weather in the Assam valley was temperamental and changeable! Most of our flights were literally VFR. We all picked up our landmarks, like bends in the Brahmaputra and other such markers, but our most important visual aids were often the tea estates with their distinctive green or red roofs. Our main navigation aid was actually the excellent monochromatic weather radar that we used in its map mode.

Strangely, there was no steamer service on the Brahmaputra. Getting overland from the North Bank to the South Bank could take as much as 72 hours, as the only bridge was at Guwahati. A flight from Tezpur to Jorhat, however, took just 14 minutes. Naturally, the Indian Airlines flight became the area's lifeline.

The crew halted for the night after landing in Chabua. There were two options for hotels: one in Dibrugarh and the other Tinsukia. Both the towns would vie for our business, and as the one who made the

choice, the Captain of any flight was the most important person in that area. Dibrugarh, the District HQ was largely commercial and trading, while Tinsukia was largely an industrial town. One crew set would go to Dibrugarh, the other would go to Tinsukia to seek the best deal.

I still remember the drive from the airport to the hotel through the forest. I was always amazed by the countless shades of green that nature could produce. Orchids of multifarious shades would peep from all corners, glistening in the sunshine that filtered through the green cover.

The cabin crew was mostly Bengali, and spoken English was not exactly their strong point. Captains usually asked the crew to decide where they preferred to stay.

On one such occasion, a new girl called Kali told the Captain she would prefer Dibrugarh. Surprised, he asked why, as cabin crew by and large preferred Tinsukia. Her answer dumbfounded him — "The cock in Dibrugarh is softer than the cock in Tinsukia." Startled and deeply embarrassed, the Captain was also confounded why her decision was not the other way around if, indeed, firmness of the 'cock' was the deal clincher. However, he soon realized that the issue was chicken and only chicken. Dibrugarh had chicken broilers while Tinsukia offered free range, country birds, which had tougher meat. The girl had literally translated male chicken to 'cock'.

My second favorite flight was IC-249 which connected Calcutta to Guwahati and the Guwahati to Dimapur, Silchar. On this flight, the layover was at the Bellevue Hotel. A quaint English era property run by Nippu and Appu Chowdary. Bellevue had an excellent kitchen with old 'Khansamas' who excelled in simple and wholesome Anglo Indian cuisine. The Bellevue Hotel night stop at Guwahati still holds fond memories for me.

Fun and games, though, were forgotten during winter and monsoon. Practically every winter morning saw Calcutta fog up, as did the Assam valley. But the Assam valley went further and displayed its own micro meteorology. Fog formation depended on the prevailing wind. The dry cold North East wind would warm up as it picked up moisture coming over the Brahmaputra, and when it hit the South Bank it would mix with cold dry "Katabatic" winds coming down the Khasi Hill and the south bank would fog up at sunrise. Guwahati, Jorhat and Chabua would get socked in. When there was low pressure in the Bay of Bengal the prevailing winds would be from the south westerly and the reverse would happen, with the North bank fogging up, shutting down Tezpur and Lilabari.

If it was not Calcutta fog it would be Assam weather that delayed early morning flights in these season. All crew would be in Movement Control waiting for the weather to clear up. In those days, we had to obtain our own ATC clearances as dispatchers were not authorized to do so. The co-pilot would go to the MET office early in the morning, get the weather brief and then go over to the communication officer and then on to ATC for final flight clearance.

What we did was to ignore the reported visibility, and focus on the prevailing wind pattern over the Assam Valley. Usually, we changed the destination to Tezpur and filed Guwahati as the Alternate Airport. This was legal and was known as "devious despatch". We would depart on time knowing by the time we were near Guwahati it was likely to clear up, and if it did not, we could sit it out in Tezpur till it did. Tezpur was just 20 minutes away from Guwahati. While Calcutta was one and a half hours away.

Such planning on the fly was important for operational efficiency. In the North East, Guwahati was the only airport with night landing facilities and we did not want to be caught out at night in any of the other locations. Had we followed the normal process, it would be highly unlikely that operations to the North East would have continued smoothly.

On one such departure, I heard a senior Airbus A300 Pilot, Capt. R.N. Rao, Dy.Operations Manager call out on RT.

"IC-211, request Captain".

My co-pilot responded "Lumba".

Then came a sarcastic reply

"Don't you assholes realize that Guwahati is below Minima. Return back to bay."

I could not hold back and responded: *"Captain, fly your fucking aircraft and let me fly mine."*

There was pin drop silence, and then we heard Robin Williams on the RT. *"Happy Landings, British Airways."* Rao had been out-ranked by the Regional Director and am told he hated my guts ever since.

The monsoon, though, was a major issue. We could not climb more than 200 ft' in the Assam valley, for otherwise we would be in cloud. So, what we did was fly over the river at or below the cloud base, and called 'airfield in sight' to take over the responsibility from the ATC. That is the only way one could operate in the monsoon period. The only places where we could land in bad weather were Guwahati, Chabua and Tezpur. The latter two airfields had GCA (ground controlled radar approach) as they were MiG operational training bases. In a GCA approach the controller talked you literally down to the ground using the radar equipment with ATC. He had two scopes one for lateral guidance and the other for vertical guidance. The controllers were superb, they had to be – and could bring one down literally to touch down.

One day, I came back to Calcutta for a posting and the Indian Airlines Airport Manager requested me to operate IC-211 instead of the scheduled Bhubaneswar Flight. He added that there was an important oil conference underway in Itanagar and the flight to Lilabari the airport for Itanagar had diverted for two consecutive days. The Ministry and Headquarters in Delhi were livid as the big wigs were unable to get to Itanagar. I had my favorite co-pilot, Maan Sahab, who had been with me at the Patiala Aviation Club and had also been trained by Ralph on low flying. We completed the mission, flying at only 100ft, and dropped off the Assam Oil executives.

God bless Ralph! I collected several visiting cards from people in the Calcutta head office who approved gas connections whenever I requested. I told Ila about the incident, and before I knew it, our friends, and their friends, started calling me to get LPG connections, which were very difficult to come by in those days. The rumor soon went around the airline that "if you wanted an LPG connection, then Captain Lumba was your man." I must have milked that one flight for 40-50 gas connections. These were some of the perks of the job.

One of my fondest memories of my time flying in the North East is of the flight from Chabua to Tezu. Ernst K. Gann, who remained one of my favorite aviation authors, had flown the Dakota DC-3 during World War II out of Chabua. In his book titled 'Fate is the Hunter', he described how he would fly from Chabua to China over the 'hump', dropping provisions for the troops. Chabua, therefore, always held a fascination for me.

Then, on government directive, the flight to Tezu was started twice a week. Tezu was, where Gann and friends had also flown. It was a small holding town for the army at the base of the hump. Surface travel time from Tezu to Chabua could take up to three days, as one had to cross three tributaries of the Brahmaputra mostly on elephant back. Flying time was just 18 minutes.

Landing there was tricky because the runway was 90 ft' wide instead of the standard 150 ft' and only 4800 ft' long. The runway thus gave an illusion that the aircraft was higher and further way than it actually was. The strip sloped from NE to SW and the right of the runway was higher than the left. Tezu borders Burma and, in fact, falls in Rangoon FIR. It rains a lot there, so the lower half of the entire runway length permanently had slippery moss deposits, forcing the pilot to use only the 45 feet dry width as far as possible.

Obviously, special training, checks and clearance was needed to fly into Tezu.

When we landed there, we were surrounded by the army jawans who needed to go on casual leave, granted maybe after a year or two of living in isolation out there. The Air Force ran a twice a week Assam Courier from Chandigarh to Guwahati, Jorhat and Chabua, and people from Tezu who wanted to take the Courier were always eager to get onto our flight, so as to be home the SAME day.

We really felt sorry for them. So, we invariably boarded extra passengers. It was never a question of load, just numbers, as all that the jawans carried rucksack only. We operated like that, and no one asked questions because it was a humanitarian service that we were doing. There was, however, a delightful karmic upside to this: a crate of rum (12 bottles) could be available for us for ₹72/- as against ₹100 for just a bottle in Calcutta. A bottle of rum to the staff at the Grand was a welcome tip. It only cost us 6 bucks but for them was worth 100 bucks.

An interesting B737 air accident in 1983 comes to mind. The flight was from Kathmandu to Calcutta. It was operated by two Captains – a pairing that I always considered unsafe. The Senior pilot "Capt. November" was carrying out co-pilot duties. The Junior "Capt. Charlie" was the Captain for this leg. Both November and Charlie did not get along with each other. Both considered themselves alpha males. The

Flight was uneventful, till the last few crucial moments. Only flight related challenges and responses were recorded. No ideal chitter chatter.

Charlie was in a hurry to land and maintained a high speed till the outer marker but forgot to select the landing gear down. The co-pilot, November was aware of the oversight, but never informed the Captain until just before touch down at about 100 ft' to go when he remarked

"Arre Chutia gear kab le ga" (You asshole, when do you intend taking the gear down). The gear was selected down by Charlie but before it could lock, the aircraft touched down. The gear folded up and the aircraft settled SOFTLY on to the engines. Seemed like a super kisser landing until the Captain tried applying brakes. There were no brakes as the wheels were up. Some passengers also clapped appreciating what they considered a kisser landing. Totally unaware of the pickle they could have been in.

This was in the pre CRM (Cockpit Resource Management) days. A scenario such as this would be highly unlikely now a days. The cause of the accident was declared as "crew not following Standard operating procedures and failing to select the gear down".

The B737 had a gear unsafe warning that sounded below 500 ft' from the ground if the aircraft landing gear was not down and full landing flap was selected. Unfortunately, in this case no warning sounded as due to high speed the landing was executed with only approach flaps. In this configuration there was no warning for gear unsafe. Subsequent to this accident the warning was modified to sound even with approach flaps selected for landing

One of the main outcomes of this near-miss tragedy was a change in pilot pairing rules. Two pilots who did not get along, could not hereafter be paired for a flight.

The DGCA restricted the ATPL of both pilots banning them from flying public transport aircraft for five years; however, they could fly non-public aircraft. Indian Airlines sacked both pilots.

Captain Charlie started flying a Beechcraft C90, which was used by politicians out of Delhi. It so happened the Rajiv Gandhi flew with Charlie often. Then he became the Prime Minister. Captains Charlie and November appealed the DGCA order and their termination in the Delhi

High Court.

The court ruled in their favor based on the premise that if Charlie could fly VIPs and the future Prime Minister, then why not ordinary passengers. For them not being permitted to fly public-transport aircraft made no sense to the court. They struck down the DGCA order and the dismissal by Indian Airlines, reinstating them with back pay.

On one of my postings to Calcutta in 1984, I met the General Secretary of the Indian Commercial Pilots Association (ICPA), Capt.

S.L. Bagchi. He asked me to come down to the ICPA offices in 54F Chowringee, and understand the kind of work that the union did. This was my first exposure to the ICPA. I started visiting the ICPA office regularly after that and got acquainted with the union members. Senior pilots would gather at the crew club on the premises and gossip. As I started getting involved with the pilot fraternity, I gained better insight and started understanding the issues.

Capt. Bagchi asked me to join the ICPA in Delhi, but I told him that I hardly had any time to devote to the union in Delhi. But he convinced me to work with him in Calcutta, and thus it was that I became his understudy. Capt. Bagchi was a legend; general secretary of the ICPA for about 15 years, and a personal friend of Somnath Chatterjee, the

ICPA general counsel, who would go on to become the highly respected Speaker of the Lok Sabha. I was introduced to the background and *raison d'etre* of the ICPA. I learned of some interesting cases.

One such case was decided by an Industrial Tribunal in 1956. Before the nationalization of airline pilot got an officer allowance of ₹100 per month. That was a lot of money those days. After nationalization Indian Airlines did not consider pilots as officers but as workmen and stopped this allowance. There was an agitation and pilots threatened to stop flying. The government set up a National Industrial Tribunal in Lucknow, headed by a gentleman called Kamla Sahi. The tribunal was to decide whether pilots were officers or workmen for the allowance to be admissible or not.

The Pilots' claimed that they were officers, like the captain of a ship, but the Indian Airlines' management held that they were workmen, as they did not have the right to hire or fire staff, and this view of the airline was shared by the Ministry of Civil Aviation. The Tribunal in its award upheld the airline and Ministry's view. Pilots were "deemed skilled workmen" and so not admissible any officer allowance.

The flip side of this dispute was, as workmen, pilots could form unions and go on strike. The irony is that years later, and till this day, the same management and ministry are trying to do everything to prove that pilots are not workmen but officers. *Karma* was now biting the airline and ministry in the arse. Had the airline giving the ₹100 allowance, pilots there would not have been an issue and pilots would not have been deemed workmen and could not form a trade union. The trajectory of Indian civil aviation would have changed completely and pilot strikes which have blotted India's civil aviation history, would not have existed.

Another interesting case from the 1950s was that of pilot fatigue, which had started becoming an issue worldwide. The British Government had set up a committee under World War II veteran, Air Commodore Douglas Bader, who came out with the first Flight and Duty Time Limitations. (FDTL). Flight Duty Limits were not recognized or accepted by the DGCA. The ICPA and Air India's pilots went on strike on the issue of quantum of work hours, inadequate rest and fatigue. Finally, the government, in a tripartite arbitration, accepted the Douglas Bader committee report in 1964, which became the basis for FDTL for

IA. In 1992 however, the Ministry and airline decided to change it unilaterally, leading to another bitter and long drawn strike.

Another instance was that of the pre-flight alcohol tests that were started in Indian Airlines on the insistence of the ICPA, not the Management or DGCA. The simple demand was: test all union pilots before every flight and after that STOP floating rumors after a crash that 'the pilots must have been drunk'.

This was instituted after Capt. Issac's training crash in Hyderabad, in which bottles of rum were found on board, which had been picked up from the Air Force mess to take home, not drink on board. Yet the investigation was able to establish, based on bar bills, that Capt. Isaac **may** have consumed beer before the flight. In my over 40-year career in Aviation, I have never seen or heard of a pilot drinking during a flight he was operating.

Reading about such cases started arousing my interest in the Union's work. So as long as I was on the Fokker, I would visit the office to learn from Capt. Bagchi. He shared his experience generously, telling

me that in this business, information is power, and the maximum information available to pilots is with the ICPA. "The ICPA files have a wealth of information because they contain the commitments that have been made in the past by the airline, the Ministry and the DGCA, which senior managers may have forgotten or overlooked, and new managers may not be aware of. In order to run union competently, you have to know these files backwards," he told me. Capt. Bagchi said that since I was showing interest, I should try to run for the Regional Secretary's post in Delhi.

I was bitten by the Union bug and my mind was veering on a path towards becoming more than just a pilot. My association with the union would only grow in the years to come and what I learned here would ultimately be utilized for the benefit of pilots and Pilot Management relations when I headed Operations Departments later in my career.

There came a time, when the Fokker fleet, overdue for phase out, could not be withdrawn because of its invaluable services to the North East. Meanwhile, pilot training on the Fokker had stopped. We were due to upgrade to the B737 but were requested to stay on for 9 months, by which time they would train more co-pilots and upgrade current co-pilots as Captains.

Capt. Chadha called in his markers and we agreed, subject to our being given carte blanche in controlling the operation. This was willingly agreed to. We controlled schedules, pilot rostering and leave planning and kept the operation going for 9 months.

True to their word, the Management moved us to the B737 and CTE for conversion type rating training in 1986, thereby ending my thrilling love affair with the Fokker Friendship. The likely end of flying by the seat of my pants.

But a new exciting chapter on flying the big jets and active trade unionism was now awaiting me.

6. SANCTITY OF THE COCKPIT

"For all professional pilots there exists a kind of guild, without charter and without by-laws. It demands no requirements for inclusion save an understanding and fair fellowship."
– Beryl Markham

The cockpit of an aircraft is a sacred place for us pilots. It is the place where we live. It's also the place where we learn to live life. There is an etiquette that is followed while in it, partly because it is standard operating procedure and partly because it's personal.

Seen from the eyes of someone of my vintage, flying has lost its charm and glamour, as it no longer presents the challenges and demands that are met only with a refinement of skills, a reliance on instincts and oodles of passion. Technology has robbed much of the magic of flying – It's nowadays like taking a highly skilled motorcar driver and putting him at the wheel of a tramcar.

Airlines now mandate maximum use of Auto Pilot and Flight Management System, leading pilots to bank more and more on visual monitoring skills, thereby losing out on honing their actual flying skills. Relying less and less on the aural and tactile senses that are crucial to safe flight, diminishing the strengths of a good pilot.

Not for a moment do I denigrate the need for procedure and safety regulations, and I agree that with the skies and airports getting more crowded by the day, there is need for SOPs and accountability. My simple point is that, first and foremost, the passion for true flying should be nurtured, along with the development of commensurate skills and the honing of instincts, before one abdicates to automation and SOPs.

Along with this transformation of the cockpit, came the change in cockpit etiquette. SOPs were cast in stone, and made paramount, First Officers were encouraged to file reports. Back in the day, the sanctity of the cockpit was inviolate, and we lived by the belief of 'What happens in the cockpit stays in the cockpit'.

Some instances dating back to the early 1980s will illustrate the old concept "The Sanctity of the Cockpit is Inviolate"

Passenger Pushback

The local Air Force MiG 21 flying exercise was in progress at the time of the normal mid-morning arrival of the regular F27 flight IC-211 into Chabua Air Force Station in Assam. The First Officer was flying and the Captain was handling the RT. ATC gave landing clearance for Runway 05 with the explicit instruction: "After landing EXPEDITE vacating runway at the END. Fighters taxiing out."

The Captain acknowledged with a "ROGER Cleared to Land". The First Officer, on landing, diligently and expeditiously cleared the runway, but on the first exit, instead of 'at the end' as instructed by ATC. The aircraft turned onto the parallel taxi track. Then the shit hit the ceiling!

The F27 found itself face to face with a flight of three MiG 21s taxiing towards it. The taxi track was narrow and both the F27 and the MiGs had no way forward or back. The aircraft just sat on the runway, glumly staring at each other. ATC was enraged.

After a few colorful abuses aimed at the First Officer, the Captain shut the engines. Soon, the little passenger ramp was brought along and the passengers deplaned.

The Air Force, naturally, wanted the F27 removed. But the problem was how? There was no tow tractor at the airport! The Captain had a quick chat with the passengers, explained the problem to them, and asked them if they were game to pushing the plane back a distance of about 200ft in order to make room for the fighters to enter the runway from the exit the F27 had used.

There was initial disbelief, then some gamely agreed, others joined in, and soon all passengers, barring two really old ladies, were heaving away, unaware that it was perhaps the first and only time in aviation history, that passengers were made to push an airplane. Jokes were made about mother-in-law's cars, about being grateful this crisis had not happened up in the skies, but they obviously did not mind.

Bashfully acknowledging the crew's thanks, the passengers were bussed to the terminal, the aircraft was started and taxied to the apron.

All in a good day's work. No reports filed, no complaints raised, no press reports.

The DGCA got a whiff of the occurrence only about six months later, and dispatched a safety officer from Calcutta to inquire. He returned empty handed as no one could recall any such occurrence having taken place.

Such was the interdependence, solidarity and camaraderie between the Air Force, the airline and the passengers on this very crucial life-line flight to the region.

"The sanctity of the cockpit was inviolate!"

Runway Incursion

Right after flight training, I was supernumerary pilot, undergoing the mandatory 100 familiarization hours.

Supernumerary pilots were at the very bottom of the food chain, and they very soon learned that they were only to be seen and not heard. Even the cabin crew treated you like dirt, so you tried your best to merge into the bulkhead panels.

Flight IC-411, New Delhi to Calcutta via Kanpur, Allahabad, Gorakhpur, was operated by two Captains through a process called 'One Way Each' (OWE), unique to Indian Airlines. Captains swapped the left seat on alternate legs and the lines demarcating the authority of the Pilot in Command were blurred since both pilots were Captains.

By tradition, the senior pilot flew the first leg. It was always my opinion that such an arrangement had serious flight safety issues.

It was a routine arrival into Gorakhpur, another Air Force station, in light rain on a wet runway with a 5 knot quartering crosswind from the right.

The cockpit buzzed with a lofty conversation on the Kathi Kebab rolls that the senior pilot wanted to take back to Delhi from Calcutta for his party the next day. The Kathi roll was then a novelty, unique to Calcutta, and had not emigrated all over India as it has now.

Next to the layover hotel in Calcutta, The Oberoi Grand, there were two restaurants, Nizam's and Badshah that specialized in making the delicious roll. Each had its dedicated and loyal clientele, and the pilots on approach were debating on which served the better one.

Both were so intent on their discussion on the Kathi Kebab roll that little heed was paid to the actual landing roll and, despite my softly repeated warnings of "Captain, look out, the aircraft is going off the runway!". Owing to the wet runway and cross wind, the aircraft gently taxied off the runway surface on to the soft and soggy ground beyond the runway edge where it got stuck.

My last warning came out inadvertently louder than intended, and as soon as the plane came to a halt, the Captain and Co Pilot turned around and glared at me. Shrinking under their withering gaze, it seemed to me that they were less concerned about the mess outside than about the fact that this supernumerary had actually opened his mouth in the cockpit!

Attempts to try and gun the aircraft out of the mud were futile. The aircraft simply settled in a bit more! Engines were shut and the argument changed from Kathi rolls to who should have been in control, who should have been monitoring and whose fault it was.

Soon an Air Force Jeep arrived carrying the Sikh Commandant of the base. As regulars on the route, they all seemed to know each other, and as one of the Captains was also Sikh, they broke into familiar Panjabi.

A winch truck was called for. Passengers were deplaned. The truck hoisted the nose wheel up and towed the aircraft out onto the runway. Passengers emplaned. Engines started and we taxied to the apron as if nothing had happened. The station engineer inspected the main undercarriages, a fire truck was called and the wheels (brakes and tyres) hosed down.

No report was filed, no entry made in the technical log, and the flight continued normally to destination. DGCA once again shook themselves awake three months later, and the whole crew, including the cabin crew and the concerned engineer were called to the DGCA for an inquiry.

All feigned bewilderment and denied that any such an incident took place on our flight. That was the end of the inquiry.

"The sanctity of the cockpit was inviolate!"

Stowaway Booze

In the eighties the only international Flights on the F27 fleet of Indian Airlines were Calcutta to Dacca – Chittagong and from Patna to Kathmandu.

Kathmandu was the favorite booze flight. Duty free booze was stowed away in empty aircraft panels and cavities unknown to the Customs.

On one such Kathmandu -Patna flight operated by two Captains as One Way each, the pilot flying without telling the other pilot, had stowed two bottles of scotch in the pneumatic panel located in the forward galley behind the left seat. The F27 had a pneumatic braking system

Unusual place, since the cavity was small and the flight control cables were routed through this panel. The usual places were below the fold-down 3rd pilot seat or below the circuit breaker panel.

It was a bumpy and rough flight due to turbulence.

During descent, the pilot flying realized that he was unable to turn the control wheel, which appeared to be jammed. He told the senior Captain that they had jammed ailerons. The latter tried, but also could not move the ailerons.

Taking control, the senior pilot informed ATC of the problem and requested a straight in tailwind landing, using only rudders for direction control. The landing was uneventful, and later, the engineers tried moving the ailerons from the wing but they would not move. The DGCA safety officer was called and the aircraft grounded. Men & Material were requisitioned from the main base, Calcutta.

Seeing the junior Pilot lurking around the cockpit, the senior asked if he had bought booze in Kathmandu and if so, where had he hidden it. The junior fellow sheepishly pointed to the pneumatic compartment. The engineer, who was still hunting for the cause of the jammed ailerons, was smartly chivvied off the aircraft on some pretext! The compartment was opened, and it was seen that one bottle had dislodged and was jammed against the aileron cable. The bottle was quickly retrieved and the crew quietly left for the layover hotel.

The next morning, they got a call from the perplexed engineer that for some reason the ailerons were no longer jammed and had full and free movement. However, the snag needed full investigation before the aircraft was released. The team arrived from Calcutta.

The F27 major Maintenance in-charge himself had come. In that era, there existed a complete trust and friendship between F 27 pilots and engineers. In times of crises, both covered for each other. The two pilots took the chief engineer into confidence.

A symbolic inspection was done and the aircraft released under observation to report if the snag repeated. It of course never did, as needless to say, the pilots never hid anything in the pneumatic compartment.

"The sanctity of the cockpit was inviolate!"

Fuck the Checklist

It was a normal 737 departure from Calcutta runway 01 right. By normal, I mean an intersection Charlie take off. In command was Capt. Kuki with Capt. Singh as First Officer. As the 737 rode down the runway and rotated, there was the sound of a loud thud, followed by the high-pitched engine fire warning!

Company policy stipulated: 'No action to be taken except silencing the fire warning below safety altitude, that is, 1500 feet above the ground.'

The crew were struggling with the engine fire warning and additionally, the loss of the hydraulic system. There was acute panic in the cabin, as passengers could see flames streaming from the reliable JT8D engines that powered the B737-200.

In those days before 9/11, cockpit entry was not prohibited and cockpit doors only shut and never locked. The Senior Cabin crew barged into the cockpit yelling, 'Captain, there are flames coming out of your right engine."

Capt. Kuki took a decision. Carrying out the fire drill from memory, he immediately did a 180 degree turn, lowered the gear down and reported finals for 19 Left, the reciprocal runway, informing ATC that he was immediately landing back as he had lost an engine, hydraulics, and had a flaming aircraft.

The whole maneuver could have hardly taken more than three to four minutes. On short finals, a very scared co-pilot's voice was said to have been heard, "Capt. Checklist, checklist!" to which the Captain loudly responded "FUCK THE CHECKLIST! We need to get back on the ground."

With the benefit of hindsight and keeping in mind the severity of the malfunction, there was enough reason to believe that had the captain delayed the landing by going through the engine fire checklist, the hydraulic failure checklist, and carried out the full SOP, the outcome may have been significantly, and tragically, different.

On touchdown, they realized that the right main landing gear was also on fire. The airplane was stopped on the runway; passengers were evacuated with no injuries. The Bengalis are emotional people, and shouts of "*Ki Bhalo Kaptan*" (What a good Captain) along with "*Capt. Kuki Zindabad*" (long live Capt. Kuki) as they carried him to the terminal on their shoulders showering him with respect and adoration.

The Deputy Managing Director, who was also Director of Safety, called up the Captain personally and thanked him for his quick decision making, seat-of-the-pants airmanship, saying how proud the airline was of such pilots and informed him that a letter of appreciation (the only reward pilots ever got) was being placed on record in his personal file.

But within hours of the incident, after the CVR was decoded, a second message arrived from the Director Training, instructing that Capt. Kuki was to be taken off command for gross violation of check list procedures, SOP and not following CRM (Cockpit Resource Management).

The Pilot Union, ICPA was up in arms. So was the Calcutta Media. Capt. Kuki was their hero. Needless to say, the Director Training's strictures were overruled and Capt. Kuki continued an illustrious, incident free career till his retirement. After his retirement from IA, he joined me in Alliance Air for 2 very satisfying years.

"The sanctity of the cockpit remained inviolate!"

There were people who faulted the Captain for poor CRM which then was basically Cockpit Resource Management, first introduced by United Airlines. It was based on the Blake and Mouton Grid that rated pilots on a score from 1-9 on two criteria i.e., task orientation and people orientation. If a person was a 1-9 pilot, he was more people oriented than task; conversely, a 9-1 pilot was more task than people oriented.

The ideal pilot as per the Blake and Mouton grid criteria would be rated 9-9, that is Both Highly Task and People oriented. Standard Operating Procedure (SOP) were designed for optimum cockpit resource management and resulted in 5-5 type pilots. In most cases requiring emergency reaction or immediate action, Captains mostly revert to 9-1 decision making mode, rather than the 5-5 consultation mode. CRM evolved from Cockpit to Crew Resource Management.

Formal CRM (Crew Resource Management) evolved much later, wherein the full cockpit crew resources were to be used for decision making and action so as to enhance safety by reducing human errors.

CRM in this true form was late coming to Indian Airlines, and served as a regulatory requirement to the point of being used as a punishment, eroding CRM as a valuable safety tool for which it has been designed.

The standard recommendations post any incident/accident from the Director General of Civil Aviation usually read, Pilots should be subjected to corrective training on simulator and a CRM module"

Sigh… What a pity!

7. THE BIG JETS AND THE PILOT UNION

"Every flying machine has its own unique characteristics, some good, some not so good. Pilots naturally fly the craft in such a manner as to take advantage of its good characteristics and avoid the areas where it is not so good."

– Neil Armstrong

After upgrading to Captain on the F27, I had started work on obtaining my ATPL (Airline Transport Pilot License). To upgrade from the SCPL to the ATPL, one needed to only to pass the written paper on Astro Navigation. It was an archaic requirement since aircraft no longer needed to navigate with the help of the stars. Yet, it was a requirement, so I hit the books and fortunately cleared my papers. I submitted my log book and SCPL for issue of the ATPL, which was issued on 17th July 1982, ATPL number was 1117. The ATPL is required to fly any aircraft weighing more than 21,000 kg which the B737-200 was.

Our batch, the 23rd apprentice pilot batch, reported for the B 737 type endorsement training in the first week of January, 1986. The training entailed 6 intensive weeks of chalk and board kind of technical and aircraft performance study of the 737 -200 aircraft, followed by two DGCA exams, one on each subject. After clearing both Exams, could one proceed for the simulator and the aircraft training modules.

In the first 6 weeks, we were familiarized with what made "Fat Albert", which the 737 was affectionately called, tick. The course in 6 weeks made one totally familiar with all the aircraft systems and their normal and abnormal operations. Key takeaways pertained to aircraft performance, that is, what it is capable of – the minimum runway length required for take-off and landing, the total weight it can carry from each runway, and the minimum fuel required for a flight, apart from an encyclopedic amount of data that one had to remember and recall, crucially during flying! I was chuffed to also learn that Boeing makes square airplanes. The length of the aircraft is almost equal the wingspan (distance from wing tip to wing tip).

In the 3rd week of February that year, I reported for simulator training and was assigned Captain Jamie, a Bombay based examiner, as instructor. Captain Jamie had booked all the 0530 am 4-hour simulator slots. This gave him enough time to also do a Hyderabad-Bombay quick return flight. He could then earn both flying and training allowances.

Jamie obviously did not realize that we flew the Fokker instead of the Avro and were not familiar with simulators! There was no briefing or debriefing, no simulator familiarization. The first sortie, 1st take offwas an engine out at V1, I rotated and crashed. The exercise was repeated and I kept crashing. Frustrated, he let me do a two-engine take-off and complete my two-hour session. My co-trainer and I swapped seats and he got the same treatment. He however managed to do 2 successful engines out take off. Jamie formed his impression about him as the leader and me trailing behind. Like many Parsis, Jamie liberally used choice BCs, MCs to describe my aptitude as a pilot.

My first session was a total disaster, and I was totally demoralized.

Next day, my second session was worse, and he terminated it after half an hour and stormed out of the simulator. Totally shaken, I went to the training section and said I wished to discontinue my training.

I was sent to the Dy.GM. In-charge of B 737 training, Capt. RL Kapur, the senior most B737 Instructor Examiner. He was called Dr Kapur BA, MA, and Ph.D. B737 and was considered a total terror. Pilots would duck simulator check rides if he was the examining pilot.

He heard me out and asked me to accompany him to the simulator. I sat on the right seat and strapped myself. He asked me to adjust my seat, I didn't know how as Jamie had not shown us. Capt. Kapur asked whether the instructor had given a briefing on the simulator and took us through the paces. I said no.

Astounded, he then showed me how to correctly adjust the rudder pedals, the seat fore and aft so that I had full rudder travel available and finally the seat height, by aligning the red and white balls. He sat himself down and put himself on the left seat and we taxied out. On the take-off run he asked me to rotate. I did and he froze the simulator and repositioned it to the beginning of take-off. He briefed me that a jet is flown differently than a turbo prop.

There are 3 speeds that dictate a multi engine aircrafts performance during take-off known as the V speeds. V1 is the decision speed at or below which a decision to No Go or Go must be taken. The runway available is enough to stop the aircraft (reject take off) or continue till one reaches Vr, the rotation speed. This is when the nose is lifted to the optimum angle for it to lift off and climb out at the safe climbing speed which is V2. The rotation must be slow to a target attitude of 15 deg (2 engines), which should ideally be achieved at the rate of 3 degrees per second.

I was rotating too fast. He demonstrated a take-off with me following on the controls. Then he made me do it by counting 1001, 1002… to reach 15 deg not before 1005. He then explained that for a single engine take off the target attitude should be 12/13 degrees only. I did a couple of take offs with him slowly powering back one engine to idle. I soon got the hang of it.

He then demonstrated the safety features of the simulator and how to evacuate it in case of an emergency. Jamie had not bothered with any of these niceties. Capt. Kapur requested that I keep our session confidential.

So, now I am back in the game and it is the third morning on the simulator with Jamie. I quickly adjusted my seat. Went through the engine start/ abort/ start procedure and taxied for take-off. Sure enough, he gave me an engine out at V1 and almost jumped out of his seat when I climbed out smoothly without losing direction. He froze the simulator, yelling *"Sala MC ne fluke kiya"*. He reset it and gave a compressor stall on rotation. The aircraft stayed smoothly on track. We completed my session without any more cuss words flying about. Now, my co-trainer performance suddenly suffered and Jamie's' sarcasm made it worse for him. I was relieved that I no longer was at the receiving end of the mad Parsi's tirades.

Unfortunately for Jamie, Captain Kapur messaged us that Jamie and his students were to report to him after the session. He asked to see our training booklets so as to review our progress. The booklets were blank. He gave Jamie a piece of his mind. Called up scheduling and ordered that when a pilot is assigned to training, they are not to be used for scheduled passenger flights, without his explicit permission.

Jamie was made to give us a full briefing on the simulator and for each session and a complete de-brief after each session, under the boss's supervision. The first two sessions were considered cancelled and the training was to start afresh next day and slots for 0930 am were booked so that we could get adequate rest.

Thereafter the training went smoothly. Jamie was at his best behavior, and in his new Instructor *avtar*, he did an excellent training job. Our Final Simulator check ride was conducted by Capt. Kapur himself.

We were now ready to move to the next phase of day and night aircraft training. This module was also conducted by Jamie followed by the day and night CA 40A checks on the aircraft. By the end of March, our licenses were endorsed for the B737 as co-pilots and we started line operations.

Captains shared their flying equally with their co-pilots to boost their handling experience. I will always remember a particular flight to Bagdogra, an air force station near Siliguri, which was the gateway to Sikkim.

On this flight, after crossing Patna, one got a clear view of the whole Himalayan range. That particular day it was extraordinarily clear and we could see Mount Everest. The New Zealand High Commissioner, Sir Edmund Hillary, was a regular on this flight. Having recognized him, I invited him into the cockpit.

My Captain, who I will not name to save him embarrassment, made a PA announcement describing the whole range and made it a point to identify Mount Everest. The High Commissioner tentatively told the Captain that what he had identified as Mt Everest was actually Mt Makalu, which appeared higher than Everest since it was nearer. My

Captain took offense and ticked off the High Commissioner, not quite realizing who he was.

When Captain said that he had been flying the sector for 5 years and knew his Mount Everest, Sir Edmund could not take it anymore and quipped, "Captain! If that's Mt. Everest, then I must have climbed the wrong mountain."

Deciding not to increase the Captain's embarrassment further, I introduced the High Commissioner to him immediately: "Captain, please let me introduce to you Sir Edmond Hillary." The Captain turned all shades of pink and apologized profusely.

After about 500 hrs as co-pilot on the B737 I was back in CTE, Hyderabad for our Command upgrade training. We were the first set of co-pilots being taken up with only 500 hrs on type. I was very grateful to all the Captains for giving me hands on flying mostly from the left seat. This had prepared me to go confidently for the Command upgrade. I always shared the flying with my Co-pilot fifty/ fifty weather permitting.

This time the training was more demanding and higher standards were expected from us. After 7 sessions each, we were up for our Command simulator check. Here again Capt. Kapur decided to conduct the check ride.

This check ride was one of the toughest and also one of my most memorable simulator sessions. Towards the end of my session, two other Examiners Harry (HR Singh) and Ravi (Ravi Kumar) jumped on board and started their fingering session.

After an engine failure (fire) after VR, I completed the take-off profile and the fire drill and checklists. I now requested a priority landing back at Delhi, which was our departure aerodrome. We were vectored to the Delhi VOR at 3500ft and after one hold, cleared for the ILS approach Rwy 28. I had decided to land. My co-trainee, advised that we would be overweight for landing. I elected to exercise my *emergency authority*, and land overweight.

We were lighter than the maximum take-off weight so safety was not an issue. I decided rather than waste time holding, to burn fuel to reduce the aircraft weight to go in for an overweight landing since after an engine failure, it is mandatory to Land As Soon As Possible (LASP) at the nearest suitable airfield. So, the LASP overrode the Landing weight restriction in this situation.

At this point, Ravi decided to give a total hydraulic failure. My stress level went up manifold! A B-737, on single engine, with total hydraulic failure is "a bitch to fly."

With checklist complete I established the localizer. We were now on one engine, with loss of all hydraulics, flying manual on raw data. Before crossing the outer marker, the gear was taken down manually and we had landing permission at 1000ft above ground.

Harry now pipped up. He announced, "Capt. the visibility has reduced to less than 300 meters and falling rapidly. Check your minima. The airfield was below minima. Every runway has two criteria stipulated – one for the minimum descent altitude and the other for the minimum forward visibility. It's illegal to fly below these unless the runway or its approach environment is in sight and a safe landing is possible. These limits are known as the MINIMA.

Co-Pilot called: "Go around, Captain".

"Negative", I responded, as it would be suicidal to attempt a Go Around on a single engine with gear down, flaps at approach and no way of retracting either due to loss of both hydraulic systems.

ATC (Harry) called out, "Training Flight, your intentions."

I responded, "Emergency landing! Request safety vehicles positioned on taxiway, no brakes." Harry froze the simulator. There was pin drop silence.

I cringed, my only thought being: 'Oh shit, I fucked up'. Then the 3 Examiners started clapping. I was told that I handled all the shit they threw at me like a proverbial cool commander! "Good decision making, congrats! You are Fit to fly in Command." Manna for my ears!

My co-trainee was chewed up for announcing a Go Around which would have been impossible, and on an actual flight could have led to a crash.

The remainder of Command training was routine and after the mandatory CA-40B and 10 route check, I was endorsed as pilot in Command on B 737 on my ALTP. Both Harry and Ravi were from Delhi base. They took me under their wings and ensured that I was cleared for

Srinagar, Leh, Kathmandu and Kabul operation just after 100 hrs of PIC time, which was the minimum stipulated.

I started enjoying flying the Boeing 737-200. It was like a jet fighter compared to the sedate F27, which had almost been phased out. Now the Boeing became my beloved mistress!

The B737 was introduced in India in the early 1970s. Its introduction was made after a lot of discussion and drama in the Indian Parliament. By the mid-1960s, Indian Airlines started looking for a jet replacement for their 4 engine Viscounts. The 2 candidate replacement aircraft type were the McDonald DC 9 and the Boeing 737-100.

A committee headed by Capt. Hulgul, the Director of Operations, selected the DC9 over the B737-100. The DC-9 had proven its chops, and was the proven main stay of most US Airlines. Like in every case of new aircraft orders, there were allegation of unfair evaluation and corruption thrown up. This time by The Boeing Company!! The issue was raised amidst considerable pandemonium in Parliament. As is the wont of all Opposition parties, they walked out. The government cancelled the DC 9 order, and Boeing was given the contract. By the time the brouhaha died down, the B737-200 was in production.

Capt. Hulgul resigned.

A most interesting anecdote related to Boeing deal comes to mind. It was shared by Capt. SL Bagchi.

A few more B 737s (High Gross weight versions) were ordered in 1972 by Air Marshal PC Lal, CMD of Indian Airlines. Before the order was signed, Air Marshal Lal demanded his Commission openly. Everyone was astounded by his open demand. Boeing allegedly offered One Million Dollars. Air Marshal Lal thanked Boeing, and then asked them to use the 1 million dollars to provide spare parts. That was the commission. Having said this, Air Marshal Lal signed the deal, leaving a flabbergasted Boeing team searching for an answer! It is possibly an entirely authentic account, but even if colored with a bit of window dressing, it adds to Air Marshal Lal's persona and fair reputation. It did indeed put to shame greedy politicians, bureaucrats and airline bosses who take cuts in every aircraft and arms deal.

My favorite flights were to Leh, the hopper via Jaipur, Udaipur, and Aurangabad to Bombay. The most coveted flight was to Kathmandu via Agra, Khajuraho, and Varanasi. This was also known as the "bootlegging" flight. Duty Free Alcohol at Kathmandu was cheap and also available in Indian Rupees, a little more expensive than if bought in Dollars.

The booze was stowed in a compartment below the weather radar. The hollow compartment could hold 10/12 one liter bottles of Scotch safely, without adversely affecting the radar's operation. Customs at Varanasi had no clue about this. After take-off from Varanasi, the booze was retrieved and placed in our overnighters.

Even one flight a month kept the cockpit crew stocked with enough Scotch. Very soon, I realized that the Customs may have been decidedly aware of our escapades, but chose to ignore us, as they got two bottles complimentary from the crew on every flight. All crew contributed towards this payoff.

This system prevailed all over India at all international custom airports. In places like Delhi, the customs would pull in anywhere between 30-40 bottles a day for their own use, given the number of International arrivals. These bottles found their way to all government Departments. IAS Babus also got their share of Scotch! I am not aware if this system prevails till today! But of one thing I am sure – there will always be one scam or another, to keep everyone in booze.

There was a group of my school friends who also joined St Stephens. There was Tariq Quareshi (Q), Manoj Joshi (Bear), Naresh Kohli, aptly nicknamed Naga and Pervez Billimoria, (Billy). We all were members of the hiking club. Once on a trek in the Garhwal Himalayas, I became the butt end of a joke. I had got lost on the way to "the Dunagiri" mountain foot slopes. For my rescue I had to forgo all my chocolate ration. Promptly, I was nicknamed *Shakleton,* after the legendary polar explorer who became a pauper after he had to pay for his rescue on a polar expedition. One night after dinner around the camp fire we were having a drink of rum when Billy stated, "If Shackleton becomes a pilot, I will cut my balls with a rusty blade."

Years went by. In a stroke of serendipity, once on a Bagdogra to Delhi flight, I looked out of the left window, and who do I see boarding? It was good old Billy from school and college! His rum-induced comment was still fresh on my mind. Once airborne. I pulled out my night kit and removed the blade from my safety razor, then requested the cabin crew to bring me the passenger manifest. Billy was on seat 2C. I wrapped the blade in a napkin and told the girl to present it politely to the passenger on seat 2C and say, Mr. Billimoria, compliments of the Captain. He welcomes you on board and says, "Billy, you know what to do with the blade." That was one embarrassed Parsi gentleman!

In early 1988, Harry and Ravi helped me get elected as the secretary of the Delhi Chapter of the ICPA. I was also nominated as the Vice President of the ICPA Central executive.

Capt. SL Bagchi had retired, but the time I spent as his understudy had given me the knowledge and confidence to handle various issues for pilots and overzealous Pilot Managers. He made me aware of the dark secret of the nexus that existed between the pilot's union and the operation's department's Managers (DGMs, GMs and Directors) This nexus existed with other unions and their department managers too. This was because their wage increase was decided only after negotiations with their respective trade unions. Unions decided managements salary. Once an agreement had been signed with a particular trade union the Manager of that department were extended the revised pay and allowance.

At times wage increase agitations were instigated by department managers. Every three years, wage negotiations were due. Managers would take union leaders aside and say "*Kutch Natak Karo*" (Start some drama) since they too wanted a wage increase. Everyone was into this game, even HR and Finance. Their own wage increases was sanctioned only after the general cadre union members got their increase.

Pilots in general and ICPA in particular hated both the HR and a finance department. This is so in almost every airline the world over. They are meanies always looking to put spokes in a pilot's life, salary and progression.

Pilot Managers were also members of ICPA and enjoyed all privileges that is pay and allowance, license insurance, annuity and voting in union elections. They were however exempted from following the ICPA calls for strikes etc. Most of them were former union leaders.

Other departments wanted the pilot agreement signed first, which set a benchmark for other union negotiations. The Pilot union always negotiated well – usually giving a little, but taking much more! They had the maximum bargaining power and nuisance value. The airline loved to hate the pilots, they could not live with them and could not live without them.

After the pilot union, followed the aircraft engineer's union, who put up a simple demand: "You did it for the pilots. Now, do it for us". The general employee unions carried forward the same modus operandi.

The "*Shakuni Mama*" in this Ramayana spectacle, was the HR department. They would drop penetrating innuendos to the CMD, warning against escalation of any industrial action as that would stir up the Ministry. Bottom line of HR warning: You could lose your job, Mr. CMD.

The interesting thing was that the Finance Department would always be able to find the extra cash to fund all demands. Decades of such activity ended up putting the airline in the sorry state it is now: a white elephant that the government does not want to maintain, given its losses and liabilities.

The ICPA's standard MO was to issue a work to rule directive such as; strictly follow the Flight and Duty Time Limitations (FDTL), no visual approaches permitted only instrument approaches, not to accept an aircraft cleared under the Minimum Equipment list (MEL). The Engineers supported by refusing to invoke the MEL, resulting in aircraft getting grounded.

In mid-1988, Mr. R Prasad was appointed the CMD. The pilot agitation was on and being from the Finance Department, he refused to give in, until it started to hurt and sinister noises started emanating from the Ministry.

One day, my Regional President and I were travelling as passengers to Calcutta in the morning A300 flight. As the flight was full, we were travelling as additional crew members. The Captain of the flight was the Central Executive General Secretary and the Co Pilot was the President. The CMD was also a passenger on the same flight.

The Captain invited Mr. Prasad to the cockpit. We were meeting after my Huns Air days. He seemed pleasantly surprised to see me there. We shared the fact that amongst the four pilots in the cockpit, we had a Central Executive quorum, and suggested we start negotiations on our wage. Mr. Prasad was game! In less than an hour, we had negotiated the wage increase. We agreed to withdraw the agitation and he agreed to issue the wage increase circular with retroactive effect that evening on his return. We shook hands. That was it.

He told me that I was wasting my talent in ICPA and I should be in management. This I did not fully believe him and laughed it off. He requested me to come and meet him in his office. Which I didn't.

On 19th Oct, 1988, flight IC-113 from Bombay to Ahmedabad operated by a B737-200, crashed while landing in poor visibility. Capt. OM Dalaya was at the helm. He was from the 22nd Batch and we had been together on the F27 in Calcutta. I was devastated as Capt. Dalaya was a cautious and conservative pilot.

On 27th Oct, 1988, the Ministry order an investigation by a judicial court of inquiry under the Chairmanship of Mr. Justice AK Mathur a sitting judge of the Rajasthan High Court. The inquiry started almost immediately. I, along with two other pilots represented the ICPA in the inquiry. The court of inquiry gave its finding on 31st January, 1989. (A more detailed account of the inquiry is in the following chapter).

I was back regularly flying Fat Albert and also busy running the Delhi Chapter of the ICPA.

The A320 deliveries were expected by January 1990, and plans were being drawn up for pilots to go for their A320 type rating to Toulouse. Five crew sets per aircraft were to be trained by Airbus at Toulouse as per the purchase agreement. Their training allowances were to be negotiated with the management. In the first meet with the Director of Operations, their offer was only $50 per day for the 5-week course. This was a pittance. Our demand was minimum $100 per day. The management refused. We retaliated by saying the union pilots will not go for training.

The first batch of 20 pilots slated were all executive pilots. We could not stop them so they went on that miserable daily allowance. The First batch was to be followed by a second batch which was a mix of 12 line Captains and 8 Executive pilots. The line pilots were directed not to go for training unless the airline increased the daily allowance. The executive pilots also decided to follow the ICPA directive.

By now they had got feedback from the first batch who were finding it difficult to manage in the $50 per day allowance. All training slots were booked and a delay could result in slot cancellation. This in turn would affect the entry into service of the first 6 aircraft expected in January 1990.

The management was adamant and we were stubborn. As the departure date approached, the matter was escalated to the CMD, Mr. R Prasad. He played hard ball, saying he had the mandate from the PM, Rajiv Gandhi, to not pay more than $50 per day which was the RBI's daily limit. We could not help but exhort Mr. Gandhi to relinquish his PM post and go for A320 training. After all, he had chosen the aircraft.

The batch was already delayed by 2 days. Mr. Prasad called us and clearly told us if it wasn't for the RBI limit he was willing to increase the daily allowance. The Director of Finance was called to confirm the RBI limit. He confirmed it, and when I demanded to inspect the RBI circular, he failed to produce one. The Finance Department did not have a circular!

A copy of the circular was obtained from Air India by Fax. The $50 limit was clearly mentioned. Seeing it in print, the President and General Secretary were willing to give in. I refused. They were both from the A300 fleet and were not themselves affected. I refused to budge.

We staged a walk out about 9pm that evening. I conveniently left my pen behind on Mr. Prasad's table. While the other members were waiting in the lobby for their transport, I returned to Mr. Prasad's office with the excuse to get my pen and sat down. He was visibly depressed.

I asked him if I could see the circular again. I studied the circular minutely and noticed an * mark at the end of the subject para that even the Finance Department had missed. At the bottom of the page, in real small print, it was clarified that the $50 limit was for Government Trainee travel where dormitory accommodation was available for trainees. I brought this proviso to his notice stating the pilots had no dormitory facilities in Toulouse. He summoned the Director Finance immediately, while I got him to agree to $75 per day. He did this reluctantly.

A peon was sent to call the rest of the Union Executive members. An agreement was signed for $75 a day and pilots advised to go for training next night on the 1st available service.

The executive pilots dug in their heels asking for the lost allowance money for the three missed training days. I advised Mr. Prasad that since they were his management boys, he had to either handle them or better still, suspend them. All he did was scowl at me since they were his blue eyed boys.

A late night call to the Director Training Airbus informed him that the pilots would be coming and if they could curtail the training by 3 days so that the training plan was not affected. He agreed. This solved the 3 missed days' allowance issue.

The dispute resolution put the Director Finance in a spot. He had committed to the PMO that the $50 allowance was an RBI limit based on which the PMO and management stand was decided. He was told to clarify to the PMO why the allowance was increased to $75 per day.

As we were leaving Mr. Prasad's office he took me aside and told me that I was a very dangerous union man and he would get me kicked out of the Central Executive. He also reminded me that I was the guarantor of an engine that Huns Air's Kilachand had taken on lease and never returned. I was legally liable. I told him to sue Kilachand and I would not be blackmailed.

I had created enough trouble for the airline with the Ahmedabad crash findings and now had out maneuvered him on the allowance. He had a lot of explaining to do to the PM also.

Sure enough, about a week later, an Emergency Central Executive meeting was called in Chennai, which I was not informed. The treasurer said that crash account of the Ahmedabad crash advance was not satisfactory and said that a ₹2000 spend from the Ahmedabad crash inquiry account made by me was not supported by bills. I was never asked for an explanation about the lack of bills. But a decision was made to expel me from that august body. I was literally sacked. In disgust, I resigned my primary membership of the union and as the Delhi Region's Secretary.

Next morning Mr. Prasad called me and calmly said: "I told you I'll get you removed from the union. You have had enough of trade unionism. It's not your profession. Come to my office around 12 o'clock. I have an important task for you. I want you to work with me for the benefit of the airline."

8. THE B737-200 AHMEDABAD CRASH

"Mistakes are inevitable in aviation, especially when one is still learning new things. The trick is to not make the mistake that will kill you."

– Stephen Coonts

Justice Ashok Mathur inquiring into Ahmedabad crash, was assisted by Shri AK Chopra of DGCA as Inspector of Accident, and 3 Assessors, Shri GS Ganesan of DGCA (Retd.), Group Captain RPS Garcha from the Indian Air Force and Shri JK Mehra, CMD of NPCC.

Justice Mathur convened the Court of Inquiry as a regular Court with all court decorum and made it very clear from the onset that he intended to complete the Inquiry within the stipulated period and will not condone delay tactics. True to his word, Justice Mathur submitted the findings of his Court on 31st January 1989, within the 3 month period stipulated by the Govt.

There were 15 Findings of the Court of which the most important were:

1) On account of not providing proper Radio/Navigation aids and Met Information at Ahmedabad Airport, the National Airport Authority failed to discharge its statutory duty.

2) Indian Airlines is also guilty of Omission that they did not insist on National Airport Authority to provide above facilities.

The CONCLUSION of the Court of Inquiry was:

The cause of the accident is error of judgement on the part of pilot in command as well as co Pilot associated with poor visibility which was not passed to the aircraft.

In addition, there were 27 recommendations aimed at enhancing the safety of aircraft operations. ALL were accepted by the Government. Of these the important ones were:

1) The DGCA setup should be totally overhauled with adequate professional civil aviation men to function efficiently like Federal Aviation agency of USA without any interference from any agency. (This recommendation was accepted by the Govt. 32 years ago and they have still not acted upon it)

2) An independent agency for going into accident investigation should be provided and it should be made autonomous. So that it can work without the intervention from any agency whatsoever. (The AIIB was set up finally after 31 yrs. Since the recommendation, but is still not autonomous, though the government had accepted it originally.)

3) The flight inspection directorate of the DGCA should have competent pilots with sufficiently more experience to independently examine the pilots (The FID was set up by 1991, within 2 years of the acceptance of the recommendation.)

4) The other 24 recommendations were accepted and implemented by DGCA quite expeditiously.

The ICPA played a crucial and important role in bringing to the attention of the court the deficiency that existed and consequent finding and conclusion. Capt. Ashok Raj, Capt. Anirudh Tyagi and I represented the ICPA, on behalf of the deceased pilots, sadly no longer alive to defend themselves. Other respondents were the DGCA, Indian Airlines, National Airport Authority, Air Traffic Officers Guild, and an Ahmedabad Passengers Association.

Each respondent was to be represented by a lawyer who was the only one authorized to file documents, intervene, cross examine witnesses, and present arguments written and oral. The basic role of each lawyer was to defend the actions of the various people connect with the crash, who in turn were represented by their respective unions.

The Inspector of Accidents presented his report along with the FDR read outs and CVR transcript. The CVR was played in court. The audio was terrible most words were drowned by the engine noise. The crew were not using their headsets so the area mike had picked up all ambient noise. In addition, the crew conversation was mostly a mix of English and Typical Bombay Hindi. From the CVR it was apparent that the co-pilot was initially flying and at the very last minute, perhaps the Captain took over. This was not picked up by the court, the assessors or the Inspector of accident.

The last moments of the ill-fated flight are in the CVR transcript (Hindi phrases are transcribed in English)

Time.	By	Text
0:41	CM1	*Kya dhik raha hai? Saaf dhik raha Hai?*
		(Can you see anything? Can you see it clearly?)
0:39	CM2	*Nazar aaraha hai Sir*
		(I can see it sir)
0:34	CM1	*Thora speed rakho.*
		(Keep a little extra speed)
0:15	CM 2	*Approach a raha sir 30/40 Doh*
		(Approach is coming. Give 30/40) (refers to flaps)
0:13	CM 1	Sound of flap lever 30/40
0:04	CM 1	*Report kar*
0:03	CM 2	*Straight Ahead Ayee hai*
		(It's straight ahead)
0:00		Sound of impact.

The transcript lead us all to believe that the pilots saw some lights which they mistook as approach lights. The approach lights at Ahmedabad were unserviceable as per NOTAM (Notice to Airmen) issued by an airport authority. It appears the crew were not aware.

The ICPA's principal argument was to show up the deficiency in the system, which instead of supporting the safety of flight operations, may have contributed to the accident due their lack, thereof. Most accidents are a result of small errors which by themselves may not be critical, but in a domino effect, could act together and contribute to an accident.

The standing counsel for Indian Airlines, DGCA and NAA (National Airport Authority) led the charge against the pilots, pointing out that it was a clear case of pilot error and they had murdered the passengers and destroyed the aircraft. From the Cockpit Voice Recorder (CVR) transcript it could be inferred that the pilots may have mistaken false light as approach lights and continued the tragic approach.

Many pilots gave witness to seeing false lights during night landings but no pilot had filed a pilot report (PIREP) about them. We carried out many proving flights at night but could not establish the presence of false lights primarily because these flights were carried out when the visibility was clear and not poor as it was on that fateful day. Worse, the lights most likely had been removed after the crash. This I believe to this day.

The honorable judge was getting influenced by the standing counsel's tirade on the pilots. At one point, the lawyer very dramatically stated. "Your Honor the pilots had 12 seconds to carry out a Go Around. 12 seconds your honor which they negligently wasted and killed the innocent passengers". With this, he finished his submission. There was pin drop silence in the court and there were surreptitious glances towards us, holding all pilots guilty.

We had done thorough research, and brought out all the ICAO stipulated requirements, that the NAA had failed to implement. NAA's stand was that the International Civil Aviation Authority (ICAO) requirements were only applicable to International Aviation and thus International airports. Ahmedabad was not an International Airport.

We brought to the notice of the court that the Government of India, a contracting state, had ratified all the ICAO conventions and to their implementation.

After a lot of analysis and unearthing data, we were able to establish that the Localizer (part of the ILS system that aligns an aircraft with the runway centre line) and the distance from runway threshold measuring equipment (DME) had not been calibrated and the DME was over reading by 1 nautical mile. The aircraft had crashed exactly 1nm from the runway threshold in line with the runway centre line.

Also, the NAA had failed to operationalize the glide slope of the ILS. Further they had failed to provide precision approach lights to replace the simple approach light.

We questioned how the airport fire service was not able to reach the crash site. In the hearing, it was established that the airport was not maintaining the stipulated firefighting category.

We challenged the reported visibility conveyed to the pilots before they commenced their final approach. Tower reported visibility was 2000 meter whereas from the CVR conversation between pilots, it was obvious that the visibility was very very poor. If the correct visibility had been conveyed to the aircraft, it would have diverted. The court appointed a retired meteorologist to do a forensic audit of the weather reports.

From the fresh forensic report, it was established that the weather consisted of mist and not a haze, and the visibility was dropping. Yet the visibility reported to the aircraft did not indicate a reducing trend. In all likelihood, the visibility when the aircraft started its approach, must have dropped suddenly due to the low spread between ambient temperature and dew point. The aircraft started its approach just after sunrise and the airfield fogged up but the pilots were misled by what the tower had reported about visibility. The court now started focussing on the airport deficiencies, but the NAA counsel kept harping on "killer" pilots.

Fortunately, on a routine flight from Bombay coming via Jodhpur, Justice Mathur boarded at Jodhpur. Capt. Ashok Raj and I were its crew. As our luck would have it, Delhi was fogged in at 300m with an improving trend.

We saw it as an ideal opportunity to show the good judge what landing in poor visibility actually appeared like from the cockpit. We invited him to come to the cockpit and he did so willingly.

We commenced our approach when the Runway Visual Range (RVR) was within minima. The RVR is the actual visibility measure along the runway. When reported it supersedes the General visibility. Unfortunately, the fog that was lifting formed a low level cloud scud layer just below our decision height (DH) of 200 ft' At DH a pilot must make a decision to either Land or Go Around. Its an instant decision. The judge was visibly nervous. At DH the required visual segment to land was not available. And Capt Ashok Raj call "DH no approach lights Go Around" I immediately executed a Go Around.

For a non-pilot sitting on the jump seat, a Go Around on the B737 is dramatic, the aircraft is pitched up rapidly and full power applied. The engines roar, the electrically operated stabilizer wheel makes a god-awful racket, there are rapid commands, gear and flaps are retracted at the same time ATC is issuing instructions and headings and altitudes to maintain.

The poor judge on the jump seat was frozen in terror. A few minutes later we were sequenced behind two arrivals and the atmosphere in the cockpit was calm. He sheepishly asked what happened. We told him that at decision height (DH), we did not see the approach lights and carried out a Go Around. He wondered aloud about pilots having to take split second decisions which MUST be right for everyone's sake. By then, we were sequenced behind another Boeing which also went around. I told Ashok that on this approach would be with auto pilot and flight director. I intended to duck under to a DH of 50ft and to set the MDA alert light to 50 ft' Radio altimeter height.

Again, we were flying in thick soup and Judge Mathur, strapped in the jump seat, unable to see anything, was on the verge of panic. We broke out at 100 ft' Ashok called "Approach lights" and I responded "Contact! Landing". Almost immediately, we were crossing the threshold. Power back, nose up and we landed. All he could see were the edge lights whizzing past and we coolly turned on to the taxied track and parked on the apron. After shutting engines and completing the checklist we turned toward him.

He was frozen and stammered, "What did you see?". "The approach lights", we said. We made a right call and unfortunately Capt. Dalaya did not. From the beginning of Ashok's calls to touch down must have taken about 10 seconds. He was astonished and said that 10 seconds passed so fast. He now understood the difference of time as perceived in flight and on ground. When a lawyer says the pilots had 12 seconds to take a decision to go around and yet they did not, it sounds like a lot of time, but not when an aircraft is moving forward at 400 ft' a sec and losing height at 240 ft' per sec.

We wished him well and he thanked us for this cockpit experience and remarked that he would never travel in the cockpit again!

That day, we both decided to attend court in uniform. The court was in session when we arrived. He held up his hand and stated: Capt. Shakti and Capt. Ashok gave me an experience in the cockpit that will last a lifetime.

Then he hauled up the standing counsel and threatened to hold him in contempt for trying to mislead the court. He asked him whether he had any experience on an aircraft in terrible weather conditions while keeping track of 12 seconds. Do you know how quickly 12 sec flashes by in an aircraft in flight? He snapped his fingers in the face of counsel and said, "Like this!'. He added that pilots are human beings not superhuman and have to take instant lifesaving decisions. If they take a wrong decision, it is an error of judgement and not pilot error.

And so, we were able to educate the court on Human Factors and their contribution to accidents. This was mainly responsible for the Courts conclusion for the cause of the crash. Judge Mathur had harsh words for both Indian Airlines and the National Airport Authority.

Next day, I rang up R Prasad the CMD and informed him that the Court of Inquiry was looking to pass strictures against the airline and the Airport Authority. He must have informed Mr. Rajiv Gandhi, the PM. Very soon a National Transport Safety Board was constituted. The chairman of the NTSB was Shri Prakash Narayan, former Chairman of the Railway Board, Capt. BK Bhasin, former Director Safety and Dy. Managing Director of Indian Airlines as member, and a third member whose name I do not recall. I appeared before the Committee.

The NTSB reviewed the finding of the Judicial Court of Inquiry and amended the cause of the Crash as "The cause of the accident is error on the part of the pilot in Command as well as Co-Pilot due to non-adherence of laid down procedures under poor visibility condition." Its job done, the NTSB was wound up and has not re-appeared since. If one was to Google NTSB India, no result is shown as if it never existed.

Since National Airport Authority was found not carrying out statuary obligations and Indian Airlines not insisting on it to do so, was considered an act of omission. A large number of deceased passenger's relatives did not accept the compensation under limited liability and sued for unlimited liability under the Carriage by Air Act 1972. The case dragged on for decades and was finally decided by the Supreme Court which finally awarded substantially more damages. It also ruled that no committee has the right to change the finding of Judicial Court of Inquiry. This could be done only by the Supreme Court after due process.

If one was to go through the various Courts of Inquiry over the last 50 to 60 years, the same recommendations keep cropping up for the safety of aircraft operations. They keep getting accepted but are seldom implemented in the spirit they were made. Truth is stranger than fiction, and it appears, more so in the case of Aviation Safety.

Safety is expensive. It costs money but it is money well spent. More of this further into the book.

9. PILOT'S BIBLE
(THE OPERATIONS MANUAL)

"It's possible to fly without motors but not without knowledge or skill"

– Wilbur Wright

Mr. R Prasad had requested that I come to his office around noon. I was at his doorstep a minute before noon.

He met me cordially and then dropped the bombshell. "Shakti, I want you to compile the Airlines Operations Manual. You will get all the support that you desire. "You will report directly to me" he said.

This was a challenge that I could not let pass and I instantly agreed. Out of curiosity, I asked, "Why me?" He smiled and said: "To keep you out of troubling the airline."

What had actually transpired was that the airline had approached The Jeppesen Company, producers of airfield approach and route navigation charts and consultancy on aviation-related subjects for producing an Operations Manual on a turnkey basis. They had quoted a fee $500,000 and a term of 12-18 months.

I came free and was given a 9-month deadline to complete a project that I did not have a clue on how to go about.

I pointed out that it would be a full-time job and that I would lose out financially since I would be unable to fly. He immediately called up the Operations Manager of Delhi Region to come and see him along with the Pilot Roster in charge. Next, he summoned the Operations Manager,

Headquarters, who was holding charge as officiating Director of

Operations as a new incumbent had not been appointed. He was requested to allot me a room along with an Operation's Assistant to assist me.

Lunch was ordered from the Princess restaurant located in Thapar House, which was the adjacent building. From here came the delicious Paneer cutlets, their speciality and from Paharganj, the best *chole bhature* I had ever had. This became the standard lunch for me.

During lunch Mr. Prasad brought up the appointment of the Director of Operations and the 3 contenders. Two of them were being pushed by different factions of the ICPA. One was Capt. VP Singh, and the other Capt. RN Tandon. Both were politically connected. The third was the Operations Manager of Flight Safety, Capt. RL Kapur.

What was my opinion, the CMD asked. I suggested Capt. RL Kapur without hesitation in my opinion he was a thorough professional and a respected instructor examiner. I added that in case Mr. Prasad decided between the other two there would be one dissatisfied faction in the ICPA, which would be a pain in his ass.

He smiled and to my astonishment called the Director Personnel and instructed him to issue the order for appointment of Capt. RL Kapur as Director of Operations. I had owed a huge debt of gratitude to Capt Kapur for his kindness during my co-pilot training for the B737.

The appointment led to much surprise and consternation among the pilots. No one expected this appointment, and everyone wondered how Dr Kapur had pulled out such a rabbit out of his hat! The conjecture was Dr Kapur had tremendous clout! That no one knew about!

On being informed of his appointment, Capt. Kapur came to assume charge and to thank the CMD. Again to my astonishment, Mr. Prasad told him to thank me. He then informed him about my assignment, and that he was counting on his support.

Just then the Operations Manager of Delhi and his roster in charge, Mr. Surinder Pal Singh walked in. They were told that the DO's office will instruct them on my flight scheduling on a daily basis.

When asked to choose a room, I quickly commandeered a room, originally belonging to Capt. HR Singh and Capt. VK Kukar, who were in Toulouse undergoing their A320 type rating. I also selected Ms Vasuda as my Operations assistant, I knew she was familiar with computers and word processing.

The first computer and printer in Indian Airlines was the IBM 286, bought for my office for a princely sum of ₹1, 75,000. I was authorised access to all files from 1956 onwards. I needed to read these so as to be able to document operational policy, orders issued and include them in the proposed Manual. To get a better grip of the subject, operations manuals from British Airways, United Airlines and Saudia were sourced.

Research and reading became my bywords. Accepting or rejecting policies and processes could not be subjective. Soon, I had a skeleton of a Manual in two volumes. All that was required was now amending operational policies identified to comply with Indian Civil Aviation requirements and converting all the General Operating Circular issued over the years as policy and standard operating procedures for which I borrowed the best practices from airlines around the world.

The United and Saudia Manuals were complying with FAA requirements and the British Airways Manual with the UK CAA requirements. The Saudia Airways Manual had been made by TWA that had set up the airline.

The ICAO, Annex 6, lays out the Standards and Recommendatory Practices (SARPs) on operations for uniformity the world over. ICAO has no regulatory powers: it cannot enforce its SARPs laid out in various Annexes and documents covering the whole gambit of Civil Aviation. It is up to the Contracting States that are signatories to the Warsaw Convention of 1944 to adopt the ICAO SARPs. States that do not, or only selectively, adopt ICAO SARPs, are to file differences with ICAO so that other States are aware of areas in which a particular State differs from ICAO. The United States does not follow ICAO in many areas and differed with it on many counts. At that time, ICAO Annex 6 did not place any obligation of pilot FDTL on the State on the operators. Later, it became a state obligation.

One day over tea, Mr. Prasad evinced a desire to completely change both the pilot and cabin crew uniforms. I thought of Rohit Khosla, (now deceased), a popular designer and my personal friend. I asked him to meet Mr. Prasad.

Rohit was thrilled. Indian Airlines as a client would be a feather in his cap. He, in fact, offered to do the designs free just to be associated with the Airline. He came up with 2 designs. A single-breasted deep navy blue jacket and trousers. Gold *zardosi* wings, stripes and epaulettes for pilots were designed. A *bund gala* suit of the same material for the male cabin crew with *zardozi* work on the collar and long flowing *angarkha* cut kurtas and churidars for the female cabin crew.

These were to be in two different colors of the same design: one in blue and the other in deep maroon. Pilot ties were of the same material and colour as the cabin crew kurtas... We both loved the uniforms. A full line for each crew was tailored for demonstration for the Board's approval.

But this was not to be.

On the morning of 14ᵗʰ Feb 1990, Flight IC-605 from Mumbai crashed on final approach just short of the runway on the KGA Golf Course, on approach to Rwy 09 at Bangalore. It devastated Indian Airlines and the nation went into mourning. Both pilots, Capt. Gopuchkar, a check pilot and Capt. Fernandez undergoing a Command route check, were killed along with 92 passengers.

Mr. R Prasad took moral responsibility for the crash and the death of passengers and crew and resigned. Till date, he remains the only CMD of Indian Airlines who had the integrity to accept moral responsibility for an air tragedy. No other CMD has ever done so and protected their own seats first. They always hid behind 'Pilot Error' verdicts after any accident.

The inquiry committee blamed the IC-605 crash on pilot error. This was supported by Airbus Industries. The conclusion was challenged by the ICPA. They pointed out flaws in the Fly-By-Wire control design and also the time taken by the high bypass turbo fan engine to achieve full power from idle. The certification limit was 8sec but the "black box" which is actually the Digital Flight Data Recorder (DFDR) showed the engines took 10 sec. These 2 seconds could make the crucial difference between life and death.

Earlier an Air France A320 had crashed on 26 June 1988 while making a low pass over Mulhouse-Habsheim during the Habshein Air Show. This crash was also very controversial. While the cause was given as pilot error, Capt. Asseline, at the helm, claimed that an error in the fly-by-wire computer prevented him from applying full power and pulling up. Then, on 20th January 1992, an Air Inter A320 crashed in the Vosges Mountains while circling to land at Strasbourg Airport, killing 87 of the 96 on board. In both the Bangalore and the Strasbourg crashes, majority of the fatalities were fire-related, leading to a common saying among pilots "if you fly-by-wire, you will die-by-fire".

The Strasbourg and Bangalore crash inquiries recommended many changes to the autopilot and flight guidance computers, which were implemented, resulting in the very safe and pilot-friendly aircraft that the A320 has now become. The A320 aircraft that Indian Airlines bought as a launch customer, and the A320 aircraft that flies today are, in reality, two different aircraft with the same name. The former was a bitch, and the latter is a pussy cat.

Pilots were hesitant to fly what Airbus called the safest aircraft. The aircraft needed modern approach and navigation aids that were sadly lacking in India, which resulted in erroneous computer guidance. Many pilots used to deselect all the fancy computers and fly it on a 'Selected' mode, just like they would on the B737, instead of the 'Managed' mode, that the aircraft was designed for.

Subsequently, the lack of aviation infrastructure became the core issue for an all-out strike by the ICPA in December 1992.

After the Bangalore crash, a delegation of pilots met with the then Minister of Civil Aviation, in the VP Singh Government, Mr. Arif Mohammed Khan, putting forth their apprehensions on the aircraft's safety. Public confidence in the aircraft was fast eroding. The Minister took a political decision to ground the total A320 fleet, stating "If the pilots don't feel safe flying the aircraft, how can the govt. permit innocent passengers to fly in it?" This was despite officers in the Ministry and DGCA advising against such action. That decision was to cost Indian Airlines tremendous losses.

How to get the aircraft back in the air again, became the great challenge. The A320 was finally "ungrounded" by behind-the-scenes activity of the French Ambassador and the Cabinet Secretary between Dec'91 and Jan'92. I got involved since my wife was the social secretary to the French Ambassador, and a Director in the Cabinet Secretariat was a close buddy from college. There were many cloak and dagger meetings, some in my house and some in my friend's house.

On 17th Jan, 1991 President George H W Bush gave us Desert Storm-1. And so the A320 was re-introduced, on the Cabinet Secretary's instructions, to carry out "The Amman Evacuation" of Indian nationals fleeing the war in Kuwait.

Earlier, the CBI had registered a case on the Airbus order. But absolutely nothing came of the case as crucial files and papers conveniently disappeared from the Airline offices and Aviation Ministry! Once the minority Congress government under Prime Minister Narsimha Rao came to power, the case just died a natural death, but the file was not closed until much later.

Airbus was back in business post 2004 when the skies opened up to Low-Cost Carriers (LCC) with Air Deccan, Go Airlines, Kingfisher and IndiGo becoming their customers, besides Indian Airlines. The flamboyant owner of Kingfisher also ordered the A380.

To go back a little, Indian Airlines had originally confirmed the purchase of the B757 to replace the B737 aircraft in 1986. However, the PM, Rajiv Gandhi while attending the Paris Air Show and was given a presentation by Airbus on the A320, a new generation, glass cockpit modern aircraft with Fly-by-Wire controls whose Entry into Service was planned for 1988. Mr. Gandhi was totally floored by the aircraft and decided to have it ordered for Indian Airlines instead of the B757 which was still using older technology.

An Indian Airlines team lead by the then CMD Captain Kamni Chadha, negotiated a contract for a firm order for 30 A320 aircraft with options for 12 more. They selected the IAE V2500 engine. Aircraft deliveries were to commence in late 1989. The airline became one of the 'Launch Customers'. Launch customers get cheaper deals, but the downside is that they are the guinea pigs for the manufacturers, as new technology can take up to 3 years to iron out teething issues and stabilise.

Capt. Chadha's favorite anecdote was that after days of haggling, they had arrived at a price that the Airbus team was not willing to negotiate further. The meeting room fell silent as negotiation stalled. Capt Chadha decided to take a loo break, and so did the Airbus team leader. Here were two senior honchos pissing away, when Capt. Chadha casually remarked, "Drop your price by $1,000,000," and, just like that, they zipped up, washed and shook hands. The deal was sealed with a piss and handshake. As per Capt. Chadha, the Airbus chap latter told him that, their piss together was the costliest piss of his life. It cost Airbus $42,000,000.

Indian Airlines cancellation of the Boeing order had created a furore in the International Aviation market. Boeing accused Airbus of using non civil aviation inducements for civil aviation sales, a violation of international agreement on civil aviation reached after Japan's Lockheed scandal where the Japan PM and Lockheed were found guilty of corruption by the US Congress.

Boeing petitioned POTUS with charges that France, to favour Airbus, offered the following non-Civil Aviation inducement for the A320 sale, which caused the cancellation of the 757 order, resulting in a loss to America.

The inducements alleged were:

–   Upgrading of the Mirage 2000 avionics and armaments platform
–   Free French assistance for the cleaning of the river Ganga.
–   Maintaining the Indian Ocean nuclear free, the largest naval nuclear presence in the Indian Ocean, then was allegedly supposed to be French.

In the US, there was a counter lobby by their aviation industry's Original Equipment Manufacturers (OEMs) petitioning POTUS that 70% of the A320 costs were actually American and while Boeing may have lost, America had not. Apparently, the issue was not taken up with France by the US government.

**(The above snippet is attributed to an opinion piece in the International Herald Tribune of that time)

In hindsight, choosing the A320 was a wise decision as it became the mainstay of the Indian Airlines fleet and one of the most successful and best-selling single aisle aircraft produced by Airbus. Of course, the A320 was Boeing's nightmare.

While all this excitement had the knickers of major aviation players in a twist, I was busy as a beaver trying to meet my deadline to produce the Operations Manual.

Mr. R Prasad was replaced by Air Marshall SS Ramdas from the Indian Air force. He took a keen interest in the progress of the manual and read through each chapter and only after his approval, could it be finalized. Capt. Kapur ensured full support, administrative and material. By October 1990, the Manual was complete – vetted, verified and approved. The manual contained the Airlines Flight Operations policies and standard procedures. It was in 2 volumes bound in fake black leather and so came to be called the Black Book. The Pilot's Bible. Each Pilot was issued a personal copy of this Bible.

During this period, Air Marshal Denzil Keelor visited Airlines House, which is what Airlines HQ was called. He was then the Inspector General of the Indian Air Force in charge of Safety. Air Marshall Ramdas introduced Air Marshal Keelor to us all. He was no stranger to pilots. He and his brother Trevor were aces of the 1965 war. Their youngest brother Gordon was a teacher in SEM, my alma mater.

Air Marshal Keelor informed us that he was on secondment to Civil Aviation to set up a pilot-friendly Flight Inspection Department to carry out assessment and proficiency checks of pilots. This had been attempted before in the 70's. Two senior officers Gamma and Grewal were deputed to standardize the Avro (HS748) pilots. Both were deliberately failed in their simulator checks by the Indian Airlines Examiners, who did not wish for anybody to rain on their parade.

The DGMs were egging him with supportive noises, on until I spoke up and said "Air Marshal, you will fuck it up, if you go ahead as planned. Don't waste your time".

There was pin drop silence and Air Marshal Ramdas turned a deep red. Just then Denzil Keelor spoke up. "Shashi, I want you to second this young man to work with me. He can help me set up the Flight Inspection Directorate in the DGCA.

I did, and also ran it for him.

Thereafter, the Indian Airline and Air India pilots selected as Flight Inspectors were good, fair and unbiased pilot instructors and Examiners. Though totally useless in writing reports, they got help (often from me) to write their reports and schedule the check rides.

Also introduced for the first time in Indian Aviation, was an appeal procedure for flight checks. Any pilot who felt he had been unfairly assessed, could file a confidential appeal with the FID. He was reassessed by another Examiner and if found fit, cleared to fly. This brought in an element of fair play and reduced victimization of pilots by Examiners from different pilot factions.

Denzil and I became great friends and in later years, we worked closely in high powered committees for Indian Airlines' pilot shortage issues, its turnaround strategy and other operational issues.

Once this task was complete, I again planned to return to line flying. Capt. Kapur was not keen to let me go back as a line pilot. He was well aware that Mr. Prasad had maneuvered me out, and he too felt that there was a danger with my return to line. He had a confidential meeting with Air Marshal Ramdas, explaining the reason Mr. Prasad had me removed from ICPA and given me the Operations Manual task. He also explained that I knew more about the Operations Department than him and that I had studied all the files and policy decisions since 1956. It was felt that it would not be in Management's interest if I went back as a line pilot.

He suggested that I be made an Officer on Special Duty to the Director of Operations, at a level above line pilot but below Dy. Operations Manager. The CMD agreed after discussion with the Director of Personnel who supported Capt. Kapur's contention.

A note was put up to the CMD on which he wrote Approved and signed it and kept it in his out tray. Coincidentally, ICPA General Secretary, the President and Vice President were meeting with the Director Personnel. The Director Personnel brought them over for a courtesy call. Whenever ICPA executives visited, Airline House would buzz with nervous anticipation: "ICPA is here". A visit to the CMD as a courtesy was a convention.

Union pilots are masters at reverse reading. Whenever one visited any airline office, they scanned all the papers on the desk for crumbs of information that they could pick up. Many a times connecting the dots from scans from different offices, they were able to guess what the management was up to and be ready with counters.

True to form the note on me was scanned. After leaving the Boss's office, the General Secretary met some of the DGMs and told them what was afoot.

The DGMs protested, fearing that sooner or later I would supersede them. The ICPA decided to confront the CMD with a threat that if Capt. Lumba was promoted out of turn, there would be industrial unrest. The CMD lost his nerve and just added a NOT in front of "Approved" and sent the note back to Capt. Kapur. (A useful tactic I used later in life when I headed Operations Departments).

This single decision changed the airlines' future irreversibly when the ICPA won a legal strike master minded by me, based entirely on safety issues that were technically Airline policy, but not followed. I knew the policies, where they were, and their implication. Of this the airline operations management was less familiar as they had recently been formulated. Capt. Kapur's fears came home to roost.

Next day, I reverted to the line and spent my time flying as much as I could. By mid- Oct 1991 I was back in CTE for 6 weeks of ground school for the A320. In the beginning, we all found the course a little tough as we tried trying to memorize all the various systems.

There was the FADEC (Full Authority Engine Control), FMGS (Flight Management and Guidance System), MCDU (Multi-Functional Control Display Unit), FMGS (Flight Management and Guidance System) ECAM (Electronic Centralized Aircraft Monitor) and FCU (Flight Control Unit) to name a few important ones.

Capt. Vijay Thergaonkar popular as Capt. Terry, was the DGM in-charge of A320 training. He finally brought in some sanity when he told us, "Forget what it means you must know what it does."

The technical information provided in the 4 volumes of A320 FCOMs (Flight Crew Operating Manuals) was strictly on a need-to-know basis. However, we needed to know more, so as to understand the aircraft fully. The technical instructors did a brilliant job in obtaining relevant information for us from the Engineering Manuals and documents. So, they were able to impart us deeper knowledge that came handy, especially when spurious messages appeared on the ECAM.

If a computer got hung mid-flight, it had to be reset; for this we had to know which CBs (circuit breaker) and in what combination they could or could not be reset in flight. On ground, there were no such restrictions. The strong foundation on the technical aspects of the aircraft played an important role in understanding the aircraft systems and how they were interlinked. This stood me in great stead till I flew the A320 on my last flight in May 2010.

After a successful and satisfying endorsement course I was back flying the B737 until it was time to go for my simulator training.

Today only very basic information is available to pilots since the 6-week chalk and board teaching is replaced by the CBT (Computer Based Training) modules of self-study that are in vogue to reduce training time and costs. It now boils down to "when this happens do that" and there is no need for pilots to troubleshoot.

On 26th of Feb '92, I reported for my simulator training. On 28th, I got a call from home that my dear Mother had passed away. I flew back next morning and drove to Rampur with my wife.

I was able to return back only in April. Capt. Lue Lingam, a neighbour and friend was also the GM Operations Delhi. He arranged for a training slot, and I was able to proceed to Hyderabad for my A320 simulator and flying training.

I was fortunate to be allotted Capt. Terry as instructor. The first thing he showed us was how to sit right and adjust the hand rest and lightly grip the super sensitive Side Stick controller that had replaced the control column, which had stood between the pilot's legs since the beginning of powered flight. The space left vacant in front of the pilot now had a sliding foldable table. Very useful.

It took only one familiarization sortie to get the hang of the side stick and the multifunctional flight and navigation displays that had remarkably uncluttered the cockpit's instrument panel.

What took getting used to, was the loss of tactile and aural inputs that we had become so dependent on while flying conventional noisy airplanes. We now had only the visual sense to rely on. We had to LEARN to LOOK and SEE.

On this aircraft both the side sticks were not interconnected. The throttles did not move, causing a loss of the tactile feedback. The engines were so silent; they could not be heard in the cockpit. One could not set the power based on the engine sound anymore. We lost the all-important aural input and we had to set engine power before finite tuning by looking at the gauges.

Pre simulator session briefing were an essential part of a simulator session. Terry concentrated on making sure we understood the logic and operation of the two flight modes 'Managed' and 'Select'. In 'managed' mode the computers controlled the airplane and the pilot just monitored. In 'Select' mode the pilot controlled the airplane and the computers monitored.

The A320 cockpit had to be managed by both pilots as per laid down task-sharing and standard operating procedures. The efficiency and competence of the pilot flying was dependent on the pilot not flying. His role was very important in the two-man cockpit. He was no longer to be a fat, dumb and happy spectator.

We completed the simulator session and check and moved on to the flying training segment. The most important tip that Terry gave was visual perception created by the large cut off angle that the top of the instrument panel, the combing provided. The A320 had excellent forward visibility due to this very large cut off angle. This had a downside. At about 200ft the amount of ground one could see seemed to increase, giving the illusion that the nose was lower than normal. The pilot instinctively raised the nose to establish the ideal picture of a runway profile stored in his brain out of years of flying experience. Now the engine computer increases power to maintain the airspeed. Coming near the ground the plane would be caught in a flatter than ideal angle causing a long flare or a hard landing if power is reduced abruptly by the pilot. Armed with this bit of knowledge, landing the A320 smoothly and accurately was never an issue. On 26th of May, my license was endorsed for the A320 to fly as co-pilot. I could no longer fly the B737.

Pilots in India are not permitted to fly two different types of aircraft concurrently. This is a safety consideration learnt after a pilot error crash. Only specially-authorized very experienced examiners are permitted to fly both kinds of aircraft by the DGCA. This does not preclude flying airplane family variants like those of the 737 family or the A320 family and mixed fleet flying of the Airbus 320, 330, 340 since they have identical cockpit flying and cockpit management procedures.

One particular air crash gives the rationale of the above stipulation. On Oct 12th, 1976, Indian Airlines flight 171 from Bombay to Madras crashed after take-off while returning to land in an emergency. A fatigue crack in the compressor caused the engine to fail, which was followed by the bursting of the compressor case and rupturing of fuel line. This caused an intense inflight fire that consumed the aircraft – killing all 95 passengers and crew.

The delayed flight was operated by Capt. KD Gupta a B737 and Caravelle pilot. Capt. Gupta was to operate the flight by B737, but the aircraft was grounded due to engine trouble and replaced by a Caravelle which Capt. Gupta was requested to operate. The Caravelle, like the Boeing, carries its fuel in the wings. In the Boeing, the fuel is fed by gravity to the high pressure fuel pumps that meter the fuel into the engine. In the case of the Caravelle, the engines were in the rear and low pressure pumps feed the fuel from the wing to the high pressure pumps which then feed fuel to the engine. The engine fire procedure is to shut the fuel pump and fire the engine extinguishers. In the case of the Boeing, only one lever that controls the fuel needs to be shut. However, in case of the Caravelle, both the levers controlling the high pressure and low pressure pumps needed to be shut.

It is an established fact that under stress a human being regresses to an older learning habit which in the case of Capt. Gupta was the B737 that he recently and regularly flew. He reacted to the engine fire as he would have on the B737 – that is, shut the only fuel lever and fire the engine fire extinguishers. But he was flying the Caravelle that need two pumps to be shut. In that high stress situation, he must have only shut the high pressure pump. The low-pressure pump kept adding fuel to the engine, which was already afire, resulting in the aircraft being consumed by fire mid-air.

After this crash, initially the Airlines, and later the Regulator, stopped permitting pilots to fly two different types of aircraft concurrently.

In August, I went on leave to sort issues with the farmland and other inheritance and legal issues after my Mother's passing. I was the youngest of five children but had to take on the responsibility of the eldest. My brother Mohan , and my sister Veena lived in Kenya and my two other sisters were married to Army officers, one on posting to the NE and the other to South India.

I returned to New Delhi in September and became embroiled in a pilot strike. I flew from the frying pan, and into the fire!

10. PILOT STRIKE ON SAFETY ISSUES

"Safety is expensive, it costs money. Everyone pays lip service to Flight Safety but no one is willing to pay for it."
– The Safe Airline

I returned to Delhi in Sept 1992 after sorting out most of the property issues in Rampur. The same evening, I got a call from a colleague Capt. Kulin Asher, a pilot domiciled in Mumbai and an executive member of the ICPA. Though I was no longer a part of ICPA after my unceremonious ouster, my friend earnestly requested me to assist the ICPA as an unprecedented crisis had erupted and the team was in need of guidance.

As I entered the room at Taj Palace hotel where the meeting was being held, I found full ICPA Central Executive sitting around the table. The General Secretary, Capt. Vilas Naik, immediately spoke: "Boss, we just served the airline an Official Strike Notice. What the fuck should we do now?" My instant reply was why you issued the notice, and whether the strike was ratified by the general body.

The reason they gave was that the management had replaced the 1964 Flight and Duty Time (FDTL) agreement with a DGCA Issued Aeronautical Information Circular (AIC) 26 of 1992 in spite of Union objection, and refused to enter into the wage negotiation that was overdue by over one year. Their decision to strike was also not ratified by the General Body. "How much money do you have in your union accounts?" I asked next. I was told that there was some money in the regional accounts but the Big Bucks which were in the Central Body's account were frozen by a court order.

Of course, this was an unprecedented crisis situation! They wanted to go on strike but had not tested the water with the General Body and did not have money to sustain a strike.

First things first, I advised them to follow the association constitution and dissolve the Central Executive and nominate a 'Strike Committee'. They could nominate themselves as long as everything was documented and minutes recorded. This was important to establish the legality of the Strike Notice, if the need arose.

I was requested to become a member of the Strike Committee. I joined as chief strategist in view of my previous union experience and knowledge gained, since I had compiled the Company's Operations Manual, which contained the Airline's Operation Policy, and Standard Procedures. As a matter of fact, I knew more about the Operations Department than the Director of Operations.

The first order of business was that each regional body was to ratify and support the intended strike and every member was to contribute ₹5000/ towards the contingency fund. This contribution was mandatory for the executive pilots.

Indian Airlines had two category of pilots – the line pilots owing allegiance to the ICPA, and the executive pilots who were management pilots in the rank of Dy.General Managers (DGMs) and above. Although part of the management, DGMs remained members of the union so as to retain the benefits of collective bargaining but were exempt from following any union concerted action. Ironically, however, they got to vote in union elections too.

The strike issues were framed as demands (since Trade Unions never *request* they *demand)*

The ICPA demands:

1) In view of the induction of the high tech A320, we demand that all runways served by jet aircraft (the whole airline fleet) be equipped with an ILS, (Instrument Landing System), a DVOR (an En route aid) that provided both direction and distance from it), and a VASI (Visual Approach Slope Indicator)

2) En routeNDBs (non-directional beacons) be replaced with the DVOR

3) Implement all accepted safety related recommendations of various courts/ committees of Inquiry that had not been implemented.

4) En route and Terminal radar coverage be provided.

5) The Trilateral Agreement on pilot fatigue and Flight and Duty Time Limitations (FDTL) agreed to in 1965 be implemented for both line and executive pilots and not changed unilaterally. (This the management had changed by an order wherein was contained fresh guidelines brought out by the DGCA in their Aeronautical Information Circular (AIC) 26 of 1992. This was an information circular and could not override a Tripartite Agreement reached in 1965 between the ICPA, Indian Airlines and the Civil Aviation Ministry with the DGCA as observer.)

6) Fixed pay and variable allowance to be increased by 50% as there had been no increase since 1989 and the revision was overdue

7) Management immediately stop victimization of pilots by keeping them off flying, pending inquiry, to hurt them financially. (They were inquiries pending finalization, for over 6 – 9 months. Pilots only earned when they flew. If they were taken off flight duty, then they got only basic pay of less than ₹10,000.)

Demands 1-5 were related to the safety of aircraft operation, which the airline, the Ministry and the DGCA were obligated to ensure. Ironically, 'Safety in the Air' was totally dependent on the skill and experience of the pilots. We were operating modern high-performance jets to airfields all over the country that had rudimentary approach aids. There was little or no buffer to cater for errors.

Mostly the world over, except in third world poorer countries The unreliable NBD had been replaced by the VOR, as it was more reliable for position finding. However, NDB hadn't been phased out in India. NDBs were totally unreliable in bad weather when thunder storms were present. The on board direction finder kept hunting seldom steady. The NDB was the main approach aid in most of the airports. Pilots had very low confidence to use it especially in bad weather and at night.

Many times when the runway light were unserviceable, kerosene lamps (gooseneck flares) were provided for night operations.

ICAO had laid down in their 18 Annexes and multiple Docs (documents) standards and recommended practices (SARPs) for safety of civil aviation. India as an ICAO contracting state had ratified the Warsaw Convention and accepted following ICAO SARPs. However, India's compliance was as good as non-existent. It was incumbent on the airline to insist on the Airport Authority and the DGCA to fulfil their statutory obligation. Accidents/incidents were routinely attributed to "pilot error", a convenient escape route for the people in power.

Pilots had had enough and decided not to fly under such primitive conditions. There were only 4 to 6 ILS equipped runways at that time – mostly for the A300 operation. The A320 needed modern navigation and landing equipment for it to be flown safely and efficiently.

The strike call was overwhelmingly supported by the general body and executive pilots. All members contributed generously.

A legal strike under the Industrial Disputes (ID) Act, 1947 is difficult. A union needs to wait 14 days after serving the notice to strike. During this period, the conciliation proceedings are initiated by the Labour Ministry, usually by The Chief Labour Commissioner (CLC). During conciliation, the Union cannot strike work. Only if the CLC submits a failure notice to the government. And the latter does not act within 7 days of the said notice, can a strike be legal. Within the 7-day cooling period the government can set up an industrial tribunal to adjudicate the dispute, during whose proceeding there can be no strike. The only window for a legal strike is if no action is taken by the government after the CLC 'failure notice'. As a result of this due process, most strikes are illegal, and strikers face financial and legal repercussions.

The strategy proposed by me was to follow every tenet of the law but use directives as guerrilla tactics to disrupt the operations. We would fly by the book, the book being the Operations Manual. This was different than work-to-rule. The Operations Manual was a relatively new addition and the operations department and other Airline sections seldom adhered to its stipulation. It was a legal document and following it in letter and spirit would not be illegal, and no one in the airline knew his way around the Operation Manual better than I did.

We directed pilots not to land jets on any runway not served by any ILS or A VASI (visual approach slope indicator). This was a system of 3 bars of 3 lights position on either side of a runway giving approach path guidance to an aircraft. If All 3 bars were Red the aircraft was too low, if all three bars were white the aircraft was too high. Ideally the pilot needed to see the top bars white and the other two red. We called it white on red.

- Pilots were not to carry out visual approaches and only instrument approaches. (Instrument approaches added 15 to 20 minutes to the flight time).

- Pilots were not to take-off or land with a Tailwind. Only into a head wind.

- They were to use the full runway length and not carry out intersection take offs.

- The ICPA FDTL was to be followed strictly and no discretionary extensions given

- No Operation into and out of the North East and J&K were permitted after 30 minutes before sunset.

- Not to undertake a flight if in the pilot's judgement he is not fit to do so or is fatigued.

This list is merely illustrative and not exhaustive.

This caused havoc in the domestic air transportation network since Indian Airline was the only domestic airline. Flights were delayed and cancelled. The Northeast and J&K were badly hit.

The airline and Government responded as expected. Quickly, mainstream media was asked to crucify us pilots for using bogus safety concerns just to serve our own financial agenda. Those days, there were no to 24-hr private TV channels. The Civil Aviation Minister, Mr. Madhav Rao Scindia, had a vice like grip on the newspapers, thanks to the owner of the Hindustan Times, and was the darling of the newspaper owners and editors, just like Praful Patel was a decade later.

Obviously, no press statements were accepted from the ICPA, reporters shunned us, and public opinion was maneuvered so skillfully that it demoralized the pilot community. We had our supporters in the

ATC (Air Traffic Control) and executive pilots who were flying under pressure and liberal FDTL dispensation given by DGCA.

We needed to get the executive pilots to strike. The Regional Director (RD) North India, Capt. RL Kapur, was earlier the Director of Operations when I was making the Operations Manual. He had also been my flight instructor on the B737. He was sympathetic but could only help us in small matters.

We identified our weakest pilots and had them put on duty on proscribed flights. They refused under ICPA directive. Got the RD to suspend them. We then gave each of them ₹5000/- bonus and made them heroes of the pilot struggle. It worked. No Pilot was willing to cross the picket line. We next got Company Security to demand identity cards from Executive pilots and those that were not carrying one, were denied airport entry. This, in a strange way, was the last straw on the camel's back.

Low and behold, the Executive pilots decided to strike and join the picket line. Now, Indian Airlines was in trouble. The Government invited foreign pilots to join the Airline. We had already been in touch with every pilot union in the USA, Britain, Europe, and Australia informing them of our demands and imploring them not to let any member pilot come to India as a strike breaker. None came.

Ultimately, near the end of the year, the government got 4 TU154 (Russian made Jets) from Uzbekistan on wet lease to maintain a basic service between the Metros. In a wet lease agreement, the plane is leased out with pilots and maintenance support.

Meanwhile, conciliation proceedings were ongoing with the Chief Labour Commissioner (CLC). His attitude was sympathetic and understanding. He refused to declare the directives as concerted action on our part much to the ire and frustration of the Ministry and Airline.

Towards the middle of November, I received a call from my guardian angel. Capt. Kamni Chadha, former CMD, who minced no words and in pure Punjabi, said, "You guys are getting your arse kicked by the press. Scindia controls the press. Be in the Delhi Flying Club Bar at 7pm. Two trusted aviation journalists will meet you. Leave the press to them."

At the bar, two gentlemen came up to me and said they were friends of Kamni Chadha and were going to help us. One introduced himself as Chaman Bharadwaj Head of PTI, the news wire service, the other Mr. CM Sahni, head of UNI, the older wire service. Both are premier wire services. I was instructed not to issue any press statements or bother to meet any journalists. It was now their responsibility

The two wire services took up our cause. Initially, it was the regional press that started bringing out our point of view, and then slowly the national papers picked up the trend of the blowing wind, and started presenting a more balanced account.

Airline House had two tele printers in its lobby – one each of PTI and UNI. They were both moved into the CMD's offices, and a public relations department officer was put on a 24 hr shift just to monitor the tele printer because they were bombarding ICPA statements and releases at all times of the day and night and the airline was unable to refute most of them.

We were at last able to tell the world the account of our side of the battle. It felt we were slowly gaining ground. Even Doordarshan carried two live episodes of our views and reason for our strike. One was by Vinod Dua and the other by Rajat Sharma, both respected and senior journalists.

Meanwhile, the CLC decided to go across to the Airline House and meet the CMD to resolve the dispute, as he considered our demands reasonable, and those demands could be met only by the government and the Airline.

Mr. L Vasudev, the CMD, was a personal friend of the then Prime Minister's son and he had been brought in from Madras Fertilisers   to whip the airline into shape. He had the backing of the PM and the aviation minister. Mr. Vasudev was not only rude to the CLC, but he also accused him of not doing his job.

The CLC came back spitting fire: "Who the hell does your arrogant CMD think he is? Tatas and Birlas wait outside my office just for an appointment. Now you proceed exactly as I advise you". Things were looking up now that the CLC was our advisor!

Just about then, we anonymously received a Confidential Intelligence Bureau report citing intelligence inputs that the insurgents in J&K had acquired shoulder-fired, heat –seeking missiles of both US and Russian make. We immediately issued a directive to stop all flights to the J&K area effectively cutting of Srinagar, Jammu and Leh, which are entirely dependent on air services, for connectivity in winter. We also suspended all flight to a Kabul, a war zone. The PMO, Aviation Ministry and Home Ministry were all caught on the wrong foot. Scindia came under immediate pressure to control the situation.

A sealed envelope was hand delivered to my home. It contained 2 ILO (International Labour Organisation) resolutions that India had ratified. This was juicy stuff and added salt to the Airline and Ministry's wounds. It gave us legal cover. One resolution dealt with not forcing workmen to work in areas where their lives could be endangered. This provided us cover for not flying to J&K and Kabul. The other resolution was that a skilled workman could not be forced to upgrade his skill if his present level of skill was adequate. With this latter ratification, we asked all B737 pilots not to upgrade to the A320 which required a higher skill level then that required for the B737.

On 6th Dec 1992, the Bari Masjid was brought down. The country was on fire. The same day, CLC summoned us and informed us that 7 days earlier he had submitted his Conciliation failure report and the government had not acted on it. Consequently, our strike was patent and would be legal effective as 5pm of 7th December.

We were in a fix to act or not to act, keeping in mind that the country was facing unprecedented chaos as an aftermath to the Babri Masjid incident. We sought a meeting with the Civil Aviation Minister. After 5pm on the 7th of December, we met Minister Scindia in his office. Also present were the Secretary, Civil Aviation and CMD, Indian Airlines. The Minister met us reluctantly. The proposal we put forth was that our strike was patent but since the country was burning it would not be appropriate to strike work now. We suggested that if all our demands were to be put up to a time bound 3-man arbitration, we would withdraw our intent to strike and start flying the next day.

Minister Scindia's reaction took us by surprise. He said "You no-good loafers and scoundrels don't have the balls or the guts to go on strike and are looking to save face. We will break your strike, your union and all of your careers."

The atmosphere got charged instantly, and accusations flew across back and forth. I can certainly admit that "hot words were exchanged". We told our CMD that he had been making shit at Madras Fertiliser, but by the time we would finish, he would be shovelling shit. We also told the minister not to screw with the Pilot Union and that it may cost him his job. There was no love lost between us.

The government's strategy at all times seemed to have been to push the Pilot's Union to strike, and crush the strike to bring the powerful union to its knees. Once they achieved this, all the other unions within the airline, would fall in line. Prime Minister, Indira Gandhi had done just this to the Railway Unions.

We walked out of the Ministry in Sardar Patel Bhavan and crossed the road to the All India Radio Head office to legally announce that we were on legal strike effective 0800 pm 7th December. All stations of All India radio carried the news. There would effectively be no Civil Aviation in India from 8th Dec, except an occasional flight by the fledging Air Taxi Operator "East-West".

The Strike Committee's job was over. The reins were handed back to the elected Central Executive to manage the picket line. I was co-opted as Advisor

The first two weeks went by in euphoria by the third week the rank and file started getting edgy. Now was the time to put the contingency fund to good use.

The strike was conducted from my flat – D1/1 Indian Airlines Colony, Vasant Vihar. Seven of the outstation members were shacked up with me. There were four of us – Capt. Ashok Raj, Capt. Shamsher Singh Capt. Kulin Asher (all regional secretaries) and me who did the ground work, lobbying, drafting letters, communication to Members of parliament, directives and written responses to the CLC etc.

One of our great supporters was the Hon'ble Dinesh Trivedi, a Congress MP. The government had started basic services between Delhi, Bombay, Calcutta, Madras and Hyderabad with the 4 TU 154 operated by Russian crew who spoke no English and communicated through a translator. Not a very comfortable operation and we went to town yelling from the roof tops that the operation was unsafe and would end in tragedy. *Our warning proved prophetic.*

Early in the morning on 9th Jan, 1993, a TU 154 on a flight from Hyderabad to Delhi crashed while trying to land in Zero visibility in Delhi. That fateful morning, we got a frantic call from Delhi ATC: "Come quick, there's a TU burning on the runway".

The tower officer on duty took 3 actions when the aircraft crashed. He activated the crash bell to alert the Fire Station, called the watch supervisor and then informed ICPA. This was indicative of the level of sympathetic support we got from the aviation industry trade unions across the board. They were well aware of the consequences of the pilot strike failing.

We called our journalist friends from the BBC, Doordarshan, Reuters, and CNN to name a few. We were at the crash site with a journalist and TV cameras. The passengers, hurt, frightened and in shock, were disembarking and trudging to the terminal almost a kilometer away. No buses could be seen. The system seemed paralyzed. Any official in uniform, seen by the passengers had shoes thrown at them, followed by choice abuses in Hindi, English and Telugu. All this was captured by the TV cameras.

Providentially, there were no fatalities and only minor injuries suffered. The aircraft had landed with one wheel on the runway and one wheel on the soft rain-soaked ground off the runway and flipped on to its back. The TU was one tough bird.

There exists a legend that the airport is under the protection of a Sufi Pir Baba whose grave is inside the airport perimeter and he protects the airport. Aircraft that have crashed within the airport perimeter have never had a fatality. Those that have crashed outside the perimeter have had 100% fatalities. The shrine is worshipped every Thursday.

The DGCA was trying to hassle the already traumatized and frightened pilots who spoke no English and expected to go to prison. That is what happened to pilots who survived a crash in their country.

We intervened and took the crew under our protection and did not permit any interview or questioning unless the crew were rested and had an Embassy representative and interpreter present. The DGCA was furious: the ICPA told the DGCA team to piss off. We had won. They had lost.

By about 10am, we got a call from the Prime Minister's Office that the PM, Mr. Narsimha Rao desired to speak to the ICPA. We put our General Secretary on the line. The PM asked "What do you want to call off the strike."

He was told bluntly, "The Head of the Minister and the Head of our CMD."

There was silence and then he asked, "What else?"

We said that all our demands should be put up for arbitration. A demand that the Ministry had refused on 7th December, he was told. He was surprised and commented that he had been misled. He then asked who the Minister of Civil Aviation should be. We told him that we had confidence only in Gulab Nabi Azad, the Minister of Parliamentary Affairs. The only Minister who kept a line of communication open with us from the beginning.

By noon, Mr. Scindia resigned, and Gulab Nabi Azad was appointed Minister of Civil Aviation. We had Minister Azad visit the holy shrine and place a "Chadar" as a thank you to the holy Pir for protecting the passengers.

Mr. MR Shivaraman, IAS was the additional secretary in the Civil Aviation Ministry. He was also the Director General of Civil Aviation. He was appointed to head the arbitration. He cursed us for making us sit on arbitration on himself as he was Incharge of the DGCA. For this, he never forgave us and got his own back when he moved to the Finance Ministry, as Revenue Secretary. He taxed the Indian Airlines pilots' flying allowance retroactively, they had been tax free since the '70s. The Finance Bill of 1989 had made such pilot allowances taxable. They however, remained exempt from tax by a CBDT (central board of direct taxes). Circular was cancelled. The allowances of Air India pilots remained tax free as they were in foreign exchange and paid abroad.

In fairness to Mr. Shivaraman he conducted the arbitration wearing his quasi-judicial hat and not his DGCA hat. Based on Mr. Shivaraman's Report, The Shivaraman Arbitration, the Government sanctioned over ₹400 Crores for the urgent up-gradation of Civil Aviation infrastructure to enhance the safety of aircraft operation.

Normalcy was restored throughout the country except in the J&K with its purported Stinger missiles in the hands of the terrorists.

The PM had informed us that he could not immediately sack the CMD and could we put this demand on hold for a month or two. We agreed in good faith and restored more than 50% Air services and the remaining 50% on 26 Jan 1993, once our demands were met. We got our 50% hike too.

The CMD resigned by February end; the Joint Secretary from Aviation Ministry Mr. Brijesh Kumar, IAS, was made the CMD.

He ask to see me. I met him in his office and he said, "You lead   a very clever campaign. We in the ministry we unable to refute every issue you had raised." Then he added that his first task was to restore air services to the J&K and added. "OK, you took J&K off the air map. Help me restore it." Restoring services were not as easy as suspending them, because of the purported Stinger missile threat. We had expected this and had worked out a feasible option. This was explained to him.

After much internal discussion within the government and Defense Ministry an additional brigade of the Indian Army had to be posted to Srinagar. The airport was encircled by two Army cordons. One covering a five-mile radius and a second a fifteen-mile radius to sanitize the area around the airport. All aircraft approaching Srinagar were required to report over head at 20,000 feet. Once the aircraft reported over Banihal, the entry point to the valley, all vehicular and human movement in the outer area was restricted. Once it reported overhead, no movement of any kind was permitted within the 5-mile radius.

Once ATC got an all-clear message from the Army, the aircraft descended in a tight circling maneuver to land. This process continued until intelligence agencies gave a confirmatory report that there was no threat to Civil Aviation from Stinger missiles.

Aviation professionals acknowledge that the pilot strike of 1992 was the wakeup call for Aviation in India, not only to modernize, but to bring the safety of pilots, crew and passengers' front and centre of the modernization.

Airline pilots of the US and UK represented by ALPA & BALPA acknowledged the ICPA effort and were appreciative of the stand taken to enhance aviation safety in the country.

The Indian Aviation Press often like to describe the '92 strike as the beginning of the decline of Indian Airlines and attribute all its ills and ultimate quiet demise to the strike. This of course, is pure and unadulterated exaggerated fiction, and I would love to rebut them. But that would take another book!

Aviation safety infrastructure in India is now world class, although now under pressure from uncontrolled growth.

11. PILOT MANAGEMENT

"Let's get one thing straight. There's a big difference between a pilot and aviator. One is a technician; the other is an artist in love with flight."

– E. B. Jeppesen

Once the ICPA Strike Committee was disbanded, the Central Executive took back the reigns of the union and I decided to remove myself from the inner circle.

Mr. Brijesh Kumar, the CMD of Indian Airlines, requested me to come work with the management. I declined, frankly citing my stint before while preparing the Operations Manual as a non-management person and the conflict that it had created.

The General Manager HR was called in to examine how I could be brought into management. A pilot's promotion to the management cadre was solely based on Seniority and before I could even be considered for a role, 30 vacancies had to be filled up in Deputy General Manager Category. The policy was that for every vacancy 3 candidates had to be interviewed. To my surprise, the vacancies were immediately approved.

The interviews were held a couple of months later, and I was number 31 in seniority among the list of suitable candidates. The first 30 were appointed and those at serial no. 31-33 were empaneled.

Meanwhile, Mr. Brijesh Kumar was moved to Air India as MD; Probir Sen, IAS, the then joint secretary in the Ministry of Civil Aviation (MOCA), was appointed Managing Director, and Russi Modi, former

Chairman of Tata Steel as Non-executive Chairman of both Indian Airlines and Air India.

Probir Sen was also a Stephenian, many years my senior. He requested me to work with him to bring the airline back on the rails. I advised him that I was a line pilot and not a management pilot but I was empaneled for promotion. The GM (HR) was brought in again and vacancies for DGMs was summarily increased by 3! The three empaneled candidates, including me were appointed.

I was now Capt. Shakti Lumba, DGM. Earlier this post was designated as DOM (Dy. Operations Manager) and they were known as the Dirty Old Men. After a Ministry mandated cadre review of all grades of the airline. Pilots were historically in a grade higher than other cadres designated by 'A', i.e., 14A Captains,16A Commanders, 17A, DOMs, 18A Operations Managers,19A Directors and so automatically were 1st in line for The Deputy Managing Director (DMD) and Managing Director (MD) positions. The cadre review abolished the additional 'A' grade thereby leveling the field between all employees in the same grade. This was considered fair but had a downside. Pilots could no longer be senior to other employees of the same grade.

After the cadre review no pilot has occupied the Managing Director's post. Earlier Pilot Managing Directors excelled as the top boss. Capt. AM Kapur and Capt. Kamni Chadha are two shining examples.

After the resignation of Mr. R Prasad in 1990, no internal employee had been appointed MD or CMD of the airline. In 1993, the top post was captured by the IAS and remains with them. The *Babus* always have a long-term strategy to look after their own. A few of the IAS officers have been excellent for the airline, admitting they were generalists who needed the guidance of specialists. Probir Sen, Brijesh Kumar and Anil Baijal were officers of such calibre. The less said about the other CMDs, the better.

A day after my appointment, Probir Sen called an emergency meeting of all Department Heads and I was requested to attend. It was my 1st experience of a high-power meeting of the airline. It was an eye opener.

There were two points on the agenda: First was that the government had decided to merge Vayudoot Airlines, which was floundering, into

Indian Airlines and had issued the notification. The airline had no choice in the matter. More on this later.

The second point was an increase the in the strength of the executive pilot cadre by another staggering 60 pilots, proposed by the Director of Operations. I was surprised that no one, not even the Director HR had any objection or any opinion on the matter. They were all sitting mute until I, the junior most in the meeting with only a day in management, spoke up to state that it would be a total disaster. The Director of Operations bristled at this presumptuous behavior on my part.

The CMD wanted to know why and how. I pointed out that the airlines did not have enough work for so many executive pilots; promoting so many more, just after the recent round of promotions, would raise suspicions. All those promoted could not be assigned supervisory duties. This would amount to Unfair Labour Practice since we would create a cadre of 'privileged workmen'.

The ICPA could also raise a labour dispute. And most importantly, if 60 more of the remaining senior and mature commanders were promoted to executive pilots, the powerful ICPA would be left in the hands of immature co-pilots. This may (and probably would) result in continuous pilot unrest and flight disruptions. Obviously, the implications were serious.

Surprisingly, the Director HR all of a sudden found his voice and stated he totally agreed with me. It appeared that he approved my temerity to speak up! The Director of Operations walked out in a huff and the meeting took a tea break.

During the break, I was quietly called by the Director of Operations and given a dressing down. I was told that their objective was to increase the non-union executive pilot strength, so that in future the ICPA could not hold the airline to ransom. I disagreed, reminding them that even the Executive pilots had joined the line pilots in the strike. I could not but add, that in his younger days, he too was an active Union leader. The airline may call them management pilots, technically they were still workmen as decided the National Industrial Tribunal. He was however confidant that this would not happen again.

After tea we reconvened, and the Director Operations explained his reasons for the mass promotions. In this, he was supported by the

General Manager Industrial Relation, his department was badly scarred due to the strike. The Director HR acceded and the Director Finance did not object since the financial impact would be minimal.

The CMD wound up the meeting by approving the executive pilot standard force increase by only 30. He further stated that the selection would strictly follow laid down procedures in this regard.

My very first meeting as an Executive Pilot ended with these two issues which were to be very challenging for the next 2 to 3 years. The airline suffered serious pilot unrest for the next few years as the ICPA was captured by unreasonable and immature co-pilots.

I got to know the truth about the large number of promotions only subsequently from GM (HQ). Both he and the Director Operations were old friends of the late Rajiv Gandhi and had maintained close ties with the family and with 'V George' of Number 10, Janpath. In a nutshell, George had desired that a "Capt. X" be promoted in my selection batch. The Director had confirmed to George that Capt. X was among the list of suitable candidates, though unfortunately not among the list of successful ones, due his lower seniority. George was upset as Capt. X had been assured of a promotion. When the vacancies were increased to accommodate list of those empaneled (which included me), Capt. X was still left out. Naturally George was livid as he had been confirmed that the promotion was through. After the standard force was increased, Capt. X was finally promoted.

As days went by, I was juggling flight duties and management responsibilities. I was losing earnings as I could not fly my quota of flights. Management related work was piling up. The merger of Vayudoot was the immediate one. The most complex issue was merging the flight operations departments consisting of cabin crew and pilots who had only flown the Dornier 228, a 20 seater turbo prop aircraft compared to the larger existing jet aircraft fleet of IA.

HR issues were more complex. The pilot union and the cabin crew unions at Indian Airlines were up in arms opposing lateral entry into their respective cadres and the Vayudoot crew were demanding inter se seniority.

Being a small airline, Vayudoot's employees reached senior management positions in 4 to 5 years whereas, in Indian Airlines, it took 15 to 20 years to get to these positions. Merging seniority and associated pay scales were complex issues likely to create airline wide labour unrest. It was finally decided to take over Vayudoot assets and employees into a separate department. The Short Haul Operations Department (SHOD). The department would operate the DO 228. I was given additional charge of General Manager, Operations of SHOD.

Vayudoot had surplus pilots and cabin crew for its aircraft. After prolonged negotiations with the Indian Airline Cabin crew union, they agreed to let the Vayudoot cabin crew be trained on A320 & A300, on the condition they would always be junior most on board a flight. They were good diligent workers and adjusted well with the Indian Airline's crew. Seniority on board is a professional and emotive issue with Cabin crew. The airline cabin crew union demanded a written commitment of the above issue. This was given by Dy. MD Capt JRD Rao and me.

The pilot issue was more complex since Vayudoot Captains demanded to be merged directly as Commanders after training, and the ICPA would not agree as seniority was the main criteria for Command Training. Also, the promotion to Commander Grade was based on seniority subject to vacancy.

I reached out to Brijesh Kumar, MD Air India, suggesting that Air India absorb the Vayudoot captains initially on deputation and train them on the Airbus A310. The entry point to Air India was for Captains to join as co-pilots and its pilot union, The IPG (Indian Pilot Guild) would not have seniority issues. This was agreed and most of the pilots got inducted into Air India. This left SHOD with a handful of Executive pilots & a few co-pilots. The Executive Pilots had declined the Air India deputation. They were given Executive pilot status in SHOD. They continued to fly the DO 228, from Goa and Cochin to the Lakshadweep Islands. A serious confrontation with ICPA was avoided.

Meanwhile Indian Airlines was losing pilots left and right. In '93-94, it lost a total 140 Captains, those from the 737 to the Air Taxi Operators (ATO), East West, Damania, Jet Airways, Modiluft etc. and a few from the A320 to Gulf Air in Bahrain and TransAsia Air in Taiwan. The Indian ATOs increased a captain's salary from ₹30,000 in Indian Airlines to ₹100,000. Mass resignations from Indian Airlines resulted thereby, resulting in an acute shortage of Captains on the B737, and A320 fleets.

The Ministry and DGCA were requested to bring in legislation prohibiting pilots from resigning without notice and joining another airline without an NOC. Both were not interested as the Air Taxi Operations was in fact a Ministry objective to circumvent the Air Corporation Act which did not permit any scheduled Airline besides the two nationalized Airlines. This is why they were designated as Air Taxi Operators and were not permitted to file a flight schedule. This restriction they circumvented by placing large hoardings before the airport and in city centers in which they displayed their flights to various cities, the timing and fare was given. This was obviously the brainchild of the aviation ministry babus who are experts at circumventing rules when it suits their bosses.

The ATO were only able to start and survive because of pilots they had poached. However, a decade later, both the Ministry and DGCA enforced a 6-month Notice Period and NOC Requirement by a controversial order dated 1st Sept 2005 to deny the upcoming LCC (low cost carriers) of a crucial resource. This circular was to directly affect me joining IndiGo.

The losses of the airline were mounting. The industry was still regulated tightly. Fares were controlled by the Government. The Ministry was not inclined to approve a fare hike. They would only agree to a minimum fuel surcharge increase.

Two high powered committees were formed. The Vijay Kerkar Committee to look into the losses of Indian Airlines and the Air Marshal Denzil Keelor Committee on Pilot Shortage. I was appointed to both the committees but focused mainly on the shortage issue. All 3 fleets were suffering due shortage of Captains.

Command upgrade was not possible on all fleets due to the pilot career pattern which basically was that a pilot would move as co-pilot from B737 to A320 and then the A300. Thereafter, for Command he went back to the B737 and then progressively to the A320 and A300. It was an inverted N pattern. It was time consuming and very expensive, requiring extensive Type Rating training twice over on each aircraft type and loss of man days for flight operation. Also, since the ATOs had poached the B737 pilots, no movement from B737 to A320 was possible.

The Keelor Committee came out with the following recommendations that were accepted.

1) Accept all pilot resignations from date of resignation.
2) Pay Market driven wage to pilots.
3) Revise the pilot career pattern.
4) Expedite Command upgrade on all fleets.

Pilots who had resigned since 1993 were still on the rolls as the HR Department did not accept their resignations as directed by the then CMD. This was a Catch 22 situation. If a pilot decided to return to the ranks, the ICPA objected and demanded he join at the bottom of the grade he left. Pilots were willing to re-join if seniority was protected. As resignations were not accepted, basic pay and PF (provident fund) were accruing, and a provision made in the balance sheet under a separate head.

The ICPA was called to start negotiations for their long-standing demands on pay and allowance, subject to a change in their career pattern. The ICPA refused to consider a revised career pattern and started an agitation on wage increase.

They started hit-and run-tactics to disrupt services. Simultaneously, there was public backlash and adverse media coverage. Thoroughly aware that CMDs of Indian Airlines could lose their jobs due to ICPA agitations and lightning strikes if the government intervened, Mr. Sen roped me in to manage the union. I agreed on the condition that there would be no direct HR and Finance involvement. The Operations Department would handle it on its own.

The ICPA had Chairman Russi Modi's ear and we would all be summoned to Bombay to find a solution for the pilots' demands which was impossible. The main tactic of ICPA pilots was reporting sick en masse. Every pilot's license stipulated that he/she could not exercise the privileges of the license if at any time their medical or physical condition fell below the limit as mandated by for the license. This is known as the Class 1 Airmen medical fitness. This was the reason pilots got extra and special sick leave that benefitted both them and the carrier, if used judiciously. However, this started getting weaponized and used against the management.

I warned the pilots that sick leave was a privilege and not to be misused. One of a pilot's greatest insecurities is passing the biannual medical check conducted by the Air Force Medical Establishments. His license validity was dependent on being found fit. And his livelihood depended on a valid license. Before each medical, all pilots start physical exercise, reduce alcohol and cigarette consumption, and so did weight, blood pressure and cholesterol. These three were the dicey grounding indicators.

The next time when about 30 pilots reported on mass sick leave, they were advised that since they were repeatedly falling sick, the Company had decided that they were to be grounded due to medical reasons and could only fly after they were re-evaluated by a DGCA approved board and found fit to fly. In fact, they were also informed that special medical appointments on priority were being arranged at The Air Force's Institute of Aviation Medicine (IAM) Bangalore. There was panic among the pilots as none was willing to go for a medical exam on short notice. The agitation ground to a halt. All 30 pilots were in my office the next day with written apologies and commitments to never report sick without cause. They begged to have the order rescinded.

I let them stew for a day or two, and then got them checked and cleared by the Company's Head of Medical Department. The threat of repercussion for using sick reports as an agitation weapon, hung heavy over the ICPA's Head. These 30 were grateful, but it was ironic that I became ICPA's 'Public Enemy No 1'.

Implementing the Air Marshal Denzil Keelor Committee Report became a priority but for it to be implemented the change in the pilot career pattern was imperative.

I proposed setting up a subsidiary to take over the Boeing 737 fleet to operate on the secondary routes and let Indian Airlines concentrate on the major routes and International Operations to Middle East and South East Regions with the A320 and the A300. The proposed airline was to operate as a subsidiary of Indian Airlines. Airline Allied Services Ltd (AASL) had been registered by R Prasad, former CMD for ancillary services. It never took off, as he resigned after the A320 Bangalore Crash in 1990. I proposed that we hang subsidiary on this nail.

Probir Sen liked the idea and wanted a project report to put up for government approval for an 'Airline within an Airline', under the trade name Alliance Air.

I proposed a flat organization run by employees on a 5 year Employment agreement to operate on private sector norms, paying market wage. I was confident to wean back pilots who had resigned, since by now the Air Taxi Operators were financially floundering. They had started serving free booze on their flights irrespective of the time of the day. This attracted passengers. Ultimately the DGCA came down hard and banned alcohol service on domestic flights as a result of a number of unruly passenger behavior.

Bringing the ICPA around to agree to a change in their career pattern for increased wages became imperative to implement the Keelor recommendation and start Alliance Air. Which could not pay higher wages then the parent company. Without market based pilot wages Alliance Air would be a non-starter.

I was the ICPA's public enemy No.1 and they would stage a walk out if I attended a meeting. Mr. Sen and I maneuvered many walk-outs to put ICPA at a disadvantage with the Chief Labour Commissioner with whom I had an excellent working relation and mutual respect, ever since the pilot strike of '92. What I would usually do at these meetings was walk in late, often wearing a red shirt (to enrage the bulls!). Seeing red, the ICPA would stage a walk-out and charge to the Chief Labour Commissioner who would roundly admonish them for their hot-headedness.

With passing days, the ICPA became secretly resigned to the idea of a career pattern change in principle, but small internal factions started infighting for personal gains, since flying allowances were dependent on the aircraft type and routes flown. Probir Sen by then had been re-designated CMD after Russi resigned. The only impression left behind of this tenure was his boast that he ate a 12 egg omelet everyday.

Probir Sen kept the pressure up to bring ICPA around. I accepted the challenge and promised him I would deliver lock stock and barrel before 26 Jan 1996. I had no clue on HOW to achieve it though! Just around the New Year Eve I got a brain wave when I was sitting *on the throne* at 4am one morning to get ready for a flight. Most eureka moments usually happen when one is sitting on *the throne:* Why have a career pattern at all? Instead of the company deciding where to place pilots, let the pilots decide which aircraft they wanted to fly in command on. This would obviously depend on the types they had on their license. The airline needed Captains on its 3 aircraft fleets.

I mulled it over, refined it and then sold the idea to Mr Sen. Director of Finance got cracking on the amount of money saved and the projected revenue increase, if each aircraft fleet's utilization increased to a benchmark of 2500 hrs per month fleet average. The figure that was crunched was substantial and even if we were to give the Pilots less than 50% of this amount as monetary productivity linked incentive, we could end up paying them more than the market wage. The take home salary was decided at ₹125,000 for a 1st time Captain if utilized for 60 hours of flying per month. If he flew more than 60 hrs he could earn more. I called it the *'Fly More Earn More'* scheme. There would be suitable increase for every year of service, days in training, non-productive duty travel etc., and fitment would be as per years of service as Captain. After getting an in-principal clearance. One morning before a flight I walked into the ICPA office in uniform to their utter shock and disbelief.

The enemy was at the gate!

I informed them that my mandate till now was to checkmate them. Now my mandate was to give them a deal of their lifetime. They agreed to listen and were astounded by my proposal which was much beyond their wildest dreams. I requested them to come see me later after my flight, with their official letter head.

I dictated a one-page letter from ICPA in which my idea was shown as that of ICPA. Doing away with a Career pattern was the key proposal. In return for change in their career pattern they expected a fair market wage. Then off we went to meet the CMD for a cup of coffee. He accepted "their" proposal and ordered negotiations to commence to arrive at an agreement at the earliest.

In house, Capt. JRD Rao and I drafted a PLI (Productivity Linked Incentive) Agreement. We bypassed HR and got the financials approved from the Director Finance and CMD. We were ready to deal.

Sen wanted me to handle the negotiations. My demand was that pilot issues were best dealt by pilots only and nobody from HR or Finance should be involved. Pilots were allergic to both these departments and the negotiations could fail. As I was only a DGM leading a crucial negotiation, I requested one Senior Executive pilot Director or General Manager to also be present with me. However, only one person could lead a negotiation, I was to be given the authority to deviate from the criteria that was set without seeking permission during negotiations. If this was granted, I guaranteed a landmark agreement within 24 hours. I give credit to Probir Sen for having the guts and confidence in me to overrule the concerns of all the Directors. In this, he was supported by Capt. JRD Rao.

Two days later negotiation started with the full Executive Committee of the ICPA. The Director of Air Safety was assigned to give me cover. The following ground rules were laid down. The Board room would be locked from outside and one could only leave the room, once an agreement was arrived at. There was enough food, water, tea and coffee laid out and the door would only be opened for *loo* visits and replenishment of supplies. Since I had the authority to take final decisions, I requested the ICPA Committee to give the same Authority to the General Secretary by passing a resolution there and then.

Each person sitting at the negotiation table had a copy of the draft agreement. We would tackle it clause wise, the clauses agreed on would be counter signed and slipped under the door to the CMD office adjacent to the board room, for final incorporation. Clauses where we disagreed on would be passed over to be tackled later.

There was lots of yelling, interspersed with colourful *BCs, MCs, MFs,* flying around. Just normal pilot lingo to which no one took offence.

Meanwhile, the Director's main contribution was of pleading with the boys to accept the deal adding "*Itne paise sapne me nahi dheke*' (I can't dream of us all earning so much money).

The CMDs team, sitting next door in his office were getting greatly concerned about the abuses flying! They feared a breakdown in negotiations. His EA popped in and told me the CMD needed to have a word. Sen expressed concern about the yelling and the curses flying about next door! Was the negotiation still on, he asked. I told him not to worry. Among pilots, such language was actually terms of endearment and loudly emphasized the particular situation. A pilot would accept them from another pilot, but not from the CMD or his managers.

Both sides threw tantrums, cooled down, discussed and spat curses – this went for 11 long hours by when we had tied up the agreement except two tricky clauses.

They wanted an assurance that the ICPA be consulted when a replacement for the A300 was finalized and who would get to fly it. I wanted an assurance that for the next 5 years there would be NO wage hike demand. They would have to guarantee industrial peace for the next 5 years in a side letter. The airline needed to get back on its feet. We accepted each other's conditions. A historic agreement had been arrived at.

Labour agreements are bilateral agreements signed in Form H under the Industrial Disputes Act of 1947. If one party decides to not honor the agreement, the issues could only get resolved by a labour court. Whereas an agreement signed in conciliation to avert a strike or resolve a strike is signed as a tripartite agreements with the Chief Labour Commissioner as a signatory. The agreement becomes enforceable.

Keeping this in mind I woke up the Chief Labour Commissioner. He was kind enough to come to the airline headquarters at 1o'clock in the morning to countersign the agreement as a tripartite agreement signed in conciliation to avoid a pilot strike. It was a win-win for both of us. He got the brownie points for averting a strike.

This was crucial, as I we could not have some bureaucrat in the Ministry raising any objections, given the huge increase in salary as productivity linked incentives (PLI) of an amount unheard of in the public sector or in government.

Only two people were not signatories, Probir Sen and me. Every Director was falling over each other to sign the Agreement that was to provide the airline industrial peace for over 10 years with one of aviation's most powerful and disruptive trade unions. In later years, these same Directors blamed this Agreement for the airline's woes.

Mr. PC Sen deserves full credit for this. The pilots were peaceful, and so were other unions. The task of turning the airline around could start in earnest.

Once the ICPA wage war was settled, the initiation of Alliance Air became an urgent priority as it was to play a major role in the turnaround of Indian Airlines.

The Kerkar Committee had made two crucial recommendations. First was, it attributed the losses of Indian Airlines to the grounding of the A320 and recommended that the Government compensate Indian Airlines ₹900 crore for this loss. I was convinced that the reasons for the losses was the low utilization of its three aircraft fleet due to pilot shortage. The 737 fleet utilization was down to 800 hrs, the A320 to about1000 hrs and A300 about 1200 hrs per month. If we could increase each fleet's utilization up to 2500 hours per month, we would be in profit.

This we demonstrated within a year of starting Alliance Air, a few months later. The airline closed 1996-97, 97-98,98-99 and 1999–2000 in profit, primarily because all three aircraft fleet were flying at higher levels of utilization.

The second Kerkar recommendation was to form a holding company under which would come Indian Airlines and Air India. They had common synergies which could be used to reduce costs. The committee recommended a 'gradual' merger over a 15-year period as against an immediate merger, which they felt would be disastrous due to clash of culture of the two airlines.

Integration of employees and management cadres would be troublesome, as both had a similar Management structure and merging of seniorities and planning employee career progression would be a nightmare. More painful would be that of creating a management structure for the combined force of Senior Managers as each airline had a Head of Department as a Director. Arriving at a common wage structure (Air India paid better wages and allowances than Indian Airlines) was a bigger problem. Finally came the tricky aspect of merging their disparate IT platforms as both used different GDS (ticket booking platform) systems.

Both airlines were as different as chalk and cheese.

The Indian Airlines Board accepted and approved the recommendations of the Kerkar Committee and sent the document to the government with its approval. There was total inaction from the government with respect to the Kerkar recommendation and reorganization of the airlines. However, the demand for compensation for losses due to grounding of the A320 was sent to the Finance Ministry.

Yet, in 2007, the government merged the two Airlines overnight. The consequences were disastrous, mainly because of the issues the Kerkar committee had warned of and had dealt with caution. Two profitable Airlines descended into chaos; the losses became insurmountable. The government threw billions of dollars into a bottomless pit of inefficiency which overwhelmed the new Air India. The LCC airlines captured majority market share and grew larger than the combined national carriers. As expected, the government finally put Air India on the block.

The Kerkar Committee recommendation on compensating Indian Airlines for losses due to grounding of the A320 became a bureaucratic hot potato. It finally landed on the desk of a Dy. Secretary in the Finance Ministry, Mr. PS Brar IAS, who had just returned from study leave from the USA, where one of his subjects was Air Transport and its economics. Brar pruned the Kerkar recommendation from ₹900 crores to about ₹325 crores and further recommended that the cash would be wasted on Indian Airlines and would be better spent giving it to Alliance Air, which I started in 1996. PS Brar later in his career joined the World Bank and was the Bank's Head for Africa, when I met him in 2018 at a party, where we got talking and the Kerkar Committee report came up.

Meanwhile, the ICPA PLI agreement gave a golden opportunity for rest of the Indian Airlines unions to demand a pay hike.

There are 2 ways Indian Airline unions negotiate:

1) We demand so and so and are willing to give up such and such. Let's negotiate an agreement. The ICPA Modus Operandi.

2) You increased the pilot wage, so we demand an increase in wages also for the same percentage increase given to the pilots.

No 2 was the most common technique that excited the HR department who would then scurry to the CMD. Having incited unrest covertly, they would persuade the CMD to comply with the demands to avoid industrial unrest. Sure enough, within a week both the Directors of Finance and HR brought up the issue of other unions raising demands for increase in wages by Productivity Linked Incentives.

I was in the meeting in which such a demand was put up, and the Director Finance who had come up with revised Revenue figures that justified an increase. HR was emphatic that other unions would have a role to play to achieve the desired revenue increases. The pilots gave up a valuable bargaining issue to kick start the airline, rest of the employees free loaded.

Not only did all employees get the PLI, but also Directors up to the level of Dy. Managing Director. The pilots flew more and everyone earned more. Little wonder that the PLI agreements fell into disrepute many years later, since the airline stopped getting the productivity it was paying for and the wage bill had almost tripled.

The Engineers were to make available a pre-determined number of serviceable aircraft and all other unions were to ensure cooperation to achieve the target On Time Performance (OTP). If the number of aircraft available fell below the fixed number, there would be an appropriate deduction of PLI. For PLI to be permissive the *OTP criteria* was fixed as no later than Departure Time plus 15mts (D+15).

There was mass fudging of data and reports, so that there would be no PLI deductions. Irrespective of the Departure time entered in the pilot trip report, departure stations never showed as departure later than D+15 from scheduled time of departure, or the revised estimated time of Departure. These timings were never crossed checked.

If an aircraft had a *'snag'*, per norms it was logged in the pilot defect report (PDR) after informing the engineer. If the snag was permissible, it was cleared under MEL (Minimum equipment list). If not covered, the aircraft would have to be grounded. So, the engineer would beg the pilot not to report the snag for if the aircraft was grounded, the engineers would have PLI deducted. If the snag was not Safety Critical, the pilots would usually agree. If it was written in the PDR, the fallout was obvious bad blood and stories from the engineer that the aircraft was fine, but the pilot has grounded the aircraft for his own ulterior motives.

Increased productivity was achieved and justified only on paper. However in reality, productivity and efficiency suffered and became a rather large hammered nail in the airline's coffin.

The solution had now become the problem.

There are no public solutions. Solutions become problems, so its an never ending cycle of solution-problems-solutions-problems…

The ill-conceived merger of two strange bedfellows led to the demise of two profit making airlines. The blame lay squarely on the failure in getting the HR departments of Air India and Indian Airlines merged, and the unbridled greed and ego of Directors and General Managers of both airlines. Add successive CMDs and the Board of Directors who were totally incompetent to the mix and you have the perfect recipe for disaster. Ministry of Civil Aviation must have junked the Kerkar Committee report and the now incumbent minister was probably not even aware that such a report existed. It went solely by the recommendation of consultants and their projections. I have always mistrusted consultants. They are kings of all trades and masters of none. Total conmen. The so called 'merged Air India' is in effect operated as two different airlines with different cultures, pay scales and internal politics.

Due to intense lobbying, in March 1994 the Air Corporations Act was repealed and started the process for the demise of the two National Carriers. Naresh Goyal's Jet Airways became the flavor of the season and the darling of civil aviation. The press in any case, is a fickle mistress. The same press was busy beating up Naresh Goyal and Jet Airways twenty-five years later. Jet Airways wielded tremendous clout and soon assumed the mantle of the National Carrier. Indian Airlines became the *national scapegoat*, seceding space, routes and slots to Jet Airways on the whims and fancies of the government.

In the summer of '96 I accompanied Mr. Sen to the Ladakh festival at Leh which was to be attended by the Civil Aviation Minister, Mr. Gulam Nabi Azad, officers of the DGCA, Airport Authority of India (AAI) and Dept. of Tourism. The issue of flight regularity to Leh due to adverse weather was the hot topic. After a white-water rafting trip, the Chairman of AAI, Air Marshal Sahul and the DGCA, HS Khola took me aside and informed me that the Minister had been briefed by some Kashmiri pilot that all that was required for better regularity of flights in and out of Leh, was to co-locate the Distance Measuring Equipment (*DME)* with a localizer having a front and back beam to guide aircraft in the longitudinal direction. The DME would give the distance from the runway for a step descent clear of obstacles. The Minister had ordered it to be done.

They sought my help to convince him that it was impracticable, dangerous and would likely lead to disaster. I explained to the Minister that while this was a good low cost idea it would be dangerous if placed in Leh. I educated him that the localizer radio beam's certified accuracy was only 10 nm. However, Leh valley was narrow with 24,000 ft' mountains on either side. The entry passes to Leh were a good distance more than 10 nm away. The localizer beam was not pencil sharp but was fan shaped and its width increased with distance. A pilot would be misguided in to thinking he was clear of obstacles and could descend into a mountain killing all on board. The wreckage would never be found. The minister immediately dropped the idea and withdrew the order. The Chairman Airport Authority was grateful.

Indian Airlines had set up two aircraft acquisition committees, one for the 100-seater aircraft and the other for the 50-seater for Alliance Air. Air Marshal Sahul was a member of the Indian Airlines board. He appointed me as board representative to the committees; I was tasked with the responsibility for providing an independent Operational report to the Board for each aircraft type considered and selected.

For the 100-seater the 3 aircraft being considered were, the MD 95, a derivative of the old DC 9, the Airbus 318/319, and B737-300/400. For the 50-seater the contenders were ATR-200, Dash 8-200 and the Fokker F 50. The 3 Turbo Prop aircraft types were largely built to provide similar ranges, max cruising levels of 25,000 & max speed 250 knts (nautical miles per hour). They could carry similar payloads.

My criteria for comparison were crash-worthiness and post-crash survival, number of accidents on each type, aircraft modifications carried out and reasons thereof, list of all Airworthiness Directives (ADs) issued by FAA, passenger and cockpit crew evacuation, noise and vibrations levels etc.

The ATR42 had the poorest safety reputation of the 3 due to wing icing related accidents and FAA had restricted it to flights in non-icing conditions. This was later corrected by ATR. Of the three, the F50 came out on top in all aspects operationally and was recommended by me. The acquisition committee however had chosen the ATR 42-200. The Board taking my report into consideration rejected the ATR and cleared the F50 for acquisition. Unfortunately, in March 1997, the Fokker Aircraft Company declared bankruptcy after all attempts to save it failed.

The whole exercise of a 50-seater selection commenced again now the contenders were ATR 42-300, Dash 8-300Q and the Saab 2000. I attended the Paris Air show along with the 100-seater committee members. Vinoo Kashyap, MD Alliance Air had advised us not to accept any manufacturers' hotel hospitality. We should pay our own hotel bills and keep all the receipts. Excellent advice. In Paris we were wined and dined by both Boeing and Airbus.

My son Shiv had accompanied me to Paris. My old buddy Kiran was our host and he had invited us to both the Moulin Rouge and The Lido. I insisted that Shiv, should accompany us to both these night clubs as it would be a tremendous growing up experience for a boy of 16. I can still visualize his dead pan face seeing stark naked women swinging and dancing at The Lido. He did enjoy the music at Moulin Rouge, though! All that the other members of the Committee had to say, was they hoped that they had a father like me when they were growing up.

Since, I was directly involved with both Bombardier and ATR, no invitations were accepted. I requested that since we would be going to Toulouse, (Airbus & ATR home) we would like an aircraft for about half an hour for circuits and bumps. So, I got a chance to fly in both the Dash8 and the ATR.

The Q in the 300Q stood for quiet. When the Q mode was switched on, reverse harmonic vibrations were created to balance the normal high vibration that could be felt in the cabin. Both aircraft were rather noisy and required noise dampening headphones to be worn throughout the flight by the pilots. Cockpit evacuation was very troublesome. The crew had to climb to the ceiling using steps cut on the edge of the circuit breaker panel. Open the over roof escape hatch. Throw it over and out and then climb out. Not an easy emergency evacuation. Both aircraft had a ceiling of 25,000 ft' and a normal cruise speed of 250 Knots. Both flew low and slow and were not suitable for our mountainous operations. There was only provision for supplemental passenger oxygen for about 25% of the passengers. This was in compliance with the FAA certification requirement for this category of aircraft, since its service ceiling was 25,000 ft'. Doing an emergency descent from 25,000ft to below 14,000 ft' hardly took enough time so as to endanger passenger due lack of oxygen.

Cross Air in Switzerland was the largest Saab 2000 operator in Europe. Saab had arranged for a visit to Cross Air for aircraft evaluation. After the first flight, I fell in love with the SAAB 2000. It could cruise at 31,000 ft' at M.70 (that *is 70% of the speed of sound. Here M stands for*

Mach pronounced mock. Aircraft speed above 25,000ft are measured as a ratio to the speed of sound and expressed by a Mach number denoted by M) and Max speed of 320 knots below 25,000 ft'. It was the fastest turboprop around and capable of flying a one hour flight in almost the same time as a jet aircraft. Its engines were not noisy and relatively quiet. It had a glass cockpit. Auto deploying individual passenger oxygen mask. There were 4 door emergency exits for the passengers. The pilots could evacuate easily through the cockpit sliding windows. I flew the simulator and did jump seat rides on the Cross-Air network. The deciding factor was a flight in the mountains to a 4500 ft' runway whose MDA (Minimum Descent Altitude) was 550 ft' above ground. The Saab had an approach propeller setting between ground fine and flight fine pitch (large *Turboprop aircraft have variable speed propeller. This is possible by changing the angle of the propeller blade, a fine pitch is used for take-off, and called flight fine pitch and a coarser pitch for climb and cruise. On ground a reverse fine pitch is used to provide braking action. This is called ground fine pitch).* If this alternate pitch is selected, the propellers produce drag which increases the aircraft rate of descent without increasing the speed. The high sink rate can be arrested easily by deselecting this propeller setting. I loved the plane. It was suitable for hot and high airfields, short runways and mountainous airfield of J&K and the Northeast.

My trip to Switzerland was memorable. On the last day, Cross Air hosted us to see the Stage version of the musical "The Phantom of the Opera". The lead singer was Sara Brighton and the music was by Andrew Lloyd Webber. This was when the seed for classical music was sown for Shiv. In later years, he went on to major in classical piano from St Mary's College in San Antonio, Texas.

The evening was rounded off with a typical multi-course French dinner in the famous restaurant on the river, the "Les Trois Rois" (The Three Kings). There were different wines for each course, which ended with a *sorbet*. The dinner must have lasted over two hours. Cross Air were the perfect hosts besides being an excellent airline.

The acquisition committee again chose the ATR. I recommended the SAAB 2000. The Board went with my recommendation. As bad luck would have it, SAAB aircraft also decided to stop civil aircraft production in Oct 1997 due to low demand.

I was beginning to suspect that I was the *'Jonah'* for both Fokker and Saab, for both closed when I selected their aircraft.

Indian Airlines ultimately ended up buying the ATR in mid-2000.

While in Toulouse, we visited the A330 & 319/320 production line. This is when I met the legendary ET, Capt. Etienne Tarnowski. Kiran Rao our Airbus host, suggested a that ET would be test flying an A330-200 in the morning and the A319 in the afternoon. If I wanted, he could ask ET if I could be on board. ET agreed to have both Capt. JRD Rao, Chairman of the committee and me aboard. JRD was an A300 Examiner, and he found the A330 easy to fly.

ET put me in the left seat of the A330 & the A319. After just a minimum brief on the length and weight of the aircraft, he said "fly it like you would the A320" and sat back.

I was comfortable and at ease in the cockpit immediately. I took off, did 6 circuits and bumps and then up to 35,000 feet over the Pyrenees, where we explored both flight at minimum speed and maximum speed and the flight characteristics and protections. The minimum and maximum speed regimes were never demonstrated in normal training. Now that I had experienced the full spectrum of protection in pitch normal law of the Airbus family aircraft, my confidence in the aircraft increased immensely. *(Airbus fly by wire aircraft provide it in-flight protection. Pitch normal law provides full protection, Pitch alternate flaw degraded protection and Direct Law no protection but only Warnings).* After the flight, all ET had to say was "You flew the aircraft at Max. Speed and Min. speed. In between it's a piece of cake."

Once on ground, a young man, who I didn't realize was a reporter, asked "Captain, how did you find flying the A330 and A319?" I said it felt no different or more difficult than the A320. Next morning, the paper had a small story of an Indian A320 pilot flying the A330 & A319 on the same day, without any special training or briefing.

His comments were that I flew the A330 and A319 like I would the A320.

There was an immediate riposte from Airbus: Doesn't it prove our case on the compatibility of the A 319/320/330. They had a point!

ET and I became great friends, and during IndiGo's early start up days, he spent many tours with IndiGo training our pilots on the line.

12. NEW GIRLS IN OLD

AIRPLANES

THE ALLIANCE AIR STORY

"Tall and tan and young and lovely
The girl from Ipanema goes walking
And when she passes Each one she passes goes, AH!

When she walks, she's like a samba
That swings so cool and sways so gently
That when she passes Each one she passes goes, AH!"
– The Girl from Ipanema

Alliance Air was conceptualized as an unorthodox solution to improve the low crew and aircraft utilization in Indian Airline, thus valuably aiding in the turnaround strategy of Indian Airlines. It was conceived as a short term solution with a life of 5 years or so, until the B737-200 were phased out.

Nevertheless, I was inordinately happy that I had thought up this idea of creating an airline within an airline, to solve the problems of the parent airline. I discussed this in a lateral thinking session in Sept. 1995. In April 1996, the idea became reality when Alliance Air was launched.

Alliance Air was in effect India's first low-cost airline at a time when the term LCC was unheard of in India. It was common sense to keep costs low. Cost control was a priority and a philosophy never a strategy. But we were not cheap and were willing to spend money for operational efficiency and **needs** of the airline, but seldom on **wants**.

Probir Sen the CMD initially suggested that I take on the project as Chief Executive. This I respectfully declined due to my seniority which I explained would be troublesome for him, and me in the long run. Vinoo Kashyap, (his former EA) now a Director was suggested for the role. He could hold additional charge as Managing Director of Alliance Air, and I was to retain Operations Control as (ED) Executive Director (Airline Operations) assisted by an ED (Engg.) & ED (Support). Both holding additional charge in addition to their current functions in Indian Airlines.

I would be on full time deputation and fly the A320 for license currency. An additional demand was I be paid for fixed 70 hrs flying, since I would suffer financially as I would not be able to fly regularly. This was an explosive issue, and opposed tooth and nail by both Finance & Human Resources Departments. I stuck to my guns and made it clear that it was a deal breaker.

Mr. Sen took it to the board and pushed through a fixed monthly allowance for 62 hrs per month. A first in the history of the airline. Paying a Pilots a fixed Salary for predetermined hours and beyond under work-more-earn-more concept is common place now.

A major decision was the selection of a small management team on deputation for starting the airline and for day-to-day management. I was keen that the team be made of junior officers with not more than about 5-7 years of experience.

Our start up team was small. There was Vinoo the MD, Ashok Bhushan ED Support Services, Pradhan for Engineering, Anjana Jain & Madhu Singh from SHOD, Rajni Rawat, my EA, Sunita Srivastava in-charge of Crew Management, Sunil Madan in charge of Operations Support. Mr. JC Chawla for network planning and Mr. ML Tufchi as Airports in charge. Ruma Sinha was Head of In-flight. Ruma was a former Indian Airlines cabin crew, who was on the F27 fleet in Calcutta. She was an exceptional cabin crew who quit the airline after she married my course mate Subodh Sinha. The pillars on which Alliance Air stood were Sunil, Sunita, Ruma, Pradhan, JC Chawla and ML Tufchi. Without them, a time bound start-up would not have been possible.

I structured a flat organization and outsourced the problem areas like aircraft loading, cleaning, crew transport etc. This again was a first in the industry. No troublesome class 4 peons, loaders, drivers, cleaners. So thankfully, no pressure from politician to give jobs to their supporters.

I set the launch flight date for the 1st flight as 15th April 1996. Following US President, John F Kennedy's example of committing my team to a deadline. He had publicly announced to the country that America will have a Man on the Moon in Ten Years. The target had been set for NASA then and now for Alliance Air.

Great emphasis was placed on computerizing as much as possible in every area, especially operations. We were using in house developed flight plans from the very first flight. I had hired retired Air Force meteorologists in Flight Dispatch for pilot weather briefing for daily operational forecasts which were their forte rather than general forecasts. These boys were worth their weight in gold.

The concept was to dry-lease B737-200 from Indian Airlines along with key young, motivated and skilled personnel on deputation for engineering, and key management functions. All being below the rank of DGM. They were named as Managers reporting to respective EDs, with two lower levels i.e., supervisors & executives. Everyone in Alliance was an officer so there would be no union troubles. Decision making had to be quick, reactive and result oriented.

The airline hired its own pilots, cabin crew, airport and support staff, maintenance engineers and technicians. Engineering spares & stores were to be got from IA under a power-by-the-hour contract. We paid the parent airline office space rental, ticket sales (on commission), booking through the IA system at a cost, and took over all their subsidiary low revenue/ loss making routes, leaving IA to concentrate on the metros and state capitals to the 4 major hubs i.e. Delhi, Bombay, Calcutta, Madras, besides the flights to the Gulf, Bangkok, Singapore and Kuala Lumpur, all on their A300 and A320 fleet. We did our own network planning, flight scheduling and obtained our own airport slots & clearances. We were accountable to the DGCA and our own Flight Safety set up.

We did everything differently than Indian Airlines and concentrated on an efficient, happy, extremely committed, highly motivated, passionate and eager work force. Most importantly we put 'New Girls in Old Airplanes', which with benefit of hindsight, was a wise decision.

Passenger acceptability was tremendous, and we fast gained the image for the best looking, efficient, friendly and compassionate cabin crew in the industry.

The airline had a humble beginning on 15th April 1996 with one aircraft, 4 Captains, 4 co-pilots, 20 cabin crew and a few engineers and technicians. The first flight was Delhi-Goa-Cochin under flight number CD 467(originally IC-467) in the first round with Delhi-Lucknow-Delhi in the second wave.

We decided to recruit only B737 rated pilots. Obtaining type rated pilots was crucial as we did not have the wherewithal to train raw pilots. B-737 pilots rapidly packed their bags from the Air Taxi Operators (ATOs) and made a bee line to join Alliance. We were paying more than a competitive market wage. The movement of this crucial resource played an important part in the grounding of the ATOs. Alliance was now doing to them that they had done to Indian Airlines, which was 'poaching' their pilots.

Alliance Air also became the employer of choice for Indian Airlines A300 and B737 pilots who were retired at the age of 58. Pilots could fly up to the age of 60 those days. They all joined Alliance Air. Some of these pilots had been my bosses and were much revered among the pilot community.

One such pilot was Capt. RP Bhalla. He was a senior B737 pilot when I was flying out of Calcutta and a regular at the Airline Crew Club. We met often when I was Capt. Bagchi's understudy. He applied to join Alliance Air and I was delighted to have him on board. Capt. Bhalla was a superb pilot by reputation and adored by his crew.

He had been involved in an A300 freak accident in 1993 and had been relegated as a co-pilot. He returned to command subsequently. The A300 accident he was involved in, was a forced landing of a passenger flight when his aircraft ran out of fuel. The amazing airmanship he exhibited in landing the A300, a really big jet – without any power from 20,000 feet on a paddy field near Tirupati, had made him a legend among pilots. The A300 was a 350,000 pound monster. Without power it fell like a ton of bricks, as it was just a very heavy glider. It could fly but for not very long.

This is what happened.

On a flight from Madras to Hyderabad, Capt. Bhalla could not land due to fog in Hyderabad. All the Air force airfields around Hyderabad were also fog bound. He made one attempt to land and during the overshoot his flap did not retract fully and got stuck. The only alternate available to him was Madras. Due to flaps not being retracted he was restricted to a lower altitude. At that time, aircraft manufacturers did not provide any information of extra fuel being burned due to extended flaps. The fuel used was at a greater rate than the flight Engineer, Mr. Sen approximated.

En route to Madras, the crew realized that they would not have enough fuel to make it to destination. Capt. Bhalla elected to do an emergency landing at Tirupati airfield. Unfortunately, the aircraft ran out of fuel before it could reach Tirupati. Capt. Bhalla had to carry out a forced landing in the open paddy fields. He landed the Airbus A300, without any power as engines had shut due to fuel exhaustion. This is also known as a dead stick landing. He chose a paddy field clear of obstacles to force land.

An amazing feat of flying. There were 262 passengers and crew on board, no fatalities and only a few minor injuries. Of course, the investigation report deemed it ***pilot error***.

It was only after this accident that aircraft manufacturers provide guidance to crew on excess fuel burn with flaps and slats extended.

When Capt. Bhalla finally retired at the age of 60 from Alliance Air, he proudly told me that the two years he spent in Alliance were the best years of his flying career. It was a moment and a compliment that has stayed with me.

The only Air Taxi Operator that took advantage of the repealed Air Corporation Act was Jet Airways, promoted by Naresh Goyal. He started Jet Airways with 40% foreign equity (20% Kuwait and 20% UAE). This Naresh did not dissolve even after he was able to stymie the Tata- Singapore bid for starting an Airline, by convincing the government to ban foreign equity in an Indian airline. Many years later, he was forced to dilute the foreign equity after the government took strong exception to it.

Air India had experimented with wet lease operations with aircraft from Caribjet and People's Express. These airlines trained Indian

Cabin Crew for this operation. Fortunately, Air India terminated the wet leases, making available adequate and well-trained cabin crew to Alliance.

By February 1997, we had taken over the complete Indian Airlines 737 fleet. Our operation increased from over 15,000 flights in 1997 and to over 22,000 by 1998 covering 47 stations, carrying 1.98 million passengers. We achieved an aircraft fleet utilization of 3000-3300 aircraft hours a month. We operated out of the four major bases of Indian Airlines where we carried out aircraft routine maintenance and checks. All major maintenance and checks were carried out in Delhi our main base.

Aircraft were rotated in and out of Delhi after mid night as "red eye flights" with a 25% fare discount. We encouraged cargo agents to accept cargo & courier loads up to 2200 hrs instead of the Indian Airlines limit of 1700 hrs. These flights became very popular as they offered the same day return option.

Revenue generation in 1996-97 was ₹ 266.72 Cr, 1997-98 was ₹ 525.75 Cr and 1998-99 was ₹ 582.87 Cr. This was a healthy sum for that day and age! All this money was ploughed back into Indian Airlines and was a major reason for its profitability in those years. The A320 and A300 fleet utilization also increased to a healthy 2800 hours per aircraft per month. The turnaround strategy was working. Indian Airlines was making good money after years of making losses.

Alliance Air was now controlling all non-metro routes and we had entered into our own inter-line agreements with Air India, British Airways, Lufthansa etc., since Indian Airlines could not issue tickets on Alliance, and Alliance could not, on Indian Airlines. The international airlines urgently wanted to interline with us as we controlled all the tourist routes.

Each interline agreement had one condition that EDs (Executive Directors) were eligible to First Class N1 status (100% free with firm space booking), Managers on Business class N1 status, Pilots on Economy N1 status, upgradable to business subject to space, all Supervisors were also eligible on Economy N1 status and Executives to Economy on N2 (100% free but subject to load). Due to the very low employee ratio all the airlines agreed to this, even Air India.

This was a major morale booster for the staff. It was a thorn in the side of the Indian Airlines Commercial Director (CD) and Indian Airlines employees, who could not get a similar deal due to the airlines' very large employee numbers. DGM's and above were eligible free firm space only on Air India.

Once Alliance Air Operation was successful, its Commercial Director wanted to club the two Airline schedules, with common inter line agreements. This, I outright rejected. To add insult to injury, all Alliance Air pilots and their families were entitled to free, firm space travel on Alliance Air flights and not subject to load as was the case for Indian Airlines' pilots on their flights. This increased the prestige of Alliance Air in the industry tremendously.

The DGCA had notified the Route Dispersal Guidelines (RDG) in which every airline had to deploy 10% of their Cat 1 (metro routes) Available Seat kilometers (ASKMs) on Cat 2 routes (to NE, J&K, Andamans) and a further 10% of this on Cat 2A routes (intra Category 2 cities). ASKMs are a measure of the certified seat on an aircraft multiplied by the number of kilometers flown. ASKM are used to measure the Cost per seat kilometer (CASK) and Revenue per seat kilometer (RASK).

Indian Airlines became totally deficient in their Cat 2 & 2A obligations. Whereas, Alliance was in surplus since it flew limited Cat1 (metro) routes. Initially, Ashok Bushan, ED (Support) and I toyed with the idea of selling our ASKMs to the highest bidder. We were willing to attach our surplus to any airline at a cost. This was much to the Indian Airline's CD's frustration, since non compliance with RDG guidelines would cause issues for the Scheduled clearance. I relented on the intervention of the CMD and attached our Cat 2 & 2A ASKMs to Indian Airlines. Jet Airways too was having trouble with their Cat 2 & 2A obligation. However, they got around this by influencing the ministry to include Bagdogra in West Bengal as part of the Northeast Cat 2 airports.

All our catering contracts were with the Taj Group. Their CMD Mr. Ajit Kerkar was well known to our MD, Vinoo Kashyap. The TAJ was the only chain that could provide us catering at over 90% of our stations. This exclusive contract gave us better catering rates, special very low room rates for crew layover and for passengers in the event of flights disrupted due weather or aircraft groundings (AOG). The crew stayed in Taj Group Hotels on "all found" basis, that is, free fixed crew meals, and free laundry, plus F and F (Fruit and flowers) complimentary. In Calcutta & Bombay, we used the Oberoi Grand and Juhu, Centaur respectively.

Whereas, Indian Airlines (IA) cockpit crew were provided 5 star hotels and cabin crew lower category 3/4 star hotels with **only** a breakfast entitlement, Alliance guaranteed yearly room nights and got better rates than IA which did not commit firm bookings for rooms. Since we had only female cabin crew, two girls shared a room; and pilots and cabin crew stayed in the same hotel. This caused problems for Indian Airlines as their cabin crew also demanded 5-star accommodation. The issue finally reached the Secretary, Civil Aviation.

I was hauled over for wasting money and providing cabin crew 5-star hotel accommodation. The Secretary realized (of course, I spoke up!) that we were paying much lesser room rates than IA was for cabin crew and were getting better facilities. After that, I was told that the Regional Directors of IA were hauled up.

Having suffered in Indian Airlines, I had decided to look after all employees to get the maximum productivity out of them. Pilots were paid up to 45 hrs fixed flying allowance and a work-more-earn-more scheme, similar to that of Indian Airlines pilots.

We had schemes for rewards in cash and kind, for a 'A job well done', and a personal "Oops, we goofed" apology from me when we were in the wrong. In Alliance Air, the management was not always right.

One key and important factor in our Juhu Centaur hotel contract was that 5% of total yearly room nights accrued back to the airline on room only basis. These free rooms were available to all employees on request during vacation or as rewards for a job well done. Pilots and cabin crew were given cash rewards for exceptional inflight performance along with a citation. This was initially objected to by Vinoo the MD but I prevailed, confident that most crew would not cash the cheques and would rather frame them as mementos. Hardly 25% of the cheques were actually cashed.

In Alliance Air, HR was just a keeper of records and Finance, a keeper of accounts. In Operations, we set up an in-house Crew Management

Section that became the single point of contact for all crew, whatever their issue. The resolution of crew issues was a matrix that was measured.

The Operations structure was flat and simple. Line operation came under a Chief Pilot, Training under another Chief Pilot, Operations Support (Technical issues, Flight Despatch and Crew Scheduling) under a Manager, Crew Management under another Manager, both of whom were Assistant Managers in IA and completely committed and knowledgeable.

Airport ground operation staff were recruited primarily from unemployed pilots. Most of them got pilot jobs later in life. I remembered my unemployment days as a pilot. I made a special provision for the children of Indian Airline category 4 employee who had graduated. Which was only possible after great sacrifices made by their parents. These families needed a break. A job in Alliance as an officer enabled these kids to jump a social level. Their children would no longer be called children of peons, drivers and loaders. They would be children of officers. This got me tremendous respect, good wishes and blessings from the under privileged I was able to help. I had a weak spot for children of widows. I was one such child. I knew the hard life a widow lives to provide for her children. All things being equal the child of a widow was given preference.

Alliance employees worked hard and partied hard due to no social boundaries… Cabin crew of Alliance need special mention. They were easily the finest cabin crew in the country. Besides being totally professional and committed, they were a good looking, caring and kind bunch. They seldom gave trouble or reported sick; when off duty, they were fun-loving and total heartbreakers, as they were unmarried. Affairs with pilots were not unusual and "bracket flying" was winked at. The unwritten law was 'discretion'. However, when issues arose with married pilot's wives, the wayward husbands were reminded of the Company standing policy of "Dipping your Pen in Company Ink". If any indiscretion became a problem for management, then the management got tough. Very tough.

I was like the conductor of a symphony guiding, directing, helping and always keeping in mind What Not to Do, which was generally to avoid how Indian Airlines did it. The general principle was if Indian Airlines went left, we chose right. Our cabin crew had the best saree designs much to the envy of Indian Airline's crew. All we had to do was select from the saris that Indian Airlines had rejected. We even got them cheaper. Vinoo was a great support ready with advice and money that was needed, Ashok and JC Chawla had a free hand on network planning, with no Director of Commercial disagreeing with them. Pradhan improved on Indian Airlines engineering productivity. He was managing the Check A on the apron overnight and Check B in 72 hrs which took Indian Airlines 6-7 days…

We had a little over 3 months to 1st Flight. There was no office timings. One kept working till the task was completed. Start-ups are fun, challenging, 'bull' sessions of ideas, screaming and yelling. At Alliance, all this was happening in one large room on 1st floor of the Indian Airline booking office at Safdarjung Airport.

When I think of it, it was amazing the amount we accomplished in that short time. Processes were developed to empower decision-making at the front-line level with emphasis on communications, quick reaction time and an informal set up on first name basis, casual comfortable dress rules. The airline offices were spread out between the Palam Airport and Safdarjung Airport. The old Lufthansa hanger at Palam housed Finance, Engineering and HR, while Operations and Commercial back offices were in the airport domestic terminal.

We had been allotted space on the 1st floor of the Palam Airport domestic arrival Terminal. It needed extensive renovation and construction to become the airline corporate office. When ready at the end of 1997, it was modern for its time, with open workstations, computers, small cubicles for officers, piped music, a conference room, a small pantry, free tea, coffee and water dispenser, a visitors' room, a modern EPABX switch board, a reception etc. The office was centrally air conditioned.

It was the envy of our "big brother" and much criticized for what they considered wasteful expenditure.

In early 1997, a female pilot candidate with only a basic CPL was referred from the Minister's office for a pilot job. This I could not honor as we only were employing Boeing 737 type rated pilots. This did not endear me with the Minister or the Secretary, both not used to hearing a "No"! The lady was however, accommodated as a flight dispatcher.

About this time Vijaypath Singhania was lobbying to join us as an honorary co-pilot on the 737 on which he was rated. I took him on board on a ₹1 contract with a quid pro quo that Raymond, his flag ship company, provide bespoke tailored pilot and male staff uniforms. This he did at below cost.

One day I suggested to his Vice President Corp Affair, Faiz Ahmed Faiz, and a fellow Stephenian, to consider training the minister's pilot protégé on the Company's private jet. They agreed and the lucky lady decided to move to Mumbai to be near her boyfriend, a powerful Congress politician.

A little after this, The Supreme Court came out with its famous "Vishakha" guidelines on female employee harassment in the workplace. One fine morning, I was confronted by Vinoo. The Minister's office had forwarded a serious charge of sexual harassment against me, by the said lady pilot.

Mr. Sen, the CMD had the charge investigated by a high-level Committee of senior male and female officers. It was chaired by Dy. MD Phillip Crasta. All female staff of Alliance were called for their statements, though the lady who had charged me of inappropriate behavior declined to attend. Ultimately, I was cleared of the charge by the committee due to no evidence and also based on the statements by all the female staff who came out in my support. The report was sent to the Minister's office.

The Secretary of Civil Aviation summoned me and verbally attacked me, accusing me of manipulating the inquiry and warning me that is there was ever any complaint against me again, he would personally ensure my suspension and termination from the airline. I respectfully told him not to threaten me, as the last time I was threatened, the CMD had lost his job and the Minister had had to resign. I walked out of his office, leaving him stuttering and stammering and totally red in the face.

I returned to office and immediately laid down sexual harassment guidelines for Alliance Air based on the 'Vishakha' guidelines. I also appointed a Sexual Harassment Inquiry Committee and made clear that any false complaint would be cause for termination.

Alliance Air was the First and only Public Sector Company that implemented the Supreme Court guidelines on sexual harassment as early as 1997. The rest of the country only did so in 2013, when the guideline was superseded by the Act on Sexual Harassment. During my tenure with Alliance, there was not a single sexual harassment charge levied against any employee.

Prompt and effective communication to employees was considered a priority to foster efficiency and quick reaction time. Mr. Sunil Mittal, an old friend, had just started AirTel, and was a great support. He suggested we use pagers for all employees. These we got from an associate company, Max. It was decided that every employee would have a pager. We initially ordered 300 pagers. AirTel threw in a free mobile phone (Nokia 2110) for every 50 pagers. So, in Feb '96, we already had 6 mobile phones. In those days outgoing and incoming calls were ₹16/min. There were no roaming cellular facilities. Each connection got four sim cards – one each for Delhi, Bombay, Calcutta and Madras.

There was no government policy on mobile phone use by PSUs or government at that time. The first four cell phones were used by the MD and three EDs and one was given to the CMD, Indian Airlines. The 6th cell phone was kept with Flight Despatch for urgent communication with Senior Management.

Except for grumbling from IA's Director of Finance about "wasteful expenditure" on the pagers, no questions were asked by anybody else. About a year later, there was a query from the Civil Aviation Ministry requesting under which provision the mobile phones were purchased in absence of any government policy. This, of course, could be easily explained – that they came free with every 50 pagers bought! This deal would have rankled the Director of Finance!

All criticism of our pager and mobile phone policy came to an end after a fire totally gutted the Indian Airlines Departure Terminal at Palam Airport on the night of 30th October, 1996, at about 0330 hrs. I got a call about 0400 hours about the fire. The terminal was completely destroyed. All our records and computers were gone. I ordered a group pager message to be sent to all Delhi employees to report to the Airport immediately to render assistance. All crew to standby at home and crew transports to wait at first pick up point.

Meanwhile, with the help of night duty staff and employees responding to the emergency, call arrangements were made to send flights from Terminal One with the help of the private airlines. Passengers were guided to terminal 1, and manual check-in started with Alliance boarding cards taken from our stores in Lufthansa hanger. Crew pick up commenced at 0500 hrs and flight despatch was shifted to a room next to the Indian Airlines crew room, where our crew reported for the mandatory pre-flight medical check.

We were able to despatch our first flight with only a 30 minute delay from scheduled departure time, and the rest of the days' flights were on time. Indian Airlines flights could only commence in the afternoon, with a number of flights being cancelled.

The pagers and mobile phones had done their job.

Meanwhile, pilots from East West, Damania, and Modiluft started joining Alliance. I concentrated on Instructors as Training Captains and got hold of Jitu Vaishnav from Damania & Daljit Virk from ModiLuft. I considered it very important to have the capacity to produce my own pilots, for which I required instructors. These gentlemen brought in with them their loyalists, and very soon we had our Line Operations & Training setup. Ruma was handling the induction and type training of the cabin crew and also hiring freshers.

SOPs were emphasized in training and line operations, but Pilot in Command authority and decisions were respected. My pilot union experience helped in designing pilot friendly, carrot and stick policies. Willful indiscipline, careless flying/ dangerous flying, willful disregard of flight safety by pilots were accorded zero tolerance. Anyone that crossed the line got sacked. No negotiations. I had to terminate four Captains for crossing that 'Lakshman Rekha'.

Pilots are human and can make mistakes. Where training was needed, instead of punishment, it was given. The policy was train to proficiency even if it required extra sessions, especially if any reduction in proficiency was observed.

In early 1998, on my return from a safety conference in Cape Town, I was met by my Manager of Safety on arrival. He advised me that the DGCA's Director of Air Safety, Northern Region, Mr. AK Chopra, was livid and on the verge of grounding the airline due to a serious safety violation, that the airline was trying to cover up.

I immediately spoke to Mr. Chopra and requested him to hold off any action until we could jointly investigate. He agreed.

It so transpired that on a flight from Leh, the pilot willfully ordered an overload to accommodate 26 extra passengers and over five tons of freight. Only 100 passengers were allowed onboard Leh flights. This restriction was necessary, as the aircraft had limited passenger oxygen available. The high terrain en route on flights to and from Leh did not permit the aircraft a descent to 10,000ft in case of emergency, as was the norm. The most critical scenarios for the Leh operation was pressurization failure and not engine failure.

First report to DGCA was from ATC at Leh, on a dangerous take off. The aircraft only got airborne just about at the end of the paved runway. The ATC was about to sound the crash alarm. When DGCA requested the flight documents, the cover up began. The flight's passenger manifest was amended, and so was the load and trim sheet, but the Cover up was obvious to the DGCA and made Mr. Chopra livid.

We started our investigation from the Indian Airlines' account section, by doing an audit of the flight's flown passenger ticket coupons. Sure enough, there were 126 coupons. When the coupon was compared with the passenger manifest, it was found that passengers that had flown were not on the manifest and for those on the manifest, their flight coupons were missing. There had obviously been inept mass fudging with active management involvement.

In case of an accident, the un-manifested passengers would not have been eligible for insurance. The truth finally came out. The Captain and agency staff handling the flight were immediately sacked.

Now the drama started. I got a call from Mr. Farooq Abdullah, the MP from J & K, to spare the pilot as the extra passengers were his relatives and had to be brought back to Delhi. I expressed regret and advised him that the pilot had jeopardized the lives of his relatives and 100 other passengers. Next was a call from Gulam Nabi Azad, our former Minister, claiming they were his relatives, and the pilot was a Kashmiri. I was asked if I could only punish the pilot without sacking him. I politely asked him if he was related to Farooq Abdullah, as he too claimed that the passengers were his relatives. Mr. Azad realized he was being used and left the decision to me.

During my tenure I terminated the service of three other Captains for willful and dangerous flying. All three were popular pilots, but they had crossed the *"Lakshman Rekha"*.

Ashok Bhushan, who was also Director Planning in IA, handled network planning and revenue management. I ran the airline and Vinoo Kashyap looked after our backs handling Indian Airlines, Civil Aviation Ministry, and Parliamentary Committees. The latter all of a sudden became inquisitive and active in our affairs.

There had always been a keen jealous interest in the way Alliance Air was being run. I remember a meeting held under the Chairmanship of the then Minister, Ghulam Nabi Azad, where Hon'ble members from Kerala actually challenged Alliance Air's bona fide as an airline and demanded its closure. All the members objected to our low-cost meals model and only snack service, and demanded full service akin to IA, an abrogation of the exclusive contract with Taj. It was obvious that both East West Airlines and the Casino Hotel in Cochin were behind these demands.

It was the Hon'ble member from Ladakh, Shri P Namgyal, who had saved the day. He stood up in our support and stated that Central Asia began from Ladakh. While Central Asia had connectivity around the year, Ladakh was a part of India, but only had land connectivity with India for 4 – 5 months a year. It was the 3 daily Alliance Air flights that gave Ladakh a year-round connectivity with India. If Alliance Air was closed, then Ladakh would be better connected to Central Asia. What he left unsaid had the desired effect. The motion was dropped.

However, we rejigged our meal planning which till then was Tea/ Coffee/ Juices & an open snack services (no boxes). The snacks were 4 types of sandwiches, croissants, cakes, *samosas, pakodas, kababs* and *tikkas* depending on the time of the day.

Meal planning for the Indian domestic passenger is one of the biggest challenges an airline faces. Food preferences differ from state to state, there are vegetarian / non-vegetarian preferences. Then there are non-vegetarians who are vegetarians, some on Mondays, and some on Tuesdays, Thursdays and Saturdays. There are vegetarians who eat eggs and non-vegetarians who only eat chicken. All these permutations and combinations make in flight meal planning impossible, since their meal preference never indicated they were vegetarian or not on specific days.

Indian Airlines could never get it fully right. On every other flight, the crew ran short of vegetarian or non-vegetarian meals and bore the brunt of passenger ire for no fault of theirs. The passengers' complaints usually escalated to the Captain. Keeping this experience in mind we had opted for the neutral open service.

Now we planned to go in for full meal service with all attendant cost and problems. The solution we came up with was to provide only a vegetarian meal on board and have an add on non- vegetarian and vegetarian open service. This reduced wastage, had passenger acceptability and there was little or no food complaints.

In Indian Airlines, soon after a plane landed, ground staff would raid the galleys and pilfer all the catering and dry stores that remained. In Alliance, we stopped this practice. Dry stores were low hanging fruit – easy to pluck. We saved lakhs of rupees per month by ensuring that the galley and catering supplies were retrieved by the Catering staff before any cleaning staff would enter the plane.

Pilfering of on-board supplies, which was rampant in Indian Airlines, had zero tolerance in Alliance. The Alliance crew had no need to pilfer on-board food as most flights ended as layovers in hotels, where all meals were provided, unlike in IA, where the crew were on only bed & breakfast basis at hotels and had to pay for their meals.

Another cost saving was the logging of flight time which was restricted "to the minute" and not rounded to the nearest 5to10 minutes. The crew knew that time was money and since their block times were protected, there was no incentive to over log. A major cost for airlines is flight-time cost and a reduction in this cost has major implication on hourly costs and dangerously increased total operating costs.

In 1996, the BJP had the shortest government of 13 days. A dashing young MP from Bihar had been inducted into the Union of Ministers, and he approached CMD Sen to provide his wife, an Indian Airlines cabin crew a ground job, as he was now a minister and having his wife work as an air hostess would reduce his prestige. Since IA had no such provision, Sen passed the buck to me, and I accommodated the lady in our marketing cell with the proviso that she could not fly in Alliance.

The Government fell after 13 days having failed the floor test in parliament. Meanwhile, cabin crew salaries in IA increased dramatically, post the pilot wage agreement. The ex-Minister now wanted his wife to fly for Alliance Air. I did not permit as her deputation was to the marketing department. There were many senior Indian Airlines cabin crew that that applied to come on deputation to Alliance. If she would have been permitted to fly, there would have been issues raised by the Indian Airlines crew being denied a deputation.

So, I offered to terminate her deputation so that she could fly in IA. She did not want this either, since the flexibility of touring the constituency with her husband would no longer be an option.

More on this later, since the wife was to cause major repercussions to my career path.

In the years when Alliance was being set up and operational, I was still involved as the trouble shooter for CMD, Probir Sen in IA. Training of A320 Captains was stuck due lack of instructors, as most of the latter left for the Gulf airlines.

About this time, Airbus had posted Mr. Kiran Rao from Washington as President, Airbus India. The VP Singh led Janata government, had registered a case on Airbus and launched an investigation into the A320 order in which, the former PM, Rajiv Gandhi's involvement was alleged. During the pendency of the inquiry, Airbus was persona non grata in MOCA (Ministry of Civil Aviation).

I met Kiran at a French Embassy reception where Ila was then the social secretary to the French Ambassador. Kiran and I soon became friends, and we still are till today. He was a great support when I was inducting the A320 for IndiGo. By then, he was the Senior Vice President Global Sales for Airbus in Toulouse.

I sought Kiran's support to get the A320 fleet fully operational. I requested him to provide IA with 12 to 15 instructors FOC (free of cost) for Captain Upgrade Training. This Airbus did with magnanimity and no quid pro quo. Kiran knew that once IA got its fleet flying profitably, the goodwill would give them a fair chance of obtaining further A320 orders. With Airbus' assistance, IA was able to train 77 Captains in less than a year. The languishing A320 fleet started flying and become profitable with increased fleet utilization.

One tremendous advantage that Alliance Air had was the level of support it got from the DGCA. Key officers of the DGCA and I had grown in aviation together, both having entered our respective organizations in the late '70s. We had worked together on opposing sides during aircraft accident investigations and had developed mutual trust and professional admiration.

DGCA was greatly satisfied by the professionalism and safety culture existing in Alliance. A very close professional relationship existed between their Air Safety Department and our Safety Section headed by Capt. SK Bhatia, a medically grounded IA pilot who had worked closely with DGCA in many crash investigations. Whenever a safety-related incident took place we would handle it on priority, determine the probable cause, amend operational policy if required, and take corrective action to avoid a re-occurrence. We would disseminate cause and corrective action within the airline and inform DGCA on priority. They usually accepted our finding, and the matter was closed. This mutually respectful relationship continued with DGCA after I joined IndiGo in 2005.

All flight crew were well aware that I was the first person to inform in case of any incident, no matter how small. Our process would immediately kick in and handling DGCA was my problem. Crew knew that they would not be victimized, even if there was just cause.

Two or three incidents are still fresh in my mind even after so many years.

Since pilots knew that if anything went wrong or felt abnormal, it was in their interest that I be the first to know. The conversation usually went thus:

"Hi Sir, This is Capt. XYZ. I fucked up."

My usual response: "What happened?

The pilot would then truthfully relate exactly what happened. There would be no cover ups, no shifting blame onto others. The Captain was in-charge and hence responsible and accountable to me and the company.

I got a call one early morning from "Capt. Dhali" which went as all such calls did.

"Hi Sir, This is Dhali, I fucked up again, I am at Cochin and I have burst all my tires after a reject take off. All four brake assemblies have seized".

I asked him if the aircraft and all on board were safe. He told me he was still on the runway and related the incident thus.

Just after the aircraft lifted off the runway he got an 'engine reverser thrust unlock' warning. He reacted instinctively by pulling back the throttles and pushed the aircraft down on to the runway and literally stood on the brakes causing all the main wheel tyre to burst and brakes to fuse. He further added that when he got the thrust unlock warning, all that came to his mind was "The Lauda Air crash".

In 1991, a Lauda Air B-767-300 had crashed after take-off from Bangkok when its No1 engine thrust reverser deployed in flight, causing the aircraft to go into an uncontrolled dive and break up in the air killing all on board.

I immediately called up DGCA's Director of Air Safety, AK Chopra, and explained the situation. I informed him that in my opinion an error of judgement by the pilot was the cause of the incident. I also added no inquiry was necessary, as the cause of tyre burst was known and that I will not be removing the Captain from Command. Further, I added that the pilot would undergo a 2 hour simulator training session on Reject take off and continued take off scenarios, after he completed the flight to Bangalore, once tires & brake assemblies were changed. Further, both Managers Maintenance and Safety concurred with me.

All Mr. Chopra said was that the runway at Cochin is only 6000 ft' long. The fact that despite getting airborne, he had rejected the take off and did not go off the runway was remarkable. He further added that the Captain must be one hell of a pilot. I agreed he was. Mr. Chopra accepted my action and just wanted a report as described for their record. Imagine the same scenario today, when both Airline Management and DGCA have such a prejudiced view about pilots.

Another incident that still gives me goose bumps is an actual engine fire after take-off from Visakhapatnam (Vizag). Here again, the runway was short with a hillock in the take-off path.

Capt. Jehangir called with the standard greeting. "Hi Sir, I think I fucked up". I had to land back after an actual engine fire on take-off. The aircraft and passengers are safe. The aircraft is grounded. "

He then related the occurrence.

Just after getting airborne, he got an engine fire warning with loss of power in the engine and a sudden yaw towards the dead engine. The fire in the engine was not extinguished by the engine fire extinguishers. With an engine out, a flaming aircraft with loss of associated generator and hydraulic pump, he had his hands full with an aircraft, whose climb performance was severely degraded. He had very little maneuver margin and had to climb straight ahead towards the hillock in the take-off path as a turn would further reduce his rate of climb.

Capt. Jehangir exhibited exemplary airmanship and skill and landed the aircraft back safely. The CVR recording was a masterpiece of professionalism. Horns, bells, buzzers were sounding and being silenced and the GPWS (Ground Proximity Warning System) was repeatedly screaming, "TERRAIN! TERRAIN! WHOOP WHOOP, PULL UP, WHOOP WHOOP PULL UP".

The cockpit was calm and under control. No panic. They were running through the checklist methodically, reconfiguring the aircraft, declared a Mayday, at the same time making appropriate crew announcements – all this with a flaming aircraft. Passengers were panic stricken, as they could see a burning engine. The cabin crew acted very professionally and were able to maintain order and calm in the cabin.

After landing, the engine was found to be in shambles – an incredible sight. The reliable JT8D jet engine had split right across the middle horizontally along the weld from the front up to the combustion chamber. The engine was like a gaping open mouth. This was probably the only isolated case of an engine weld giving way in the service life of the JT8D engine. The cause of the reduced climb rate was due to the immense drag the dead engine caused. The aircraft cleared the hillock "by the skin of the crew's balls" as Capt. Jehangir said.

I despatched our Safety Manager Capt. SK Bhatia to Vizag and informed Mr. Chopra who ordered the Air Safety Officer in Madras to get to Vizag immediately.

The full crew were rewarded in both cash and kind. Each given two free international tickets along with a complimentary stay for 2 nights at the Mumbai crew hotel with spouse/companion.

The DGCA wrapped up the inquiry within 48 hrs. In the inquiry, they complimented the crew, a rare occurrence in today's aviation environment. The present adversarial role of the DGCA, egged on by the media is neither healthy nor safe. DGCA is no longer run by professionals that grew up within the system and understood how things work or studied human limitation and behavior in the extremely trying circumstances of tackling an emergency in flight. What a pity.

Then there was the curious case of Capt. 'Kookie' Thind. Kookie was a lovable, hippie Sirdar, totally mad, but an excellent pilot. We had been apprentice pilots together in Hyderabad, although he was a batch senior. While I was undergoing training in Hyderabad, Ila had come to visit me for the New Year of 1978. Kookie decided to give us a grand evening, and as a member of the Secunderabad Club, invited Ila and I for the New Year gala there. It was a wonderful night!

Kookie left Indian Airlines in 1993 to join Saudia. I was surprised that with his quirky personality, he lasted with them for over 3 years. He suddenly quit Saudia, and one fine day presented himself in my office. All he said was – I have come to join your airline. When can I start? Luckily, in Saudia, he had been flying the B737-200 and his Indian License was also current. I signed him on and packed him off to Hyderabad for recurrent training.

In Alliance we had an exclusive Aviation fuel contract with the Indian Oil Corporation (IOC). In those day IOC did not have refueling facilities at all airports. The exclusive contract gave us a 10% discount on fuel if we paid our bills on time. Which we did.

The only downside was that we had to move extra fuel by tankers for airports that were not served by IOC. On one such flight, Kookie had to divert to Gwalior due to bad weather at Bhopal. Here he needed to refuel as he had less than the minimum fuel required to go back to Bhopal or continue to Delhi. The problem was that IOC had no facility at Gwalior. It was a Hindustan Petroleum station.

We were looking at a long delay at Gwalior as IOC would have to send a fuel bowser from Bhopal. While we were trying to arrange this, I was informed that the flight had departed Gwalior, after a quick refueling and that Capt. Thind had paid for the fuel with his American Express Gold credit card!

How he sweet talked HP to acccpt his credit card remained a mystery. He later told me that since the aircraft was still in its Indian Airlines

186

livery, the Hindustan Petroleum bowser turned up to refuel. Without explaining too much, Kookie told them how much fuel he wanted and the refueling happened. It was only after this that HP realized that this not an Indian Airline flight and they had no contract for fuel credit with Alliance Air. Kookie bailed himself and the HP guys out by offering to pay with his credit card.

Kookie was a favorite Captain with the Cabin Crew. He treated them courteously and was always the gentleman. The pilot roster loved him as he always helped out.

In the monsoon, landing at Goa is tricky as low clouds and passing rain showers suddenly reduce forward visibility. On one flight, while approaching to land at Goa, Kookie had to carry out a missed approach as he lost sight of the runway due to a passing rain shower. Observing another rain shower coming in from the sea he cut short the missed approach procedure, did a 180 degree turn and reported finals. The ATC was caught on the wrong foot. They had opened the runway crossing and there were people, cyclists and cars on the runway. The aircraft had to carry out a second missed approach, after which the airfield fell below minima, due to heavy rain, low clouds and strong gusty winds. Kookie's only option was to divert to Cochin.

He was riled with the Goa ATC and the Indian Navy for blocking the runway during his second landing attempt and made an announcement cussing the Navy, while apologizing to passenger for the inconvenience caused by not landing at Goa. I could not fault the ATC for opening the runway crossing since they expected the aircraft to carry out the complete missed approach procedure, but Kookie had cut it short.

To Kookie's bad luck, among his passengers were three Navy Admirals dressed in their finery. They were bound for Cochin. The Captain's announcement must have caused them great embarrassment.

The next day, I got a call from Naval Headquarters. Commander Theoraj, the DNAS (Director Naval Air Services), responsible for all civil flight clearances to Naval airfields and also an ex- Semite, was on the line. He informed me that the Vice Chief (one of the passengers on Kookie's flight) had instructed him to inform Alliance Air that Capt. Thind is not allowed to land at any Naval airfield either as Captain or co-pilot. All Alliance Air Flight have to inform Naval ATC the name of the Captain and Co-pilot on first contact. I suggested that this was too drastic and the Navy should reconsider. The airline would handle Capt. Thind internally and the MD and I would apologize formally to the Navy. The Indian Navy refused to budge.

In an internal meeting I kicked Kookie's ass and told him to stop behaving immaturely. I also took a stand that I will not be bullied by the Navy. Despite Vinoo's objection, I called up Theo at Naval Headquarters and told him since the Navy had banned one of my captains landing at any Naval airfield, Alliance Air will not be landing at any Naval airfield thereon.

This effectively took Goa, Cochin, Vizag and Port Blair off the air map. Instructions were issued to cancel all flights to these Naval airfields. Once the individual airfields got the notification, the shit hit the ceiling. Theo was back in contact. I reminded him of our school motto which was *"Certa Bonum Certa Men"* (FIGHT THE GOOD FIGHT). He caught on and by the evening the Navy withdrew its ban on Capt. Thind and I reinstated flights to all Naval airfields.

Keeping the Navy's sensitivities in mind, I informed Roster that Capt. Thind should not be rostered to any Navy airfield for at least a fortnight. I informed Mr. Chopra to keep him looped in and also Mr. PC Sen, just in case there were any ripples later. All he said was: "Shakti, that was gutsy but you are lucky it went your way, and the matter did not escalate to the Civil Aviation Ministry."

When Air Marshal Denzil Keelor got to know, he called saying, "This is what leadership is all about. Leaders stand by their boys." Off the record, he told me that that one of the Admirals involved in this issue told him that the Navy brass was surprised by the stand taken by a civilian airline manager. Such stands are usually taken by Defense service Commanding Officers.

Two different perspectives on the same incident.

The winter of 97-98 was severe and there were many fog-bound days, the most crippling being a 2-week stretch with fog setting every day after midnight and only lifting for a few hours after noon. Flight operations to Delhi were severely affected and the Ministry was concerned.

The Minister called an emergency meeting of all airline heads and Operations Chiefs. The Minister asked Mr. Khola, the DirectorGeneral of Civil Aviation, why Indian aviation was not geared for such weather. Mr. Khola instantly attacked the CMDs of Air India and Indian Airlines stating that the DGCA had repeatedly asked both airlines to train pilots for Cat 2 ILS operations and both airlines had ignored this directive. Had the airlines trained sufficient pilots to use Cat 2 ILS, the disruption would have been minimal. The Minister lost his shirt and took off on both Probir Sen of Indian Airlines and Michael Mascarenhas of Air India. Given my nature, I could not stay silent. I interrupted politely and suggested that the minister was being misled. I further added that even if the airlines had trained pilots for Cat 2 ILS, it would have made no difference to productivity. My team proceeded to explain, using graphics, our computerized data of all half hourly airport weather reports. It was explained that for the 12-16 hours of fog each day, the visibility was in Cat 2 range for only about half an hour. Most of the time, visibility was below 100 meters, and then transited through Cat 2 range to Cat 1 limits. Hence, ILS Cat 3 training was the solution, not Cat 2.

On the spot, the minister asked the chairman of the Airport Authority to make Delhi Airport be certified and ready for ILS Cat 3 Operations by the winter of 1998. He further instructed that all operators were to train pilots for up to Cat 3 operations and submit monthly reports to DGCA, which was to conduct meetings before each winter to assess fog operation preparedness by all concerned. The meeting was adjourned.

Delhi Airport became Cat 3 compliant by the winter of '98. The Member, Operations of AAI, Mr. Robey Lal, did a tremendous job to ensure that AAI delivered. The DGCA however had a problem. They had no background information on the pilot training, assessment and approval criteria. My old friends from DGCA came calling and requested we provide them with either FAA or British CAA regulatory material as the Ministry desired the Civil Aviation Requirement (CAR) for CAT 2 and 3 operations be issued immediately. We were the only organization that was computerized in the industry. My Operation support wizard, Sunil Madan, quickly accessed the FAA website and downloaded the relevant AC's (Advisory Circulars) for Cat 2 and 3 operation. These were copy pasted into the CARs.

On 12th of Dec 1996, Saudi Arabian Airlines Flight 763 a B-747 collided in flight with Kazakhstan Airlines flight 1907, an IL 76, killing 349 souls on board both airplanes. The collision occurred over Charki

Dadri in Haryana when both airplanes were under positive control of Delhi Air Traffic Control (ATC).

The Judicial Court of Inquiry faulted the Kazakh aircraft for the accident. It had been cleared to descend only to FL 150 (15,000 ft') whereas the Saudi Arabia Aircraft had been cleared to climb to FL 140 (14,000ft'). The Kazakh aircraft however descended below FL 150, to FL 140, resulting in the collision.

After this tragic accident, the DGCA made it mandatory for all public transport aircraft flying in and over Indian air space to be fitted with S-mode transponders and an Aircraft Collision Avoidance System (ACAS). This order resulted in enhanced safety of flight operations and since then, there have been no mid-air collisions. Another recommendation of the nquiry report was that inbound and outbound route to and from major airports be bifurcated. The realigned in-bound route to Delhi resulted in a slight reduction in the Indian Air Force local flying area (northwest of Delhi) much to their dissatisfaction.

Herby lies another tale.

There were some in the Air Force that could not stomach this and decided to create a scare by contriving a near miss between an Alliance Air flight from Jammu and a fighter, so as to highlight the danger if a civil aircraft strayed outside the 5 nm wide safe limit of the airway.

The captain of the Jammu – Delhi Flight reported the near miss to ATC; in his statement he stated that he was flying dead on track at FL 290 and a fighter appeared from nowhere and performed a "Vertical Charlie" maneuver just ahead of his flight path. This is the same as showing someone your middle finger (   ). Both aircraft could have collided with disastrous consequences.

I brought this to the attention of the DAS (Director, Air Safety) DGCA who desired an immediate near miss report filed. We were both of the opinion that it looked like a mischievous attempt of the Air Force to regain their lost local flying area. I leaked the incident to an Indian Express reporter buddy.

Next morning, the front-page carried a report something to the effect that another Charki Dadri tragedy had been averted. Suddenly, the establishment woke up!

The Minister of State (MOS) of Civil Aviation was Ms. Jayanti Natrajan. She immediately called a meeting, in the Ministry's Conference room, of Director General HS Khola, Vice Chief of Air Staff, and Alliance Air. Meanwhile the DAS had procured the tapes from the MLU (Military Liaison Unit) located in ATC Delhi. An MLU coordinates air traffic between Civil and Air Force air traffic control units. As per rules every incoming and outgoing radio telephony and telephone conversation is recorded and kept secure for a pre-determined period.

On the day, the Air Force put up an impressive performance. Officers in crisp blue uniforms, striped rank epaulettes and hats with scrambled egg marched in, smartly saluted the Minister and then made a very impressive presentation.

They had a sort of radar plot that indicated that the civil aircraft had deviated port (left) of track and infringed the Air Force local flying area which resulted in the near miss.

We disputed it and gave our presentation on a moving map display showing the aircraft was within the Pre-Determined Route (PDR) at the time of the incident. It was a Mexican standoff.

The minister desired that the incident be investigated by a 3-man committee consisting of the DG, Mr. Khola, the Vice Chief of Air Staff, and myself. Before the meeting was called off, I requested the Minister to please listen to a MLU recording. The recording was in Hindi and mainly was of the conversation between the MLU's unit at Palam and the concerned Air Force base. The gist was, I paraphrase:

"We had informed you of the civil aircraft on air route flying at FL 290 from Jammu to Delhi, now there has been a near miss reported by civil aircraft".

The base unit replied, "We informed the fighter pilot, but he disregarded our information and continued into civil airspace. These fighter pilots think they are gods. We are reporting the incident to concerned air traffic unit."

The Air force gentlemen sat there red faced. The Minister graciously quipped in, "Let's not embarrass our Air Force friends any further. We sincerely hope they will take the necessary action so that there will not be another such incident in future". The matter was closed.

Yet, the Air force did get back to us. The Commanding officer and the concerned pilot were reprimanded (polite way of saying got their butts kicked) for their over zealousness in trying to regain the lost airspace, which now was lost forever.

Alliance Air opened the following civil stations at Air Force airfields: one at Jaisalmer, Rajasthan, and the other at Thoise, in Ladakh. We also inaugurated Lengpui Airport in Mizoram, giving Aizawl a much-needed jet connection to Calcutta, Guwahati and Imphal. Earlier Mizoram was served by Silchar Airport, as the old Aizawl airport runway was too small for jet aircraft.

Both the Home Minister, Sri LK Advani and the Civil Aviation Minister were on board the inaugural flight to Lengpui. An opening ceremony was planned at the Airport. The ministers were aware that the flight would carry on to Imphal and land back at Lengpui after about an hour and forty five minutes. It would be carrying passengers connecting to the A300 flights to both Delhi and Mumbai as per their schedule. They were advised that a Do 228 would be positioned at Lengpui for their return to Delhi if the ceremony was delayed. The scheduled flight could not be delayed.

While taxiing out from Calcutta, the Home Minister's private secretary approached me and said the flight had to turn back, as the weapons of the Minister's Security Detail had not been loaded in the hold. This would cause a delay. I went up to Mr. Advani and apprised him of the situation and asked if he desired to turn the aircraft around. Without any hesitation, he said, "No please continue the flight without the weapons". We landed at Lengpui and there was a huge welcoming crowd to greet the VIPs. The flight had to be parked on the runway. Most of the tarmac was carpeted and had chairs laid out. A small stage had been erected for the VIPs.

Ceremonies at the airport got prolonged and before the VIPs realized, the scheduled return flight from Imphal was preparing to land, circling overhead. I approached the Home Minister and politely pointed out that the flight from Imphal was landing and as the ceremony was far from over, the Do228 was available for their return to Delhi. Mr. Advani decided to cut short the ceremony and said he was ready to return to Calcutta on the Boeing flight. I was greatly impressed by Mr. Advani. He was polite, courteous and soft spoken. He did not stand on formality and exhibited none of the arrogance and self-importance normally associated with Ministers.

When the aircraft was ready for departure, the VIPs boarded followed by the commando carrying flowers, presents and packages. It was a once-in-a-lifetime sight. The Home Minister of India's Security Detail Commandos carrying flowers and not deadly weapons.

After landing at Calcutta, while waiting for the IA flight to Delhi, Mr. Advani and Mr. Ananth Kumar, were in the AAI VIP lounge and we underlings in the IA business class lounge.

Unknown to us, MOCA held a press conference at that very time, in which it was categorically stated that IA would procure the ATR for Alliance Air. Meanwhile in an informal conversation with a journalist in Kolkata, when asked if Alliance would ever fly the ATR, I casually remarked "over my dead body" since it had not been found suitable and had been rejected twice by the Board.

To my horror, a Calcutta paper next day carried this Headline: "Civil

Aviation Minister say Indian Airlines to buy the ATR aircraft for Alliance Air.

Alliance Air Executive Director Capt. Shakti Lumba says "Over my dead body".

Oops! I goofed and how! After that incident I became very wary of "off the record" conversations with journalists. Some could be trusted. One or two not so easily to my great dismay and disappointment.

It soon came to pass that Minister Ananth Kumar insisted that Indian Airlines order the ATR. Mr. Probir Sen, the CMD, attempted to explain that the Board had rejected the ATR and no plane could be ordered without the Board's approval. He was called to the Ministry by the Secretary of Civil Aviation and told that the Minister wanted Mr. Sen sacked and replaced by Shri Anil Baijal, IAS, who was the Jt. Secretary monitoring Indian Airlines. Along with him Vinoo Kashyap, Alliance Managing Director, was also removed. Indian Airlines ultimately did procure the ATR for Alliance Air but only in 2003.

"The Ministry posted Mr. Anil Baijal, as CMD Indian Airlines in place of Mr. Probir Sen. Mr. Baijal started with a review of Alliance Air and observed that it should be classified as a Class D, Public Sector, since it had only a ₹5 crore equities. My gut told me that would be the beginning of the end of Alliance's independence and efficiency, if this came to pass.

I was called in by Mr. Baijal and asked to take over the MD's position. I politely declined again and suggested that the position should rightly go to either a Dy.MD of IA or a Director, and suggested that Capt. JRD Rao, the Dy.MD of IA should take over. JRD was given additional charge as MD, Alliance Air.

Alliance Air kept flying without a hitch. Until one morning JRD called to see me, and informed me that the CMD on request of the PMO desired that the spouse of THE minister (who will remain unnamed) should be made in charge of Alliance Air's Inflight Department. I refused point blank. I considered it to be a disastrous move. We had the best inflight department run efficiently and there was no way I would replace the current incumbent. My sentiments were conveyed to Mr. Baijal. A few days later, Mr. Baijal called for me. In the meeting, he explained his dilemma regarding appointment of the minister's wife since the request came directly from the Prime Minister through his Principal Private Secretary (PPS), and it was inappropriate that I refused to comply. I clearly stated that I would comply with any written order from the PMO, the Ministry or his office but not a verbal instruction. I naively requested a written order.

The Prime Minister's PPS, also a Shakti, ultimately spoke to me and I requested him for a small note to help me comply. He expressed his inability to do so and added that in his career he had never come across such an arrogant officer.

My stubborn attitude had placed my CMD in an awkward situation with the PMO. I respected him, so offered the only solution to the impasse which was, that I resign. He was taken aback and asked if I was willing to give up the most powerful position in Indian aviation at that time. I was the only one who could hire and fire as I pleased and ran the airline like a benevolent dictator. Something even he, in his position, could not. Was I willing to give it all up on a principle? I told him that a competent pilot never loses power as long as he has the left seat. I wrote a short resignation letter describing my exact reason for resigning. The CMD wanted me to change the reason of resignation. I refused. That was the only resignation he would get from me.

He kept it aside and wanted to know who I would recommend taking over from me. Alliance Air now needed a more diplomatic hand to steer it. I could only think of Capt. Ron Nagar, a likeable man, not bull-headed like me. The airline was established and needed a different personality to steer it. So, I recommended Ron. He met Mr. Baijal the next day and was appointed ED (Airline Operations). Mr. Baijal requested me to work for him as an Officer on Special Duty (OSD), which I very willingly accepted.

I closed the Alliance door behind me towards the end of 1999 and moved to my new role. I had briefed Mr. Baijal on the raison e'etre for the 5 yet limit I had set for Alliance Air and that its employees had been hired only on a 5 year contact. Alliance Air had fulfilled the role for which it had been created, the turnaround of Indian Airlines. This was totally disregarded by both Indian Airline and the Ministry.

Very rapidly Alliance Air degenerated into an over staffed airline with departments similar to Indian Airlines and a similar pyramid structure. It became a mini Indian Airlines.

Initially Air India was up for sale with Alliance Air excluded from the sale. Fortunately, the Tata Group's bid was the winning bid. The government was able to off load Air India after 3 yrs of waiting for the right buyer and the right price. Both Tata's and the Government seem to have got what they desired. The Tata's got back the Airline that was stolen from them 68 years ago.

As per news reports dated 11th Oct it seems that the government has changed its mind on keeping Alliance Air and have decided to sell it too. A prudent thing to do. Otherwise the mandarins in the Civil Aviation Ministry would have used Alliance Air to do their bidding and deploy its aircraft as they desire. It would have become a white elephant and a thorn in the Ministry's backside.

As OSD to the CMD no specific work was assigned to me. I had to create work for myself.

On 24th December 1999, Indian Airlines A300 flight from Kathmandu to Delhi was hijacked. The handling of the hijack by the concerned agencies was disastrous primarily because of poor information flow and subsequent decision making at the highest level.

After an accident the authorities must take control of the media and information within the first hour. If they lose the initiative to the media, then one is only reacting to public opinion, or a false narrative created by the media.

This is what happened in the case of this hijacking. The media had the initiative and the government only reacted to public opinion, resulting in the disastrous outcome at Kandahar, and the release of terrorists in exchange for passenger hostages. The fallout of that decision has snowballed into something far more sinister in Kashmir today.

On doing a WHY analysis one can conclude that the main failure, in this case, was the fact that the airline did not have an Emergency Response Plan nor a Central Operations Control. I offered to formulate a Policy Manual for the airline. This was a demanding task which took almost 4 months. The Manual on a Central Operations Control and Emergency Response Plan was submitted around April 2000.

About this time, the ministry came out with an advertisement in the newspapers for the post of Managing Director, Indian Airlines. I jokingly mentioned to Mr. Baijal that although I was just a Dy. General Manager in the airline, I met the qualification criteria because of my Alliance Air experience. He suggested half-seriously that I apply. I made out the application and gave it to the Director Personnel to forward to the Ministry "through the proper channel". The Director outright rejected it.

Thoroughly annoyed with this rejection, I called the Director of Personnel a postmaster and that he was only required to forward it. The matter was escalated up to the CMD, and the Director Personnel marked my application to him for approval. Mr. Baijal apparently recommended and approved the forwarding of my application.

I remember it was a Friday, and the next day Mr. Baijal was posted to the Andaman and Nicobar Islands as its Administrator. I reverted to normal flying in the Northern Region.

13. THE EMPIRE STRIKES BACK

You'll be bothered from time to time by storms, fog, snow. When you are, think of those who went through it before you, and say to yourself, 'What they could do, I can do.'

– Antoine de Saint-Exupéry

Mr. Anil Baijal's replacement was Mr. Sunil Arora IAS, joint secretary in the aviation ministry who was given additional charge of Indian Airlines. I was informed reliably that the first file he probably saw was my application for the job that he was keen on taking up full time. Mr. Arora was to become my "*bete noire*" for the next 3 years.

The Manual I made on Central Operations Control and Emergency Response Management never saw the light of day in Indian Airlines.

The work, however, was not wasted. After I joined IndiGo, it formed the basis of IndiGo's Operations Control Centre (OCC) and Centralized Flight Dispatch. The first Airline to have an approved OCC and Centralized Flight Dispatch which played a crucial role in its efficiency and lowering costs.

Petty jealousies, internal politics and back biting in the hallways of Indian Airlines had convinced Mr. Sunil Arora that I was a double agent who had one foot in the union and the other in management. I had created trouble for the airline through ICPA and then had come up with the solution which was the Pilot's PLI agreement.

This resulted in the pilots' earning a higher salary not only than the CMD but also the Cabinet Secretary. As per them, this agreement had imposed such a great financial burden that it was breaking the airline's back.

Of course, they failed to point out that 90% of the airline, ended up freeloading on the pilots agreement and received commensurate raises, as a consequence of that agreement. The agreement had played a crucial role in the turnaround of the airline and given years of industrial peace with the pilot's union. This too they failed to mention.

On 17th July 2000, an Alliance Air B737 crashed while landing at Patna killing all on board. I flew the relief flight to Patna with Mr. Sunil Arora among others as passengers. He asked me to accompany him to the crash site. I declined saying that I was on duty and had to operate the return flight.

I had seen crash sites and the tragedies had affected me psychologically. The smell of burnt fresh would haunt me for days. Undoubtedly, the tragedies had an adverse effect. I frankly told him that for the sake of the safety of the passengers I was to fly, it would be prudent I did not go with him. Without any comment, he simply asked me to visit him at his office.

I just forgot about the incident, but quite obviously, it set the ground for a strengthening of the negative opinion Mr. Arora had of me.

In subsequent incidents, he assigned blame on me as the mastermind behind critical comments on TV about Alliance Air by some pilots. Why I would deliberately badmouth my brainchild is something that never occurred to Mr. Arora. He chose to believe the rumor-mongers and gossips.

Once such an adverse perception was created and enforced, there was little I could do to change the CMD's mind.

It soon came to pass that interviews were held for the Posts of General Manager, Operations. Most of the DGMs being considered were a couple of batches senior to me. I ended up tutoring everyone on the Financial and Administration powers of a General Manager, along with a broad review of the airline's performance and its turnaround strategy etc.

Air Marshal Denzil Keelor and Robby Lal were the external members of the interview Board. Despite the fact that I was not as senior as the other candidates, I had 5 recent yearly appraisal ratings as "Outstanding" by the Airline's CMDs. The most recent by Mr. Anil Baijal. In such cases merit and not seniority become the criteria for promotion. I am told I was number one in the selection.

When the list was put up for approval, Mr. Arora declined to approve it as my name was on it. He desired it be removed from the list of selected candidates.

Air Marshal Denzil Keelor and Anita Mitroo GM (HR) informed me that the CMD would not clear the file as long as my name was in the selected list. I had obviously fallen from grace.

I asked them to knock it off the list. I had been there, and done that.

To add insult to injury I was made to undergo a third vigilance Inquiry on my tenure and decisions taken in Alliance Air. This one by the Director of Vigilance of the Airport Authority of India. I had earlier undergone two inquiries. One was by the Director Vigilance of Alliance Air, another by the Director Vigilance of Indian Airlines. I was exonerated by all 3 Inquires of any wrong-doing, misappropriation of funds, or favoritism. One Inquiry pointed out that it found me to be a fair, just and equitable officer.

Life carried on. Mr. Arora ignored me and I him. His many requests on his visiting card to upgrade passengers from economy to business I refused to do, unless the passengers agreed to pay the fare difference. Since, it was cause the company revenue loss. None agreed.

On one occasion, I off-loaded Mr. Pramod Mahajan, the then Minister of Communication and Information Technology from a flight from Mumbai to Delhi. We were ready for an on time departure with all passengers on board. This is when the duty officer came to me saying there was a message from the CMDs office to delay the flight indefinitely as Minister Mahajan was delayed.

I believed I owed a duty of care to our fare-paying passengers and the airline for maintaining on time performance. Employees PLI was at stake. The Minister was a 'no show' as per the rules. I refused to delay the flight and ordered the flight to be closed. The process had taken more than 15 minutes and the passengers were getting restless. As I was pushing back, I saw the Minister's cronies on the aerobridge, waving frantically and signaling to stop and return. I ignored the ruckus and continued to push back. I can imagine the report that was sent to the CMDs office on the Minister being left behind!

What happened next was a test. There was an unwritten understanding and practice that stood the test of time, which was that pilots could not be transferred unless on promotion. Not only was I deprived a promotion, but to add insult to injury, I was transferred from Delhi to Chennai with immediate effect.

I was in Mumbai that day, getting ready for my return flight to Delhi when Anita Mitroo, GM (HR) called me on my mobile and dropped a bombshell. She informed me she was holding my immediate transfer orders to Chennai signed by the CMD. I requested her to hold them back till after lunch as would be landing back by 1200 hrs.

The only punishment that IAS and government employees are given is "transfers". I guess old habits die hard.

On landing, I immediately applied for 13 days leave, giving a death in the family as the reason. The General Manager, Operations of Delhi approved my leave. With the approval in my pocket, I informed Anita to release the transfer order.

I now had time to think and went underground. Unfortunately, the Thelka scam hit the headlines the next morning and everyone from ministers to bureaucrats who owed me favors went underground.

I was later informed that the Director HR and Director Operation came with my transfer order and instructed the GM (ops) region to release me immediately and send me to Chennai by the evening flight. These were the CMDs orders. He told them he could not as I was on leave which he granted earlier. They informed the CMD who summoned the GM's presence immediately. My letter for leave was shown to him. He is said to have smiled and remarked that I was a clever man as even he could not reject a 13 day leave request on a death-in-the-family case.

To fight fire with fire, was the only way to counter an influential officer who had the backing of powerful State and Central politicians. He was their blue eyed boy.

The fire I chose was the good offices of the Vice President of the Vishwa Hindu Parishad (VHP). My family knew Mr. Vishnu Hari Dalmia intimately. My father had died when in the service of his father Jai Dayal Dalmia. We were like family. My sisters tied "Rakhi "on Vishnu Hari since childhood. We called on him and I explained my problem. He asked me who he speak with to get the job done. I told him that the best bet was The Vice President of India, Mr. Shekawat. He was a former Chief Minister of Rajasthan and Mr. Sunil Arora had not only served under him directly but was also his protégée. The Vice President should speak to my CMD.

Now the CMD was looking for me desperately, but I had to remain underground for at least 13 days. After which I surfaced and went to meet him. His attitude towards me had completely changed and he wanted to know my connection with 'Vishnuji.' I explained. The CMD then requested me to report to Chennai and then put in request to reverse the transfer order on compassionate grounds. He would then reverse it.

The transferred was reversed but I chose to spent 2 weeks in Chennai with old friends, Ashim and Indra Mitra. The two weeks were spent well. I was able to fly to Colombo and Male and build a booze stash.

Thereafter, the persecution stopped. I too, had learnt a lesson. I simply laid low till my badly placed Saturn's malefic effects waned. Shortly thereafter, the gentleman got promoted and moved back to Government.

Since discretion is the better part of valor, I have ruthlessly kept myself from spilling out many other devious shenanigans of the powerful. In my twilight years, it would be a foolhardy exercise to try to take on the still very powerful junta.

14. MY INDIGO JOURNEY

"I've never known an industry that can get into people's
blood the way aviation does."
– Robert Six

My IndiGo journey started in Feb 2005, when an old friend Anil Chanana, invited me for a drink at his home in Sultanpur farms. I had actually met Anil through Sunil Bharti Mittal. I knew Sunil since 1986. In fact Sunil had sponsored a trip to Australia for my son, Shiv to compete in the Taekwondo World Championship held in Sydney in August 1991. In those day we could not afford the fare even on a pilot's salary.

To his credit, Shiv won the gold medal in the under 21 kg Bantam weight category. He was only 8 years old. He must have been the youngest Indian to have won a Gold Medal in an International Championship. I subsequently met Sunil again with Anil and Raza Bilgrami in the early in 1995. At the time Sunil was starting Bharti Airtel in which Raza was initially involved along with his brother-in-law, Bashir Karimji, who was already running cellular services in Mauritius. Both Anil and Raza were international commodity traders.

Anil had specifically called me to meet his best friend, Rahul Bhatia. I had earlier met Rahul during my Alliance Air days. At that time, he had been keen to buy out SK Modi's stake in the then defunct ModiLuft that had stopped operations as an Air Taxi Operator and did not pursue a scheduled airline permit after the Air Corp Act had been repealed.

I had discouraged him then, pointing out the challenges in starting an airline in those days. Rahul's dad, Kapil Bhatia was a contemporary of Naresh Goyal, and Rahul was very keen to diversify their large Travel business into an airline business as Goyal had. However, at that time, the senior Mr. Bhatia was not keen.

By 2005, Rahul had expanded his company Interglobe Enterprises, into many successful companies all in the periphery of the airline business. Rahul came straight to the point. He wanted to start a world class airline and was now ready to do so with his father's support. Aviation had been deregulated and the government was keen to encourage more airlines aiding to the rally of the economy. His initial questions led me to list out the key ingredients to start a successful airline. These were, in order of importance, endlessly deep pockets full of money, powerful political contacts, and hiring professionals with proven track records to run the airline. (To be successful the promoter should never micromanage the company but let the professional run it.)

So my questions followed. How much money was he willing to invest? The regulatory equity of ₹30Cr would be totally inadequate for a sound venture, where only the minimum start-up capital required would be to the tune of ₹100cr. The promoters needed patience along with deep pockets, as no profit could be expected for at least 3 years as these are highly capital intensive. Rahul informed me that between him and his US based Indian-American financier, they were willing to invest up to $150 million (about ₹600 Cr those days). I was impressed.

Next Question: Did he have the political contacts in the UPA government? This was essential if one wanted to acquire the NOC to start an airline. Furthermore, if the government fell, did he have enough political clout in the NDA if they seized power? He said he had. The last question was what about contacts in the aviation bureaucracy. He was totally confident. He was serious.

Why approach me? I was told that a former CMD (Chairman and Managing Director) of Indian Airlines had recommended me, as the person who started and ran Alliance Air very profitably and efficiently.

Rahul got to work on procuring the NOC. Till then, further discussions were futile. Subsequently, I met Rahul a number of times, and learnt about his proposed partner, Rakesh Gangwal. At this point,

I was convinced that Rahul's proposal was worth considering Rakesh had had an exemplary aviation career and a reputation as a hard and demanding task master. He had been with United Airlines and also had been the CEO of US Air. He and Rono Datta were two Indian Americans that had held top job in US Airlines. Rono in American Airlines and Rakesh in US Air.

In a meeting in May, Rahul asked my recommendation on the aircraft type the proposed airline should consider. For a domestic operation, there were two serious contenders – Boeing's B737NG and the Airbus A320. Both had almost similar economics and performance. "Choose the one for which you get a better deal and support", I said.

However, I added I would prefer the A320 as I currently flew it. Getting qualified Manpower should not be a problem. Further, since their main base of operation was going to be Delhi, then for operations in winter the A320 had a tactical advantage. Being "Fail Operational", it could land and take off in very poor visibility up to ILS category 3B minimums whereas, the B737NG, being only certified "Fail Passive", was limited to the CAT 3A minimums. The A320 was capable of providing better regularity in the crucial fog months.

In June 2005, the international aviation industry was still undergoing the negative effects of the 9/11 terror attacks. The aviation world was surprised when Airbus announced at the Paris Air show, an order of 100 A320 aircraft by an unknown Indian Company, InterGlobe Aviation Ltd. Shock waves reverberated in Indian and international aviation, as this was the largest aircraft order at that time for the aviation industry.

Later, when we met with Rakesh Gangwal, he regaled us with this anecdote. At the Air Show the Boeing Chalet was nearest to the entrance so he walked into the Boeing Chalet and at the reception stated he wished to place an aircraft order. "How many aircraft would you desire to buy", came the response from the gentleman at the counter. Rakesh replied, "One hundred aircraft, initially."

The Boeing representative must have thought he was a joker. He did not take him seriously and told him that he could order five or ten aircraft only at the Air Show. Rakesh walked out and went into the Airbus chalet. He was immediately recognized and Airbus CCO, John Leary soon came up to him saying, "How many aircraft do you wish to order, Rakesh?"

"One hundred," Rakesh said.

"ONLY one hundred?" John responded,

The rest is history.

Rakesh was very experienced in the art of aircraft buying and leasing, having bought many for United and US Air, and was an old Airbus customer. During those difficult times that the aviation industry was going through, the 100 aircraft order was a life saver for Airbus, and Rakesh was able to extract a real honey-deal, not only from Airbus but from all Original Equipment Manufacturers (OEM), who were suppliers of essential associated equipment.

One hundred aircraft meant 200 engines for Roll-Royce to name just one. It was a lifeline for the suppliers struggling to survive during the aircraft sales famine post 9/11. Rakesh drove a hard bargain, resulting in very low aircraft and spare parts costs, which normally are the killers for start-up airlines.

It was clear that Rahul Bhatia intended to be a serious player in the Indian aviation market. I sent him a congratulatory message and confirmed that I was willing to quit Indian Airlines, to join his new venture. He was pleased. He asked me to be on standby for the Company's Chief Legal Counsel, Mr. Aditya Ghosh to sign an employment contract and confirm the role.

I immediately got in touch with Indian Airlines Acting-CMD, Sushma Chawla. I knew her well from my ICPA days when she was the Controller of Financial Rules. I met her next morning and informed her that I had a challenging offer to start a new airline. I was looking for Voluntary Retirement (VR), as I had completed 25 years of service, was above 55 years of age, was in a dead-end job and due to retire after 3yrs.

She immediately called the Director HR, Anup Srivastava, told him of my intention and to immediate draft a VR request on my behalf as per rules. He was back in no time with two copies. I signed and submitted one to HR and the other for my record. I knew Anup from before: I had chosen him as Head of HR in Alliance when he was but a DGM in Indian Airlines.

Sushma sat me down and made me note down what salary and perks I should ask for. A high basic, company accommodation, key-man insurance, medical insurance, company vehicle and stock. My release date was fixed as 31st August 2005.

I immediately informed Rahul that I was available to him from 1st September. News of this spread like wildfire in IA and Alliance. I got a call from Mr. Patel, the Aviation Minister, requesting me to reconsider the offer as he wished that I take over Alliance Air which had gone into decline and had become a mini–Indian Airlines. I thanked him for the offer but respectfully declined.

Although, I had not signed any contract, I had given my word to Rahul. Ever since I had started working, I was known as a 'Man of my Word', which had a higher value than a written agreement. Yet, in this, I am also quite naïve, I trust a man's word before a written commitment. But not everyone keeps their word.

As promised, Aditya Ghosh, Chief Legal Counsel of InterGlobe called in first week of August and on my next off day turned up at home. I was amazed at the patience and perseverance of this man. He sat through all the confusion of people and other guests going in and out of our home which, usually was like a busy thoroughfare.

He kept on fine tuning all my demands. We were finally finished, a good 6 hours later, during which time he had nursed a glass of Coke. We shook hands. It was done!

I signed my contract a week later, I guess I was one of the airline's first few employees, the Head of Operations. It was a priority for Rahul to sign me on as one of his biggest challenges would be getting enough high-quality pilots who were in short supply, since Air Deccan, Go Airlines and Kingfisher had opted for the A320.

Once officially on-board, I invited Rahul, Bruce Ashby the designated CEO along with Aditya, for dinner at home to meet the family. Rahul made it a point to assure my wife that she was not to worry about her husband leaving the secure Indian Airline's job. She need to have no worries as he was giving her his assurance written in blood that he would be taking care of me.

Later I learnt that the dinner was not taken too kindly by the Indian Airline top brass, who all lived in the same apartment block.

Meanwhile, I found a suitable independent bungalow in Palam Vihar and gave up my company allotted accommodation in Vasant Vihar.

In the 3rd week of August, I received a bombshell from Indian Airlines, rejecting my voluntary retirement. I was confused and angry as I had been honest and open with the airline. The CMD and Director HR had themselves supported and encouraged me. But when I called to speak to Sushma, she said she was busy and the decision was out of her hands. Anup Srivastava avoided my calls.

I informed Rahul of this development. He was visibly upset. I *had* to be there for the operational start up. I assured him that I had given him my word and I would join him on 1st September come what may. I operated my last flight with Indian Airlines on the 30th of August; the pilot roster was out for the first 15 days of September, and I was not on it as everyone knew I was exiting on 1st Sept. All the boys in pilot roster were my Alliance Air boys and they had my back.

Rahul had hired a house in Vasant Kunj as an office and equipped it with computers, printers and scanners, I had already chosen my team. Both former Alliance Air colleagues, Sunita Srivastava and Sunil Madan who I had mentored as Managers and developed into independent professionals. After their period of deputation was over, they were just Deputy Managers in Indian Airlines working well below their potential and capabilities, totally frustrated. Rahul had met them and approved their hiring. I got them appointed as Directors on a salary of ₹100,000/- a very major jump from what they were getting in Indian Airlines. They had also served notice. Both walked out with me and started working on the crucial manuals for InterGlobe Aviation.

I came to know later, that the ICPA, egged on by pilots who were immensely jealous, had approached the Minister and told him that if I was released, I would take with me many pilots from among my large following. This apparently was what had tied Sushma's hands.

To add insult to Injury, on instruction of the Ministry, the DGCA issued a CAR effective 1st Sept 2005 on Notice Period, as per which no pilot could resign from an airline without giving and serving a 6-month Notice Period and then too, without an NOC from his company. Indian Airlines was confident that I was hog-tied, and Rahul Bhatia's Airline would be a non-starter. They expected me to stay back.

I received numerous dispatches by dispatch rider to operate flights & report to office. I ignored them totally. My boys in roster made sure each flight was covered and no delay or cancellation could be attributed to me. Indian Airlines issued suspension letters and Show Cause notices and used the DGCA CAR of 6-month Notice insisting that I had only given 3 months' notice. Finally, they initiated disciplinary proceedings against me which I refused to attend. I was untraceable.

My work on the new airline continued. Both Sunita and Sunil were also informed that their resignation was not accepted, and they were absent without leave. They too, encouraged by my stand, ignored all threats. Their leaving was not as much of threat to the Airline as mine was. They ultimately negotiated their release.

I had filed a writ petition in Delhi High Court and within 3 months got my release from the Airline, but had to forego all my hard-earned post-retirement benefits.

Hiring for the airline was in full swing, Bruce Ashby, a former colleague of Rakesh Gangwal, was the CEO, Rahul Bhatia was the Managing Director, from InterGlobe came Sanjiv Ramdas for Airport Services, Vineet Mittal for Finance, Shalini Singh as EA to the CEO, Suman Chopra was hired to Head In-flight, SC Gupta who was former Director Engineering of Indian Airlines was to Head Engineering, with Ashwini Acharya to assist him.

Bruce had brought in a New Zealander, Adrian Hamilton for route planning. Capt. KPS Nair, a former Director in the DGCA was taken as Chief of Safety.

Both SC Gupta and I, with our experience in Indian Airlines, were totally familiar with the requirement for our areas of expertise and knew *"What Not to do"* which was the way Indian Airlines did it. It was inefficient, expensive, time consuming and labour intensive.

We both desisted from taking the easy way out which was copying and pasting all Indian Airlines' manuals. This is what had happened with Air Deccan, Kingfisher and Sahara before them. In my opinion, this was one of the main causes for the poor performance, high costs and inefficiencies of these carriers. Their copy-pasted manuals had embedded in them all the inefficiencies, work culture, high-costs, procedures and policies of the national carriers that had a social, but no economic, obligation. Indian Airline's legislated mandate was to connect the country with an air transport network that was safe, regular, comfortable and lastly affordable. But economy of Operation was their lowest priority.

By November of '05, we moved out of Vasant Kunj into the proposed corporate office in Tower C, Global Business Park, Gurgaon. The whole building belonged to InterGlobe Enterprise. IndiGo had the 3rd Floor. The office was open floor, arranged in clusters of work stations. The CEO and the heads of Departments were allotted a standard Cabin 8ft' by 8ft'. Real estate costs were high and the space did not come free

In the first meeting of the Leadership team with Bruce, we were informed the airline's name chosen was "IndiGo" that its business plan was to fly a single aircraft type, the A320 and we were going to be a Low-Cost Carrier with no frills. IndiGo intended to connect everytown with an airport having a population of one million or more.

The question on every one's mind was the dotted arrow logo. We were told it was multifunctional and could be used also as a direction indicator. The logo was an 'arrow plane' in the same proportions as the A320. Why 'arrow plane'? Simply because the Hindi speaking population called an aeroplane an 'arrow plane'. We were also informed that our IATA code was 6E and Radio Telephony call sign 'I Fly'.

Cost control would be the company's overriding philosophy. The guiding principles were: do we need it, or do we want it; can we manage without it? Each department would be a cost centre with a budget. Initial wants were laptops and Blackberry mobile phones. It was decided that only those who would be expected to work from home were to be allotted laptops and those required to be contactable 24 hrs, the Blackberry.

In my previous avatar in Indian Airlines, laptops or emails were never used. The airline management system was based on subject files, hard copies, note sheets and written approvals all on file that were kept in a central registry. I was basically computer illiterate and being allotted an Executive Secretary was a demand that had been agreed to.

HR had short listed some candidates and I selected a young girl, Nidhi Dhingra. I would be lost without Nidhi until I slowly got the hang of using a computer and emails.

My first priority was to structure the Flight Operations Department. The proven structure developed for Alliance Air was used. We kept it flat with decision making delegated to sectional heads. The structure was simple.

The Vice President Flight Operations would be responsible for the safety of aircraft operations, operations policy, discipline, and compliance with all regulatory requirements. Reporting to him were the Director Operations (Support), Director Crew Management, and three Chief Pilots. One each for Training, Line operations and Standards & Quality Assurance. Each Chief Pilot was supported by a Fleet Captain & Fleet Supervisors.

An aircraft has a large number of equipment redundancies. The Manufacturer's Master Minimum Equipment List (MMEL) lists all items that can be unserviceable without effecting the aircraft's Certificate of Airworthiness (C of A). From the MMEL is derived the airline's Minimum Equipment List (MEL) by both flight operations and Engineering. It then needs DGCA approval for its use in line operations.

The Flight Operations Department rested on 3 pillars. They were Sunita Srivastava, Director Crew Management, Sunil Madan, Director Operations Support and Capt. PK Sinha, Chief Pilot, Training. Each of these pillars were internally supported by their teams. I was responsible for all Flight Operations policy, guidance, motivation of each team, and conflict resolution. We never considered anything a problem but a challenge. If anyone came up against a brick wall, he or she was not to come to me for a solution but with at least two options on how to overcome the challenge. This principle was applied down the line by each sectional head. I would then choose the option that would be cost effective, efficient, and easy to implement.

I had learnt this from my previous boss Mr. Probir Sen, CMD of Indian Airlines.

The challenges identified now were:

1) Recruitment of pilots

2) Training of pilots

3) Obtaining DGCA approvals and Permits

4) Cost effective and efficient Operations Support

5) Oversight for safe operation was important part of safety culture that we wished to instill. For this it was imperative that we ensure proper adherence of our and DGCA policies in our day to day operation. Risk identification and elimination or mitigation to an acceptable level was to be our mantra.

It was made clear to my team that we could not even afford to scratch an aircraft, leave aside break one. So, safety culture needed to be inculcated among all personnel of the Flight Operations Department along with effective quick communication. There would be no 'Boxes' in which different departments got insulated, but there should be an awareness among every one of the responsibilities of each other's areas and their interdependence on each other.

It was realized from the very inception that one of our greatest challenges would be staying ahead of the aircraft induction program with respect to having enough pilots to fly them. The induction dates for the 100 aircraft were fixed. The pilot requirement needed to be achieved. Flight cancellation / reduced utilization due to shortage of pilot was not an option, nor was deferring aircraft deliveries because we did not have enough pilots. Based on projected utilization we would require 5 sets of flight crew per aircraft, 'Ready to Fly'. It was my responsibility to, recruit and train pilots for the Airline requirement.

Bruce and I, together worked to form a comprehensive pilot agreement that would cover all issues clearly with each party's responsibilities and obligation clearly spelt out.

I used my old reliable formulae for pilot compensation. The principle was having 2 categories of co-pilots, those with experience and having an ATPL were senior pilots and junior co-pilots were those having low experience and only a CPL. The senior co-pilot was pegged at 75% of the captain's pay and the junior co-pilot at 60%. It was decided to scale the salary on a fly-more-earn-more principle, but the baseline would be a fixed guaranteed amount per month at 70 hours assured, as long as the pilot was in 'good standing' and 'available to fly'. These two terms, their applicability was clearly defined in the individual pilot agreements. This was a very American concept Bruce probably borrowed from "Jet Blue", as was most of the clauses.

There was a drastic difference in the way airlines in America and airlines in India viewed pilot-management relations. In the US, pilots were a paradox - "Impossible to live with and impossible to live without". A US Air Pilot once told me that in the airline's crew rest room, there was a dart board with the photo of Rakesh and Bruce for pilots to throw darts at. In contrast, in India the pilot had a good standing with the company and in society. He was treated well and handled with kid gloves. These two differing perceptions were the cause of friction between me, my team and our expat American colleagues.

The foremost priority was to obtain the Airline Operating Permit (Air Operators Certificate or airline license) from the DGCA. Each item that was required was identified for each department, listed with a completion date and its progress capture in green. Each departments progress was tracked. The CEO, Bruce held a meeting every Monday of the Leadership Team, so that everyone was aware of each other's progress. Slowly the spread sheet that was a sea of red started filling up with green as we progressed.

All this while the crew management team and I were busy hiring pilots. I concentrated on Bombardier CRJ pilots who were flying for Air Sahara. During one of my visits to Toulouse Capt. ET had mentioned that the Airbus team that had done the development of the A320, had moved to Bombardier and had designed the CRJ using the same principles they had for the A320. He was of the opinion that CRJ pilots would find it easiest to convert on to the A320.

One of the first pilots to approach me for a job was Capt. Hardeep Malhotra, an Instructor Examiner on the CRJ with Air Sahara. He signed up in Nov'05. Along with him came other Captains and co-pilots. Pilots were required to serve the 6-month notice period to their employer as required by DGCA. They committed to join 6 months later and were each given a month joining bonus. I got the company to agree to pay the A320 Type rating costs with the proviso that each pilot would sign a 3 year Training Bond and surrender 3 un-dated cheques of ₹500,000 covering the ₹15,00,000 cost of training. After each year of service, one cheque was returned. In case they left earlier, the cheques would be cashed to cover the cost of training.

Slowly the ranks of pilots kept increasing. The industry was surprised that pilots were willing to give up airline flying jobs to join a new airline that did not even have the Airline Operator's Permit. The salary we were offering was not the best in the industry. In fact, it was lower than what Spice Jet, Kingfisher Airlines and Go Airlines were offering. Rahul's confidence in me and my reputation was paying off.

I hit a snag in April when pilots started signing in after their six months' notice required by DGCA. I had instructed Finance that all pilot salaries must be paid by the last working day of the month. Come hell or high water. Any salary delay would seriously affect my hard-sell to pilots that HR and Finance would have no role to play with regards to them. They would only interact with HR for joining formalities and later on exit.

Finance contacted Bruce. He called me out saying he will not pay pilot salary until they started flying. I should lease them out to Kingfisher, Go Air or Deccan.

I was aghast. This guy had no idea of the ground reality of pilot availability. At any point of time there were four airlines trying to attract any available pilot, with bagfuls of inducements. Without understanding the pilot shortage position in India, he was asking me to hand over precious pilots to our competitors on a platter.

I immediately barged into Rahul's office across the road and told him to abandon his project if they were not willing to pay pilot salaries. He spoke to Rakesh, explained the issue and they immediately released a million dollars for pilot and employee salaries. Bruce could not have been very happy with me.

Believe it or not, Finance made no effort to pay salaries on time as demanded. There were fireworks in the Leadership meeting and payroll was handed over to HR who subcontracted payroll to a specialized company and from the next month till this day each employee's salary is credited to his/her account before the last working day of each month. Most Companies paid by the 7th or 10th of the succeeding month. When financially stretched, salary was delayed by months. IndiGo's salary credit before the last day of the month became a major selling point for me with pilots.

The Operations Manual was being completely rewritten as were Standard Operating Procedures. The most important part of the Operations Manual is Part D, the section on pilot training. This is the only part that the DGCA actually approves. The rest of the Manual is accepted by them as the Airline Policy. This policy cannot supersede any DGCA rule, order or CAR (Civil Aviation Requirement).

It is imperative to ensure that part D is never copy pasted from another airline's Manual, just to ensure ease of approval. This is what all the existing airlines actually did, thus increasing their costs of training. Once Part D is approved then reducing any training requirement is an uphill task with the administrative Babus.

In IndiGo, Cost Control was a fetish. It was the company's philosophy. Cost control as a strategy never yielded desired results. Pilot training is high cost and easily plucked 'low hanging fruit'. We looked at the best and modern training practices which mostly did away with training on an aircraft and substituted this with more training on advance simulators referred to as Level D training devices. These simulators replaced aircraft training with Zero Flight Time Training (ZFTT) on simulator.

IndiGo only carried out the mandatory 3 take off and landings on the aircraft required by the regulation for a new type rating. This amounted to a huge training cost reduction not only with respect to the initial 100 aircraft order but the 400-500 aircraft that were to be ordered subsequently. The other airlines had copy pasted the Indian Airlines' Training procedures which involved 10 hrs by day and night of actual aircraft flying per pilot, a colossal waste of money and aircraft hours.

Airbus was at that time charging $55,000 (US) per crew set for a standard type rating. This we rejected. There was a CAE/Airbus joint venture located in Dubai. Sunita, Steve and I were able to negotiate the ZFTT training with additional sessions ensuring all DGCA requirements were met. I also insisted on two additional sessions for low visibility training up to ILS Cat 3 C level. Every pilot was to be trained for low visibility operation and Captains needed to be right seat qualified. This was just in case two Captains were rostered together. The whole package was at a cost of only $42000(US). This too by Airbus instructors and Airbus's Manufacturer Training Certification.

We also got CAE hotel discounts, free airport-hotel transfers with priority immigration and gratis transport for training and a complimentary 24-hour snack bar, well stocked. The feather in our cap was an innocuous clause I insisted on, stating that all IndiGo training would be only during "social hours". The advantage of this was to dawn on CAE once the IndiGo training started. Pilot training slots cover the whole 24-hour period. IndiGo slots could never be before 8am and never after 8pm. Other customers ended up with the unsocial slots from 8pm to 8am.

The Operations Control Centre (OCC) was also being set up. It was to have operations controllers to maintain flight watch, commercial controllers, pilot and cabin crew schedulers, flight dispatchers, meteorologists and an integrated Maintenance Control Centre (MCC) and for Emergency Response Management.

OCC was to be the nerve centre of the airline that was to control the operations, manage disruptions, recover diverted flights and maintain a communication with the aircraft via Aircraft Communications Addressing and Reporting System's (ACARS) High Frequency (HF) data link. The Very High Frequency (VHF) data link connectivity was very poor; VHF communications were limited by range. It was only HF data link that met the crucial flight supervision requirement for the DGCA to approve our OCC. We were under their scanner to ensure all their requirements were complied with.

With this in mind, I had insisted that an HF (High Frequency) set with data capability was included in the purchase order along with ACARS, which would use the HF datalink for two way communication between OCC and the aircraft.

For Operations Controllers, I insisted on retired Air Traffic Controllers; for weather expertise, I chose retired Air Force meteorologists, their expertise lay in accurate small window forecasts more useful than the general area Meteorological forecasts. Initially the Retired ATC controllers played a key role in IndiGo's OTP (On Time Performance) reputation. By the time we started, airfield congestion was becoming an issue causing delayed departures and arrivals due to congestion. Aviation passenger traffic was growing at more than 15 to 20 percent.

Getting start up clearance was like entering a bar brawl. I worked out a system. IndiGo aircraft would give one call for start-up. ATC would say stand by. Each aircraft by tail number had a dedicated mobile phone given to the Captain before a flight. The aircraft would call the Ops controller and give him his bay number and that he was fully ready. The controller would call the tower controller, often who was his junior and voila, one heard the beautiful words "I-Fly123 cleared to push and start."

But I'm getting ahead of myself.

While setting up OCC, we needed to procure state-of-the-art software. I put Sunil and Sunita on the job and finally they came back with their choice, costing about ₹80,00,000/- to buy with an additional monthly cost. They were a little apprehensive it was too expensive, given their Indian Airlines background which gave any contract to the lowest bidder.

Since, software was not my area of expertise I put it up to Bruce.

It didn't take him long to walk into our work area saying, "We are not going to buy such garbage. This will collapse beyond a 25-30 aircraft fleet. We may be low cost, but we are not cheap. To handle our fleet requirement, the software we require should cost not lesser than a million dollars. You guys should get out of your Indian Airlines mode and start thinking BIG not small". He later informed us that the company would be ordering the Sabre-Rocade combo. It cost a bomb, over a million dollars and a huge yearly fee. We learnt our first lessen which was to go for the best and then negotiate. Never go for the cheapest. It will let you down.

The final specs for the Airbus purchase agreement were being finalized. Rakesh and Bruce were looking at ordering a product that would be acceptable in the lease market. The reason behind this I learnt later when we were in Toulouse to pick up our first aircraft. Airbus had agreed to a buy back each aircraft after 6 years. This way the airline fleet would remain young, reducing maintenance costs.

The principle was to go for all that was essential and needed, avoid *wants* which end up making the airplane more expensive than required for a low-cost operation. Vijay Mallya had ordered the A340 and filled it with his wants, considerably increasing the aircraft weight and cost. The A340 was a beautiful aircraft and much in demand but configured for Kingfisher it bombed. It was unable to carry out the task for which it had been bought due to its higher weight and consequent higher fuel consumption. Later it became difficult to sell.

At the onset, we in IndiGo had an understanding that whenever there was a difference in opinion between the promoters and a Department Head on cost of a high-end item, the department that required it, had to make the final call. I needed ACARS for the Centralized Operations Control and Flight Despatch. Without them the DGCA would never approve our concept. ACARs is an Aircraft Communication Addressing System. It uses a data link for communication between the aircraft and its ground unit, automatic reporting of an aircraft's position and also aircraft in flight faults as they occur. It works on both HF and VHF frequencies. I had already discussed this project with Mr. AK Chopra who by then was the Joint Director General. He was agreeable to approve our Centralized Dispatch and OCC. The first in the country as long as we had assured communication between the ground and the aircraft to exercise flight supervision also called Flight watch. He said that with ACARS and HF data link he would approve our concept. So, when ACARs and the HF were being discussed, I said "My call. It's a need, not a want". The issue was settled. (So I thought).

A similar situation arose when the galley confirmation was being chosen. Because of weight consideration Rakesh had decided that there would be no hot meal service and so ovens were rejected. Rahul was a foodie and was keen on good hot food service. But obviously, it was a want, and he was overruled by Rakesh on the LCC decision. Rakesh made the call.

Another call I made was not to accept all the FOC engines that the Rolls Royce-led consortium, International Aero Engines (IAE) was offering. I preferred to keep them in their General Engine Pool in Singapore. An engine should be made available whenever/wherever an engine was required on AOG (Aircraft on Ground) basis. To my surprise they agreed. From experience I was aware that there was no aircraft in India with a large enough cargo hold to ferry a fully dressed A320 engine. Blue Dart was the only Cargo Airline. It was flying the B757 cargo version. Even this could not carry an A320 engine. Ferrying an engine by air was a problem. The good engine had to be dismantled into 3 modules to be carried. Once it reached its destination it had to be reassembled before installing under the wing. Similarly, the dud engine also had to be dissembled so as to be carry back. This whole process took 2 to 3 days and had huge cost and time implications.

The first occasion that my call was tested is when after a bird hit, an engine changed was required at Bhubaneswar. Within 5 to 7 hours a fully dressed engine arrived by IL 76. The dud engine had already been removed. It was loaded on to the IL 76 and sent on its way for damage check etc., under the Guarantees and Warranties (G&W). The replacement engine was fixed on the wing and aircraft was serviceable within 10 hours. IAE must be rueing the day they agreed to this arrangement. They had to fly in engines at their cost whenever and wherever an engine change was required. Indigo saved both money and time.

Although the call for ACARs was made under ***need to have,*** Bruce informed me that because of its very high cost it was removed from the list of components ordered at the end.

I was shocked. My whole centralized OCC & Dispatch and its approval was dependent on our using ACARs. The DGCA approval was expected accordingly. I dialed Rahul, who suggested that I take it up with Rakesh. I contacted Rakesh at his home in Washington and explained the issue and suggested that the whole aircraft induction plan be deferred by six months as a centralized OCC and Dispatch would not be approved without ACARs. I would now need to set up mini Dispatch units at all layover stations and have Dispatchers trained and approved by DGCA. The costs would go up and efficiency down.

Rakesh quickly understood the implication and cost saving with a centralized OCC and Dispatch. He instructed Bruce that ACARs must be fixed from the first aircraft onwards. Rockwell Collins (its manufacturer) must deliver the equipment and Airbus wire the first aircraft for ACARs, otherwise we would not accept delivery of the first aircraft as planned. Bruce was not happy again.

I immediately called Kiran Rao and briefed him to get cracking with Airbus on getting this done. Needless to say, that the first flight had ACARs as standard equipment. The ACARs automatically triggers a report when an aircraft moves out of bay, it gets airborne, touches down and parks in the bay. These reports are called OOOI (OOEE) reports.

1st O stood for OUT is triggered when the aircraft departs from its bay

2nd O stood for OFF is triggered when the aircraft gets airborne

3rd O stood for ON was triggered when the aircraft touches down

I stood for IN was triggered when aircraft parks in the Arrival Bay.

Imagine the jubilation in OCC back home when first O was triggered out of Toulouse. Our aircraft had departed. There after they kept getting position reports every half hour of the flight's progress. Everyone loved the ACARs.

The LCC concept with no food service and buy your food was alien to us all as we had come from full-service backgrounds. We were concerned about passenger acceptability. Not so much as for me, since

I had started Alliance without meals, with only snacks, but free. My gut told me passengers would fall in line if the air fare was low enough.

In a meeting on the issue Rakesh asked, "When you go to a restaurant to have dinner does the restaurant give you a free air ticket?" Of course not. Then when you buy an airplane ticket, why should the airline give you a free meal? You want good food to go to a restaurant, you want to fly at the cheapest fare, come fly with us.

It made sense. I knew that it was not the cost of the meal that was the issue, but the infrastructure and manpower cost of providing the meal. It is my opinion and experience from decades in the airline business, all airlines serve bad food. Airline food differs only in its degree of badness. The scale is from bad to awful. The reason is that the food is prepared 8 to12 hours before, then flash frozen which it remains till loaded on board. Then its flash heated in the airplane oven. The flavor and taste gets killed.

In Alliance, I never did food trials in the flight kitchen, but on the aircraft by heating the frozen food. All the flight kitchen chefs hated me. The culprit was the ovens that heats everything in the casserole to the same temp. Eggs get over cooked, Chicken and meat dry out. So, I supported the concept of cold snacks which were more palatable.

Many may not agree but the acceptance of the LCC concept in India, proves that people travel to go from A to B as cheaply, safely and on time, and not to enjoy the food on board.

One savings head that airline's fail to take advantage of are enforcing Guaranties and Warranties with aircraft component providers. Rakesh insisted on tracking and claiming these for which a large cell was created specifically. He arm-twisted suppliers to keep spares under bond at Delhi. If a component was required, it was taken from the bond under a power-by-the-hour agreement and the unserviceable part send for test. Most were covered by the G&W agreements thus reducing maintenance costs immensely.

Meanwhile, the promoters decided to bring on board a Chief Operation Officer. They hired Steve Hearst, a former US Navy pilot who had flown the F14 (Tomcat) and had gained Civil Aviation experience of management in an American Supplemental carrier.

Steve was introduced to the leadership team, and we all gasped when he walked in. He was a really good-looking dude. A total showman. It was inevitable that he was nick named 'Tom Cruise'. I was now to report to him.

We did not enjoy a cordial relationship. We were both Alpha males in the same kennel. He loved to hate me but could not live with me or without me. The crucial Airline Operators Permit was still to be got from the DGCA and my role for this was crucial. He did not think so, but Rahul did. Our American bosses kept aloof of us 'Kalu Indians'. We only interacted during working hours. I made many attempts to try and get them to integrate socially but was kept at an arm's length. They were the superior race and we the inferior.

By May 2006, we were ready to submit our application to the DGCA for grant of the Operators permit. The process is formal. The DGCA is represented by the Director General along with Joint and Deputy Director Generals who headed the various Departments which were, Training and Licensing, Flight inspection, Airworthiness, Air Safety, Air Transportation among the crucial ones. They would have studied the proposed Manuals, procedures etc. for compliance with all other DGCA requirements.

All of these would satisfy the Authorities that the airline was ready and capable to provide safe, efficient and regular air transport services.

We were given an appointment in the first week of June to meet the Director General and his board which would have reviewed all our documents and would wish to clarify or amend anything they were not satisfied with.

We met with the Director General and his team. Before leaving for the DGCA Offices we were briefed that Bruce would do the introduction and Steve will give the audio-visual presentation and answer queries. We were only there to be seen and only heard if Steve required one of us to give any clarification.

Our American bosses were gung-ho, as if they had it in the bag already. And we were just going through the formality. Poor suckers did not know the DGCA, their egos and how they worked. I was very apprehensive.

Rahul called me just before we were entering the conference room and asked if we were ready and how confident I was. I told him we were ready but with Bruce and Steve's attitude and arrogance, Mr. Kanu Gohain, The Director General would kick our ass. I knew Mr. Gohain well. We enjoyed each other's mutual respect. We had grown in the industry together and we had very close interaction and cordial relationship since my Alliance Air days.

Sure enough, Bruce introduced himself and Steve giving their back grounds, he went on to say, how they were well equipped and prepared to operate an airline. He handed over to "Tom Cruise" who started his presentation on the wonderful passenger boarding ramp that IndiGo had designed, which was going to be the game changer. Then he went on about how we had even exceeded the FAA requirements which were the most stringent in the world, implying that those of the DGCA when compared to the FAA were not stringent enough. That was the wrong button to press with Gohain.

The DG interrupted the presentation and stated that they were neither interested nor impressed with the passenger ramp. The application was not for a ground handling license but for an airline licence and they needed to be assured that we were capable of complying with their Operations, Maintenance and Air Safety requirements. IndiGo had to satisfy the Indian regulatory authority who would issue the permit and not the FAA. He ended the meeting by saying you obviously are not prepared. You can apply for another meeting after a month.

Bruce and Steve's faces turned red with embarrassment. They were in a fix. The one-month delay would be a huge screw up as the 1st aircraft delivery was at the end of July and the inaugural flight on 4th August. I got out of the room and called Rahul and in real street Hindi told him how Gohain had thrown us out with a kick on the back side. He requested me to swing via his office for a full debrief.

I briefed him on the meeting and told him that he should immediately call on the Minister to intercede with the DGCA for another appointment within a week. Also, Bruce should only confine himself to introducing his team and that we would satisfy the Authority on our readiness. Under no circumstance should Steve speak unless addressed directly. He should be seen, not heard. A COO is not a regulatory post. For the DGCA the regulatory and accountable people are the Heads of Operation, Maintenance and Air Safety.

Thankfully, the second meeting was reconvened within ten days. Before Bruce could open, Gohain started by welcoming 'Mr. Bruce' and 'Mr. Steve' and their IndiGo team and asked for the record, "Who is your Head of Operations?"

"Capt. Shakti Lumba" Bruce replied. Gohain looked at me and asked, "You made the Operation and Training Manual?". I confirmed. He turned to the Chief Flight Inspector and asked if he had examined it, but before he could respond, Gohain added, "We are pleased that Shakti is the Head of Operations, DGCA has full confidence in him, his integrity and commitment to Flight Safety.

He next queried about Head of Maintenance and also complimented Mr. SC Gupta and had a good word for him. Next it was the turn of Flight Safety. He nodded approvingly at Capt. KPS Nair remarking that Capt. Nair was a veteran from DGCA's Air Safety Department from where he had recently retired as Deputy Director. All Departments confirmed that they had studied all our Manuals and were ready to give their approval. The Operators Permit meeting was over. The Minister's intercession worked. With that Director General Gohain, got up thanked everybody and announced that our application for grant of permit was accepted and approved.

"Congratulation! The permit will be issued after due process." The meeting took all of 30 minutes.

The look on Bruce and a Steve's face could be described only as 'shock and awe'. They learnt that day that it was best that people responsible for particular departments deal with the DGCA and not flaunt FAA to their face.

We had adequate crew sets trained. However, there were Captains who had never flown the A320. The only A320 type rated pilots were Capt Amit Singh and I. Capt. Amit Singh, an A320 Captain had joined us from Indian Airlines, the only one that I took willingly. I was not keen on any Indian Airlines' pilot, knowing that they would find it difficult to adjust to working in an LCC. Bringing them in from the beginning could have adversely affected the start-up. Amit's licence and ratings were current. The regulation required that in order to be certified to fly in command a pilot needed at least 100 hrs experience as a co-pilot on a particular type of aircraft. As per our training manual these 100 hrs were to be done with a Training Pilot as Initial Operating Experience (IOE).

My problem was I had no A320 training pilots on board. With this limitation we need Airbus instructors do carry out the IOE of all pilots we had trained to meet regulatory requirements and for standardization of training. Airbus agreed to provide 120 man-months of free of cost line training support with a proviso of an increase to 240 man-months if required. One-man month was defined as 100 hrs or 30 days which ever came first for one Instructor pilot. If there were two instructors assigned it would amount to 2-man months. This solved my initial pilot line training and recurrent training issues.

If it was not for Airbus's support, IndiGo could not have been ready for induction of almost an aircraft a month. Each aircraft requiring minimum 5 set of flight crew line ready and available to fly. Sunita did a terrific job as Director Crew Management and because of her competence, persistence and dedication I relied on her the most, for all pilot issues.

As we needed type rated pilots desperately, Steve and Sunita roped in half a dozen pilot providers, and we started hiring expat captains from the US, Europe, South America, Southeast Asia and Philippines. For this, I hired Capt. Blue Petersen a former Eastern Airline Pilot, as Chief Pilot (Expat Provisioning). Blue travelled the world looking for pilots. He got us a large number of Filipinos, who we housed in an apartment building in DLF 1 Gurgaon, which got named "Little Manila".

DGCA, India does not accept any ICAO pilot licence for conversion to an Indian Licence for airline pilots. Instead, they issue a Foreign Aircrew Temporary Authorization (FATA). Airline submit the crew's licence, ratings, logbook extract along with passport and visa details for Security clearance, after which each crew had to undergo an interview on Indian Air Legislation, Operations Manual etc. for issue of the FATA. Only after obtaining the FATA could the Airport Entry Pass (AEP) be issued by the Bureau of Civil Aviation Security (BCAS). Many a times, due to some delay, mostly for the AEP, a pilot would be sitting on his ass on full pay, for months.

An Expat pilot's Cost to Company (CTC) was almost $16,000 US with instructor cost up to $18,000 US per month. Pilots were paid in equivalent Indian Rupees, after tax deducted at source, and were entitled to furnished company accommodation up to $2000 per month, work rotation of 8 weeks 'ON' and 4 weeks 'OFF'. With a company provided economy class return ticket home every 8 weeks. The Expat Pilot's CTC was huge – almost double that of national pilots. All pilot provisioning contracts were done by Steve and were implemented by him, Blue and Sunita.

The delivery of the first aircraft along with Transfer of Title (TOT) was scheduled for the end of July. However, my flying license had expired. I was in a fix on where and how to carry out my recurrent training. Indian Airlines was not willing to do my recurrent training on their A320 simulator at any cost. I approached Capt. Vinod Sharma, Head of Operations of Go Airlines. Vinod had joined me in Alliance from East West he was also the Secretary of the Delhi Flying Club. He agreed to arrange for an aircraft check ride on their A320. They had a training flight arranged after two days at Hyderabad with an A320 Airbus Instructor Examiner. I had agreed to pay for the cost of training. Go Airways however, provided me with a complimentary return air ticket from Delhi to Hyderabad for this training. After I had done my check and license was renewed. Vinod informed me that Go Airways would not be charging me for the training. Apparently, he had approached their Managing Director, Jeh Wadia, on how much to charge. Jeh acted the perfect Parsi gentlemen and said that there will be no charge. His airline would not charge the Head of Operation of a new start up for just one check ride and a ticket. I was grateful and promised to return the courtesy anytime they needed a favor.

I was in contact with Kiran Rao, who by then was the SVP sales under John Leary, Airbus's CCO and in charge for hand-holding IndiGo. I had a problem with crewing the 1st ferry flight, as I and Amit were the only two pilots qualified to fly but the flight required 2 sets of crew due, Flight and Duty Time Limitations (FDTL). The normal route was not available and the flight had to take a longer route over Africa.

I suggested to Airbus that their instructors who were coming on the ferry to commence the IOE of our pilots fly the 1st leg. Airbus agreed and the Toulouse Sharjah leg was flown by Airbus pilots. From Sharjah Amit and I would take over for the flight to Delhi.

IndiGo's team for Toulouse were cabin crew, Amit and two Chief Pilots, Capt. PK Sinha, Capt. VK Verma, Bruce, Steve, SC Gupta, a host of Engineers, Finance officers, and me. Of course, there was Adrian Hamilton who had designed the flight and cabin crew uniform, cotton white shirts and cotton indigo colored trousers and skirts. A really low-cost uniform that neither fit nor draped well. We all looked shabby; none of us wore those uniforms with pride.

We were wined and dined by Airbus, and Kiran was the perfect host. The pre-delivery acceptance flight was crewed by Airbus pilots with Steve and me on the jump seat. The flight was routine and ready for Transfer of Title (TOT).

It was only after the TOT, that I got to know that IndiGo was not the owner but the lessee of the first (and many subsequent) aircraft. Rakesh had tied up Sale and Lease-back agreements with Lessors who paid for the aircraft and leased it to IndiGo for 6 years. Airbus got paid the contracted amount. The Lessor got an aircraft below sticker price and IndiGo made a pretty penny on the sale. I thought it was a brilliant idea. A first for any airline in India.

Since, we were going to take delivery of an aircraft a month, I realized that it would not be possible to spare pilots every month for ferry flights, given that most were under line training. I had a chat with Kiran explaining the problem and suggested that since Airbus was going to be positioning up to 6-8 Instructors every month, then we should set up a rotation in which Airbus pilots, instead of flying commercial, could ferry the aircraft. They would save one-way Business class fare too. This flight would count towards their man month. This Airbus willingly agreed to, without really catching on to my devious plan.

I also requested full details for all their instructors even those on contract from Sabena. This group also included American pilots working with Airbus in Miami. Since we did not know which instructor was coming, when and from where, I had all of them security cleared and got special permission for them to fly the ferry flight without a FATA. DGCA agreed as they were "Manufacturer Pilots" and did not require detailed vetting. IndiGo's start would not have been smooth if we did not have the support of both Kanu Gohain and AK Chopra and their confidence in me.

The upside of this arrangement was that all our ferry flights were henceforth flown by Airbus at their cost. Each aircraft came with a full tank of fuel. IndiGo only paid for the minimum fuel required from Sharjah and overflight charges. This was not in the contract but became the accepted practice. After all, Indigo was a special customer and I had an excellent rapport with their Directors Training and Customer support thanks to Kiran. He was the ace up my sleeve.

On the day of the first ferry, all pilots were in the Airbus Delivery Centre. We were there, as well as crew from Go Air, Kingfisher, and Qatar Airways, each taking a delivery. Capt. ET walked in and remarked, "Am I in Airbus Delivery Centre or is this the Indian Airlines Flight Dispatch?" All the pilots were ex-Indian Airlines and knew ET well.

The ferry flight had left Toulouse a little later than planned, being delayed by last minute paperwork and a big, insulated box of some of the finest cheeses that I had Kiran pack for Rahul, the foodie.

We got into Sharjah very late at night and after about an hour and half turn around, Amit and I took over from the two Airbus Pilots.

Now that it was their own crew flying, everyone made trips to the cockpit – some to sneak a few puffs since they knew I was a heavy smoker those days. For most it was their first experience in the cockpit, and they were thoroughly curious on how things worked.

It was a little after sunrise when we were overflying Pakistan about an hour out of Delhi, when Steve barged into the cockpit without the courtesy of either knocking or asking permission. The American stewardess from Delta that he had hired as cabin crew training in-charge, apparently told him that there was a party on in the cockpit and everyone was smoking. He came in yelling, "How dare you smoke in my brand-new airplane?". Actually no one was smoking at that time. I told him, "No one is smoking." And I added, "It's my airplane, as I am the Pilot in Command." On board, I out rank him. Next time he wants to enter the cockpit it would only be with my permission.

He stormed out. That was the first of our many flare-ups. He had made it clear that he did not like me, and he would have me replaced as Vice President Flight Operations. I also made it clear that we were too small an airline to have a CEO and COO and that his position was actually redundant.

We landed quietly at Delhi. No Welcome from ATC, there was no fancy water cannon salute, and we parked in a remote bay. There was a reception committee of the leadership team and officers of flight operations who had worked hard to see this day happen. Rakesh Gangwal and Rahul Bhatia were there too. This was when Rakesh Gangwal took me aside and told me, "Shakti, I am confidentially designating you the 'conscience' of the company. Do not let anyone ride rough shod over you. And don't let anything happen that will adversely affect the company, safety or its reputation." I took this to be my sacred duty. This gave me the confidence to stand up and be heard on mostly safety issues.

The aircraft had to clear customs which mainly meant that they measured the fuel remaining in the tanks on which customs duty would be charged. Customs releases the aircraft after inspecting all the documents, import license etc. That's when the DGCA takes over and converts the temporary Certificate of Airworthiness (C of A) given for the ferry flight to a regular C of A and the Temporary Certification of Registration (C of R) to a permanent C of R. Thereafter, the aircraft is entered into the Air Operators Permit (AOP) also referred to as the Air Operators Certificate (AOC). Now the aircraft becomes legal to operate scheduled services for the airline.

For all future deliveries, IndiGo refined the process. The ferry flight from Sharjah, with Jaipur as alternate airport was scheduled to arrive by 7am. The fuel remaining on board would be to the tune of 4500 kgs, for which Customs duty was pre-paid. As a result, Customs released the aircraft before 10 am. Thereafter, the DGCA's inspection took place. All formalities were completed by 5pm with the aircraft endorsed in the permit, ready for a scheduled flight on the next day.

In those day and even today it takes others up to a week to get customs' clearance and DGCA formalities completed.

The Inaugural party was held for the industry at the ITC's Maurya Sheraton. A real low-key affair compared to the 3-day high profile bash held by Vijay Mallya for his Kingfisher Airlines. Ours was so low-key that the Civil Aviation Minister, Mr. Praful Patel, jokingly remarked during his speech, that "it was a real low-cost party of a low cost airline." The biryani from ITC restaurant Dum Pukht was excellent and the only thing worth remembering of that evening.

Before the aircraft's first flight, a 'Puja' and 'Havan' were done in the office after the aircraft was blessed and a coconut broken. There were no lemon or green chillies hung on the aircraft. This ritual was repeated for every single aircraft. The Bhatia's were a religious and God-fearing family.

IndiGo's first flight was from Delhi to Guwahati to Imphal and back. Most people were surprised by the choice of route, we were not. After all, Adrian was in-charge of network planning. Sometime later, Adrian quietly exited the airline and we started getting issued decent uniforms. For the pilot stripes, I had insisted on the "Nelson Knot" which formed one of the stripes. For some reason the company decided to go for silver instead of the more common gold stripes.

Once we had adequate instructors, we had the capacity to 'produce' our own pilots, and so, line training was carried out on a war footing. Sunita was given 90 days to ensure that a Captain was ready for line release within 90 days of him completing his simulator training. This was a Matrix that was measured. Sunita hounded both our training section and crew scheduling to ensure this deadline was met. This got her a rating of 5 in the bell curve.

As pilots' salaries at IndiGo were lower than in other private airlines, it was tough to convince Captains to join at a lower salary than they were earning. I wanted to increase their salary by only ₹50,000 per month. This was resisted by Rahul, Rakesh and Bruce.

When Rakesh made his biannual visit, he met the leadership team. In his first such meeting, I brought up the issue of the captain's salary. His response closed that chapter forever on my watch. He categorically stated if we increase the salary to a million dollars, he could fill the airline with Captains. He didn't have a million dollars to pay the Captains and not even the ₹50,000 desired. However, a couple of years post my exit, IndiGo had to increase pilot salaries substantially to enable it to fly the number of aircraft being inducted, at times 3 in a month.

Only option open to us was to hire pilots with an ATPL as Senior Co-pilots who after 300 hours on type and stringent assessment checks on simulator and line, could be sent for Command upgrade. The number of Airbus Instructors at any time on property was increased from 6 to 10. Airbus resisted, but with my dear friend Kiran's help, we prevailed.

Airbus hired more instructors on contract to enable them to meet their commitment to IndiGo and other customers.

For Command upgrade, I had stipulated the minimum 300 co-pilot hours. I knew from experience that a pilot coming from a conventional aircraft, required a minimum of 300 hours to get comfortable in the A320 fly by wire glass cockpit.

Some airlines had higher age and experience limitations for Command. Such restrictions equated the horse with a donkey. We introduced stringent upgrade testing and simulator checks prior to Command up grade. The horses in our stables made the grade, while the donkeys did not. Thereafter, the latter pilots were paired with experienced Captains till their weakness was ironed out. They were tested again for command upgrade. I insisted that each pilot due for upgrade, spend one working day with ATC and one with company airport services. This is so they would understand the limitations that these areas had and that better coordination and communication was key.

Rakesh kept a close watch on the CASK (Cost per Available seat kilometers) for every department. Flight Operations was the airline's biggest spender. So, if the Flight Operations CASK even increased by half a cent he would 'kick my ass'. The SOPs (Standard Operating Procedures) were fine-tuned always keeping safe operation in mind and that a buffer to cater for error existed.

We modified many Airbus procedures. Every change was after a meeting with the Airbus instructors so that everyone was on the same page. These meetings were long, loud and protracted. It was in one such meeting that I brought in Crew advocacy in the Operations Manual. I viewed subtle pilot incapacitation as a clear and present danger. The A320 cockpit is designed for two crew operation for which task sharing is assigned. It is not designed for single pilot operation. Both pilots are responsible for safe operation.

Pilot incapacitation is an in-house threat to safety. There are two kinds of pilot's incapacitation. Obvious and Subtle. Obvious incapacitation, is clearly identifiable such as a heart attack etc. However, subtle incapacitation is not so easy to identify. It may cause skills or judgement to be lost with little outward sign. The pilot may not react to stimulus, his piloting skills may degrade so could his decision making. Subtle incapacitation can be triggered in a high stress or workload situation. Here the pilot may appear to be functioning but his brain may not be.

I think it was United Airlines that came out with the two communication rule somewhere in the early seventies. If the pilot flying did not respond to two successive call outs to a flight deviation by the pilot not flying, then subtle incapacitation was to be suspected.

In IndiGo, I went a step further and in the Operation Manual after the standard Two Communication rule, I added that if the airplane was seen to be in an obvious unsafe flight condition then the pilot not flying (co-pilot) was authorized to take over the control of the aircraft to establish the safe flight condition. Allowing the co- pilot to take over control was considered controversial especially by senior Captains. I stuck to my guns, as the safety of a flight was a higher priority than the ego of Captains. This saved an aeroplane when the copilot took over after the captain was attempting an off airport night landing.

Every employee's contract had no yearly increment clause. Those days the Bell Curve was the favorite theory of HR all over. Bruce had introduced it. I hated it and fortunately the pilots were not under its purview. Instead, they were given 5% of their annual salary as bonus. I queried HR why was no yearly increment admissible to me. He had instructions from Bruce that I was not eligible for an increment as my contract did not have a mention of it. I protested saying that no other employees contract had an increment clause.

Rakesh in a meeting specially instructed that shares should be issued to those who had been promised. I politely informed Rahul that I had not been issued any shares that were due on joining and also none after completion of the 1st year with them. He told me that I had ***his assurance*** that they will be issued in due course. I took him at his word.

This did not happen. I ended up regretting placing my trust in Rahul and his WORD.

Bruce and Steve concentrated on hiring expat pilots. I was of the opinion that their cost to company was almost 2 times that of a national pilot. If a salary increase was permitted, then we would get adequate pilots. Their logic was that the expat pilots were a short-term solution for which the higher cost was acceptable. Increasing national pilots salaries would be a long-term cost. Their short-term solution ended up with IndiGo employing increasing numbers of expat pilots for over ten years, adding substantially to the CASK.

I found innovative ways to give the national pilots a fairer deal. I was able to wheedle out of Rahul ₹25,000 per Captain per month as longevity bonus, which came to ₹300,000 per year, payable only at the time of their exit.

The toughest period was flying the initial 15 aircraft. We required 5 sets per aircraft but had to manage with 3 sets per aircraft. This was possible only with pilot friendly scheduling, requiring a quid pro quo from both pilots and schedulers. This reduced pilot-to-aircraft ratio resulted in utilizing pilots to the limits of the FDTL. Thankfully, with AK Chopra as the Joint Director General of DGCA, who was also overseeing air-safety, I was able to extract a concession on the weekly limit of 30 hrs. He agreed to my 35-hour request, after I assured him that pilot would only do a 5-day week and be provided 2 consecutive days off.

One October after launch, Rakesh held a review of the operations. He started off by stating that he was surprised pleasantly that the company was able to operate its existing fleet efficiently, safely and on time. He had several complimentary things to say about my performance. Needless to say, it was welcome! Bruce and Steve of course did not appear so happy Praise coming from a hard task master was indeed high praise, but it had its downside too. This was the start of back biting, petty politics, character assassination and increased jealousy.

One of the main reasons that we were able achieve the industry's best On Time Performance (OTP) was because of being able to operate in the winter of 2006-2007, during Delhi's notorious fog. While the other airlines except Indian Airlines were grounded due to fog related poor visibility, IndiGo was able to operate as we were already ILS CAT 3 approved, within 5 months of our launch, much to the irritation of Spice Jet, Go Air, Jet Airways and Kingfisher Airlines who had been in operation much longer. They played by the rules, I played the system.

As per the rule, an airline could only apply for ILS CAT 2 certification after 1 year of operating experience and 6 months thereafter, apply for Cat 3 certification.

Every airline had, by and large copied the Indian Airlines Training Manual, which stipulated the above time frame and the associated simulator and aircraft training. Indian Airlines always over trained as cost was never a consideration. Economy was its last priority. On the other hand, I had only stipulated in the Operations Manual Part D, that our pilots will be trained in low visibility operations as per the Airbus program that was EASA (European Aviation Safety Authority) compliant. The training was as per Airbus syllabus that was informed to the DGCA. Every pilot was trained up to and beyond Category 3 level visibility conditions. This was stipulated in our approved Training Manual.

Every year Delhi would get fog bound around mid-December. The Director General himself held a monthly review in the first week of each month on how many pilots each airline had trained up to CAT 2 and CAT 3 levels. A confirmatory list of pilots trained by name and license number was to be submitted for their record. This was as per the Ministry's instructions in 1998 when Delhi was to be upgraded to a Cat 3 airport.

In the DGCA meeting held by the DG in early September of 2006, I listed the names of pilots trained by Airbus up to CAT 3 along with the manufacturer's certification. A list was submitted in Oct., Nov., and Dec. These were always submitted to the office of the DG under receipt and not in the central registry.

I gave Rahul copies of the 4-letters addressed to the DG and told him that they HAD to be kept in his car. I further told him at about mid-December, fog as usual will hit Delhi. This would result in mass chaos at Delhi airport due to diverted and cancelled flights. The Minister would then react to the adverse press reports and summon the owners and Heads of all airlines and give them a dressing down on why they had not trained adequate pilots for low visibility operations. This was the time he was to politely bring to the Minister attention the four letters stating we had trained pilots up to CAT 3, at great additional cost, and informed the Director General himself. (Unfortunately, the DGCA had not even bothered to respond to our letters.)

It happened just as I had predicted it: the fog came, flights got disrupted, the minister threw a fit, and Rahul acted as directed. The minister questioned the DG. Mr. Gohain immediately rang up the Chief Flight Operations Inspector, Capt. Samant, who was responsible for Cat 3 authorizations, roaring in panic, "Samant, immediately call Capt. Lumba and ask him to bring all training and practice auto-land reports and grant IndiGo ILS CAT 3B authorization".

Having anticipated this response, I had all the files ready along with the Flight Recorder readouts for each landing. As per our SOP pilots were required to carry out practice Cat3 auto landing in clear weather when landing at Delhi. They were to record all auto lands and file a debrief report showing a satisfactory auto land. I was in Samant's office by 3 pm and back in my office by 5 pm, fully authorized for low visibility operation to the Cat 3B landing- minima. I handed over a copy of the authorization to Bruce who looked at it casually and passed it back. His reaction indicated I had wasted his time, not realizing the impact of it, or what I had achieved for the airline. This authorization permitted us regular operation in in adverse weather and notched up our On Time Performance that became IndiGo's catch phrase "On Time Every Time".

Next day, when news of our CAT 3 authorization spread, the Heads of Operation of the other Airlines also demanded CAT 3 status, but since their application was only for CAT 2, it was granted in accordance with their training manual. About six months later I was summoned by the Capt. Samant and asked to explain how IndiGo had applied for Cat 3 authorization with only 5 months of operating experience. I politely told him we NEVER applied for authorization and had only submitted the list of pilots trained as required. In the panic and confusion caused by the Minister's reaction they had accorded us the much deserved authorization. It could not be withdrawn as we had operated the winter season safely and successfully and we were only the 2nd operator besides Indian Airlines capable of CAT 3 Operations. Gohain remained pissed off with me for a couple of months and refused to speak with me. But our association went back more than 20 years and so we were soon back to cordial relations again.

In January '07, Harinder Singh Punia (Dirty Harry) retired from Indian Airlines at the age of 58. He joined IndiGo as Chief Pilot, Standards and Quality Assurance. This is when our FOQA (Flight Operations Quality Assurance) program took off in earnest.

We were doing 100% flight recorder monitoring, not for punitive reasons, but to quantify flight parameter that exceeded the laid down limits. Initially we just collected data, both aircraft-wise and pilot-wise and looked for trends; thereafter we examined our SOPs. It was only when Capt. KPS Nair brought to our attention any alarmingly abnormal flight exceedance, would the pilot be requested to visit my office for a cup of coffee.

Very gently Harry would explain the reason he was called, what could be the worst consequences of the exceedance and the pilot was counselled. This usually was enough. KPS and I had excellent coordination and cooperation. We understood what made a pilot tick and that first he was a human being with human limitation and a pilot second

We proactively investigated even the smallest of incidents and took corrective action. Then Mr. AK Chopra was informed, who was usually satisfied. Like pilots of Alliance Air, the IndiGo pilots knew that whenever any incident or abnormal event occurred I was to be the first informed. Then the pilot was assured that I would have his back. However, if a pilot tried to hide or suppress an incident and if the DGCA got to know first, he was on his own.

We discussed the exceedance instances with the Airbus instructors and decided if it was a training issue or a policy issue. I remember being overwhelmed by one particular exceedance for Calcutta Runway 19, where the pilots were stabilizing only by 500 ft' instead of the stipulated 1000 feet. We immediately increased the initial approach altitude from 1500 ft' to 2000 ft' Voila! The exceedance disappeared. In many cases, a change in policy usually was the corrective action required.

I firmly believed that Operations Policy was not cast in stone. We regularly amended policy in the light of operating experience and encouraged pilot feedback. There were however certain incidents of a serious nature that were not reported and only came to light through the monitoring.

There was a case of what turned out to be a loss of control due to pilot disorientation in a night approach. It was the last-minute intervention of the co-pilot who executed a go around and avoided an off-airport crash. It was a matter of great concern that the incident was not reported to the safety or operations department.

The crew were called for an interview. The captain was from Peru and the co-pilot was a national. The captain denied any incident, but finally the co-pilot let the cat out of the bag. I had to let the captain go.

In another case, we found that an aircraft in the landing configuration, Gear Down with land flaps extended at 35,000 ft' 150 miles away from Delhi. The captain was a Filipino expat. I had him come over for "cup of coffee". Invitations for a cup of coffee with the Vice President Flight Operation meant they were in the shit house. I sat him down and asked him what the gear and flap extension operating limits were. He promptly answered that correctly. I then asked, "What the fuck were you guys doing at 35,000 ft' in the landing configuration, practicing touch and go on the clouds?" His prompt response was "Sir, ATC told us to reduce to minimum approach speed immediately." I was astounded. Here was an obvious case of a communication gap because of nonstandard phraseology.

I explained the meaning of the terminology "reduce to minimum speed". It was the speed ATC expected during cruise and during approach. In his case, he was expected to reduce to Green Dot (210 kts). His punishment for exceeding Gear and Flap limits was 10 "Murgas" as well as to write a hundred times that he will not take gear and full flap, unless on final approach.

It must have been a sight to see a Captain in uniform holding his ears and doing squats. Later I took him down to China Club on the ground floor, gave him a beer and lunch and off he went, relieved that he was not sacked. Later I received an "Oscar" statuette for BEST BOSS from him.

When pilot managers issue stern memos to pilot demanding explanations, it is a big blunder. This really pisses off pilots and demoralizes them. The poor chap goes around asking people to help him with a reply. It is best to call them over for a cup of coffee, bawl them out, and then take them out for a beer. Understanding pilot psychology is very important for harmonious pilot – pilot management relation, pilot morale and motivation. Pilots are humans and not machines, and human fallibities play an important role in their professional lives. There are times one has to be tough and others when you have to be understanding. There are certain zero-tolerance lines that cannot be crossed. Be tough, only when regulatory or flight safety issue are involved. If not, then be a father figure rather than a school headmaster.

In IndiGo, dangerous flying, blatant violation of company or regulatory rules and reporting for duty under influence of alcohol or drugs were zero tolerance. Pilots lost their jobs.

The pre-flight breathalyzer (BA) test mandated before every flight was a contentious issue. Airlines, the world over, DO NOT conduct pre-flight BA test nor do regulators mandate them. Only if a pilot is obviously drunk or at times, when random post flight testing is done and the pilot found over the limit (usually the Motor Vehicle limit) the pilot is declared FUI (Flying under Influence) and is treated according to the law.

The DGCA has stipulated a ZERO alcohol level for pre-flight testing. So even a 0.001 BAL (Blood Alcohol Level) meant that the pilot was drunk as per them. The media plays up these incidents giving pilots and airlines a bad name.

I had set the limit for punitive action at a BAL 0.10. First time offender with a Test up to 0.009 was allowed to rest, knowing from experience that the BAL level dropped by 0.003 every 20 minutes. So, a BAL of 0.003 would reduce to 0.000 before the next confirmatory test and the pilot was cleared for duty. The 2nd time offender was advised to take a break and seek medical counseling.

The expat pilots were very vulnerable. They usually stuck to the "12 hours between bottle and throttle" rule, but even after only 2 to 3 beers they were found to be over the 0.000 limit. We found the problem was the high alcohol content in Indian beers that got them into trouble. During pilot induction, it became my practice to warn pilots to avoid the Indian high alcohol content beers and always keep in mind that a *healthy* liver can only metabolize 1 ounce of alcohol in 3 hours. If a pilot suspected he would not clear the pre-flight alcohol test it was better he reported sick then come for a flight.

Steve brought in two expat Directors into OCC – one for Operations Control and the other for Pilot Scheduling and Flight Despatch.

On a number of instances, I had to tick these guys off for taking extended lunch breaks from 1pm to 4 pm. They did not appreciate being ticked off and took the matter to Steve, who without even speaking to me, moved the OCC from Operations under me to Airport Services. This resulted in the breakdown of coordination between pilot schedulers and pilots. The quid pro quo was stopped. The schedulers took their cue from the expats and their attitude towards pilots which started pissing of pilots.

Pilot utilization was now almost to the FDTL limits. Their work life balance was getting adversely effected by 2 and 3 back-to-back layover flights week after week. New bases were being opened and pilots domiciled in Delhi and Mumbai were required to go on TD (Temporary Duty) for 3 to 5 days. Places like Jaipur, Ahmadabad etc. were given aircraft parking slots. Crew scheduling was on a high. This resulted in many Captains quitting because of burnout from continuous flying. I would recruit and train a Captain and another would "bite the dust". Both Bruce and Steve were totally indifferent.

Their solution was to hire more and more expat pilots, who in their opinion, did not mind the flying load, as they were here to earn money and most did not bring their families over. These pilots obviously had no issues, since after 8 weeks on duty, they got to go home for 4 weeks. They had no cumulative fatigue issues.

The issue of cumulative fatigue was building up in the case of Indian Captains logging over a hundred hours per month. Flying so much they would reach the regulatory limit of 1000 hours a year in 10 months. After which, they could not fly and would have to be put on a "gardening holiday" with full pay for 2 months.

I meanwhile came up with 11 weeks ON and 2 weeks OFF scheme for national pilots, and despite resistance from HR and Crew Scheduling, pushed it through. This broke the cumulative fatigue issue and also broke the monthly cumulative hour's cycle since a pilot could no longer exceed the 1000 hours a year limit.

Pilots loved it and lined up to sign the contract amendment. Now they could plan holidays with their much-neglected families, without crew scheduling raining on their parade. I received numerous messages from pilots, they said it like they saw it. "What an idea, Sir ji. Thank you". To a large extent, this reduced the captain exodus.

We came up with many innovative schemes to make sure that there were always two bums in the cockpit. Our pilot line training requirement could not have been met even by Airbus dedicating 8 instructors exclusively to IndiGo. We had used up the 120-man months of free instructor time and had exercised the option to go to 240-man months.

Steve signed an agreement with EasyJet for line flying of their cadets on IndiGo flights and another agreement with Storm Aviation to provide their cadets a minimum of 500 hrs of line experience.

The only condition I made was that their respective cadet line training would be done by their instructors. Further their instructor would also carry out line training of IndiGo pilots – 60% of their instructor time would be with their cadets and 40% with our pilots.

I was back in DGCA convincing them to permit type rated expats co-pilots to fly on FATA. Initially, this suggestion met with a point-blank 'NO', but slowly we were able to bring AK Chopra around and the DGCA agreed.

After two years, the DGCA withdrew their permission to let expat co-pilots fly on FATA, as unemployment among CPL holders was increasing and DGCA came under valid pressure.

Among the Airbus instructors that were assigned to IndiGo training, there were two from Airbus Miami, Capt. Chris Parker and Capt. James Harbinson. Two great pilots and gentlemen, they were Examiners on the A320. After one tour of duty they called me from Miami with a strange request. They wished to resign from Airbus and come work full time with IndiGo. I immediately send them a contract and with a letter to the Indian Embassy along with their DGCA approvals for granting an Indian Employment visa. Within a month they were back with us full time.

One of the pilot providers had sent us the CV of an American pilot who had worked in the FAA administrator's office. He was an A320 Instructor with North West Airlines and was also an FAA Designated Examiner on the A320. He had respectable experience and all his documents and FAA certificates appeared kosher.

Very soon, Capt. Michael Doherty was flying for us. Michael was a typical fun loving Irishman. He drank hard, worked hard, flew well and was a good instructor.

Now we did not need to send FAA certified pilots to the US for recurrent training. We could do it at CAE Dubai on their FAA certified A320 simulator. I happened to meet the FAA guy attached to the US embassy in New Delhi and enquired about getting Chris and James certified as FAA designated examiners, just like Michael Doherty.

He suggested I send him the papers, certificates, logbook extract and instructional experience details of all three pilots and he would put them up to the concerned office. After about 3 weeks, I received a bomb shell from the FAA. They stated that the pilot certificate of Michael Doherty was forged. All the FAA certificates were forged. They added that the pilot's name was actually Michael Fay. His licence had been cancelled by the FAA and that this was not his first instance of producing fake documents abroad.

Fortunately, Michael was landing back from a flight at 4pm. He was asked to swing by the office on his way home.

When he dropped in, I told him that there were some doubts raised about his pilot certificate and would he come in next morning with all his original documents so that we could clear up the matter. I also told him that until the issue was sorted out, he would not be flying and asked him for his AEP (Airport Entry Pass) to be deposited with Sunita.

He did not flinch a bit and said he would be in office by 9 am next morning with all his original certificates.

Next morning, there was no Michael Doherty. His cell phone was switched off. I send two guys from training to see if he was at his apartment. They returned saying the flat was empty. As per the building security, he had booked a taxi for the airport for 11 pm the night before.

Michael had jumped ship.

I reported the matter to DGCA with a request for the cancellation of his FATA. We did an internal review of the existing expat status and notified all the pilot providers of the incident and emphasized the importance of the due diligence clause and their responsibility in this regard.

One day, I got a call from our office security that a gentleman wanted to meet me urgently but would not give his name. I asked to speak to him. At first, I could not connect his first name but when he gave me his last name, I realized who he was. He requested if we could meet outside the office.

I went down and took him inside the China Club restaurant, as it was about lunch time. It was the ex-minister whose wife was the cause of me leaving Alliance. He opened with the remark that we both had history, but he had come for my help. He had got himself a CPL and was keen to do an A320 type rating and I was the only one who could make it happen. I could see that he was on edge. I assured him that I never held a grudge. I had closed the Indian Airlines door and that was another life.

I had two conditions. One was, he pay for his own type rating and not get it sponsored. He said he could. Secondly, he would have to dedicate all his time and effort and not let his political career affect his training. He was willing to leave for training at short notice.

I called up Henry George in the Miami Sim Centre for a type rating slot. There and then, I negotiated a training cost of $25,000 as against the normal $30,000. Within a week, he got the I-20 for his visa and was in Miami within 15 days of our meeting. He returned after 4 weeks and I signed him in as a Junior Co-pilot on a ₹1 contract and made it very clear that he would only be line released when he was fit to be. This would depend on the time he could spare towards flying.

Rahul was a little upset that I didn't consult him. I told him that I had never consulted him on pilot hiring but he was assured his airplanes would be safe as the gentleman would be cleared to fly only when he was line ready. Also, he had an ace up his sleeve in the opposition party. The gentleman was a charismatic up-and-coming popular young politician who could be useful one rainy day.

About this time, my personal equation with both Bruce and Steve were at its lowest point. I had also heard from the grapevine that Rahul was scouting for my replacement. He had by now used me to get his airlines flying high and running. I was also aware that Corporates used you till they squeezed out all you had and then would ease you out.

He had contacted two of my friends who both refused to even consider stabbing me in the back. As far as I was concerned, I had set up a Flight Operations Department that was efficient, safe, economical with a very low contribution to CASK, having the lowest number of incidents, safety violations and no accidents (minor or major). Every pilot was certified for low visibility operations. The only black mark was pilot scheduling where I myself gave the airline just a passing grade.

One of our largest expat pilot providers was Aero Personnel based in Canada. As per them, the talk in the industry and among Airbus pilots was that I was running the best A320 Operation in Asia. But my bosses were still not satisfied. I was now spending 60% of my time countering both Bruce and Steve and only 40% in running the operation that was running smoothly because of our processes. IndiGo, because of its proposed size, had to be process based.

On another afternoon soon after, I got another call from security that there was a foreign lady demanding that I go down to the ground floor to meet her. She refused to come up to the 3rd floor. I spoke to her and knew why. The lady was Steve's wife. Steve was in office.

I rushed down and steered her away to a café in the next building and asked what had happened and how I could help. I told her that she had put me in a very awkward situation. She said she knew that Steve and I did not get along and that's why she had come to me.

She handed me his personal mobile device and spoke. "This has everything in it that the company should know." I refused to touch it. I called up Rahul, briefed him and asked him to advise me about next steps. He immediately sent Harish Gandhi, the group Vice President for HR to the café. Harish took the device and left.

Meanwhile I had contacted my wife to come urgently. I introduced them to each other and left Steve's wife to pour her heart out to Ila. I returned to my office just in time for a meeting with Steve. Ila never told me what they spoke about. I never insisted.

About 15 days later, Harish handed the device back to me and I gave it to Ila to return it.

A month or so later, we were informed that Steve's contract was not being renewed as he wished to relocate back to the States. In May 2009, Bruce's contract also ended and it too was not renewed.

Everyone was surprised when Aditya Ghosh, the Chief Legal Counsel for the InterGlobe group of Companies was appointed as the President of Indigo. There was no CEO appointed.

I was confident that I would have a better working relationship with him. Aditya had mentored himself into aviation. Being an excellent lawyer, he was very good and quick on the uptake and very intelligent. He imbibed everything he heard from Rakesh, Steve and Bruce. As Chief legal counsel he had vetted all the agreements that IndiGo had entered into, and like a sponge, he had soaked in all the aviation knowledge and jargon.

By now I too was burning out. I had been on the job 24x7 since we started on 4th August 2006. Instead of things getting better, they only got worse. My health was now going downhill fast. I was hypertensive and impossible to live with at home. The wife and kids tiptoed around me because of my short fuse. The stress and pressure of the job was now getting to me and making me not a very likeable husband, father or boss.

The pressure on my pilots was building up. Aditya adored only the cabin crew who were his darlings. Soon the authority of the Pilot in Command started being challenged. Pilot morale was declining alarmingly. Low morale, overworked, under paid pilots were a recipe for disaster.

I decided to come out with an all employee circular reminding everyone of the authority of the Pilot in Command and the legal and regulatory consequences of anyone challenging it. It ended with "The Authority of the Pilot in Command is inviolate and is irrespective of the rank of any of his passengers."

Aditya threw a fit and ordered me to withdraw the circular. I responded with a letter of resignation dated 30th June 2009, demanding my immediate release. In the letter I told him to "Stop shitting on my Pilots. Cabin crew were not the be-all- or- end-all of an airline. Its pilots were".

I guess I walked right into the game plan of moving me out. Aditya cultivated yes-men and he knew I was not one. I had set up their Airline and he no longer had much use for me. This could not have been his decision alone. It must have been with Rahul's blessings.

Like most Corporates it was Interglobe's modus operandi to seldom tell a person to leave but to create a condition in which he would resign after he had outlived his usefulness. This way they kept the door open. Just in case they could tap the person for future use. (In fact they did in 2017 about 8 years later!)

I was asked to continue till the end of the year to handhold the new incumbent. Aditya had already selected Capt. Saleem Zaheer to take over. During this period Saleem was basically incharge. I was there to smoothen the transition. Saleem was an old friend who had joined IndiGo from Air Arabia for a short time then moved to Kathmandu to start a joint venture for Air Arabia in Nepal. The economic downturn of 2008-09 resulted in the venture not taking off but he decided to stay on in Kathmandu.

I had to undergo a six month cooling period as per my contract which I did as an advisor to Aditya. I was not needed in office. IndiGo needed no advice.

During this period, I finally realised how naïve and trusting I had been in my dealing with IndiGo. Rahul had never been my friend, but my employer. As per my contract, on joining I was to be assigned 25,000 shares at a strike price of $1.50 and an additional 5000 shares after every year of completed service. These were the shares that Rahul had earlier committed would be assigned, when I had asked after I had completed one year with IndiGo. I had believed his word. What actually happened was that in my exit agreement, Aditya had made me sign away all IndiGo's contractual obligations in a very cleverly drafted document.

Finally, IndiGo only issued me a miserly 84 shares at a face value of ₹1000. Even these were held back and only became a reality when they were converted to ₹84,000 at a face value of ₹10 per share at the time of the Company IPO in 2015.

Rakesh and Rahul became dollar billionaires and Bruce and Steve dollar multi-millionaires. Serving Vice President got issued ESOPs in excess of 100,000-250,000 shares and became *crorepattis*.

IndiGo may have taken away my equity shares but could not ever take away my honor, pride, integrity and legacy. I had started IndiGo's most crucial and important Department of Flight Operation that stands on the rock-solid foundation that I had built, the Best Flight Operations department of any airline in the country.

During my cooling period, I had given up my company accommodation and moved to our Farm, Laksh Farms nestled in a beautiful valley, deep in the Aravali Range south of Delhi. It was SO NEAR AND YET SO FAR.

15. EPILOGUE: LAKSH
FARMS – MY SLICE OF PARADISE

"Those who are looking for paradise on
Earth should come to see... Laksh Farms".
(Apologies to- George Bernard Shaw)

A few weeks after the ICPA agreement was signed in Jan 1996, Mr. Probir Sen and I were having an informal chat in his office. He was on his favorite subject, Maslow's Hierarchy of Needs. As they say in Hindi *'Roti,Kapda aur Makaan'.*

Once a person has acquired the basic human needs of food, shelter, wealth, he then desires power. Once power is attained, then it's a constant desire to retain power at any cost. This is very obvious in the case of politicians and bureaucrats who dread a loss of power, and some will sell their soul to retain it.

So, prior to retirement, they start lobbying with and sucking up to Government for post-retirement appointments, where they can exercise a semblance of power. This disease is now also affecting honorable Judges and retiring Generals.

In the middle of that discussion, Probir Sen advised me to plan my retirement early on. This got me thinking and I came to the conclusion that for me, the best post-retirement option would be agriculture. As an agriculturist one could fit into most strata of society, from a farmer upwards.

Besides, my mother also used to tell me to invest any money I got from my salary or from selling any property into land. Else, the money would vanish and I would wonder where it went. I had just received my share of inheritance after my mother's death in 1992 and decided to invest it in land, not more an hour away from Delhi.

When flying into Delhi from Bombay, when about 50 nm out, the Delhi Approach Radar would give the flight a right turn towards the Badarpur Thermal Power Station. When the aircraft was 25 nm from Delhi the flight was descended by radar to 2500 ft'.

I had noticed that this track took the flight directly over a large lake about 15nm South East of Delhi Airport. The lake was surrounded by a thickly wooded ridge which in months of March-April was studded with patches of red. These were the 'flame of the forest', flowers of the *'dhak'* tree, indigenous to *Aravali* range. The *Aravali* protected Delhi from creeping desertification by the Thar Desert.

On one such flight, I noted the GPS coordinates of the lake and decided to try and locate it on ground. It lay south of the Gurgaon-Faridabad hilly road. I made many attempts to locate the lake with the aid of a handheld 'Garmin' GPS. I could never find an access through the ridge to the lake. These were pre Google Map days. I soon gave up the search.

A number of pilots had invested in one acre plots with a builder who was touting eco-farmhouses in Faridabad District in village Mangar just across the border of Delhi a hop step and jump from Dera Mandi Farms.

I got conned into buying an acre for ₹2,50,000. A month later, I received the registered sale deed for the plot along with the title deed known as the *'Jammbundi'*. The developer disappeared. I later found out he had bought it at ₹50,000 per acre. He had made a quick buck. I was later able to sell my plot for double the price. I advised others to also off load their plots. Some pilots held on expecting steeper appreciation. Unfortunately, the land no longer has any commercial value as it was protected as forest land after the National Green Tribunal. Which had banned all commercial activity in the Mangar Aravali of Faridabad.

One day at a gathering of friends I happened to mention that I had bought an acre of land with a group of pilots in a place called Mangar. Our good friend, Dhiren Navlakha, asked if it was on the ridge or in the valley. Ridge, I said.

He mentioned that there was a beautiful valley with a lake in which a Mr. Shaukat Rai had purchased land. I was intrigued. I called Indira Rai, Shaukat's ex-wife and asked her if she had heard of this place Mangar and if Shaukat had land there. She said she and her son Aman had land there next to a lake. She gave me the contact of a Mr. Bir Singh, a property agent.

I contacted Bir Singh, and one Saturday he turned up to show us land in that area. He got to Mangar via Faridabad from the Faridabad Sohna road. We turned right at Village Dhauj and after about 3 km we came to a *'Bund'* (embankment). Low and behold, beyond the Bund, was a very large lake. It was a stunning sight. I check my 'Garmin' GPS. This was the lake I had identified from the air and which I was unable to locate. It was called the *'Dhauj Jheel'* locally.

Ila and I decided that this was where we would build our home. I had found the place where we wanted to invest my inheritance.

The valley was the catchment area for rainwater runoff from the ridge that covered 3 sides of the valley; the fourth side was open and this was where the embankment was constructed in early 1940's. It had a sluice gate and a canal that could irrigate the fields downstream in the East. There was a strip of raised land called a *'Tilla'*. It was higher than the valley by about 20 ft', measuring about 30 acres. It was a strategic place between the lake and the valley.

In the monsoon the *'Dhauj Jheel'* flooded the whole valley and the *Tilla* became like an island surrounded by water on 3 sides. The water would cover most of the valley with over 5ft' of water. The Haryana Fisheries Department would auction off the whole water body to fishing contractors. *Mangar ki Machli* (fish) was in great demand in the then wholesale market in *Jamma Masjid* area.

The *Tilla* was always above the water. So, I identified its most scenic part which gave a good view of the valley to the west, the lake and Dhauj Rocks and ridge to the north and south. The land was however, totally degraded on which only thorny bushes, and local grass grew. There were only two *desi jamun* trees in the portion I had chosen. The land was mainly used by goat and sheep herders.

This piece of land belonged to the Village *'Sarpanch'* (Headman) and his extended family. I tried to convince all my friends to pick up an acre or two, because I saw a lot of potential due to the natural beauty and proximity to Delhi, Gurgaon and Faridabad.

Mangar valley was very scenic and the ridges surroundings were covered with a variety of indigenous trees, and medicinal herbs. Only Captain Ashim Mitra and Captain Indira Sharma, both co-pilots in Alliance Air agreed to buy an acre each. I was able to bargain a price of ₹3,00,000 per acre for the prime part of the Tilla

In times to come, the value of the sweet water below the land would be worth more than the land. Agricultural land on the Jaipur highway or on the road to Pataudi was priced around ₹9,00,000 per acre with mostly brackish water.

On the western end of the valley is a sacred forest, *'MangarBani'*. This is where a very spiritual man once lived. He is revered to this day by all the neighboring villagers. He was *'Gaudariya Das Baba'*. There's an old temple dedicated to him in the forest. To the believers he grants boons. The forest is believed to be protected by him. To my mind he was, besides everything else, an environmentalist. He had decreed that no tree, not even a branch was to be cut nor cattle grazed within the forest, and people paid heed. This is the reason why MangarBani is supposed to be the last of the original Aravali forests that still exists.

It is mainly populated by the *'Dhau'* Tree. The intricate root structure of this tree channels rainwater into the ground. Surprisingly, the Haryana Government refused to recognize MangarBani as a forest. What was an ancient forest seemed useless shrubs to them. Scrub land full of kikar trees however, they considered a forest. It took an order from The National Green Tribunal (NGT) to protect the Mangar Bani along with a half kilometer buffer area around it from land developers and Government sharks.

My investment in this land was the best investment I could ever make. Its value increased from ₹3,00,000 per acre in 1997 to ₹3,00,00,000 in 2020.

After due diligence of the land records, we had the land transferred by a sale deed and got it mutated in our individual names in the land records. Converting the degraded land into arable land was a challenge and expensive. A farm sucks resources like a bottomless pit during the development phase. I first had it leveled and laid down an irrigation system.

When we were leveling the land a very large number of lead shells were dug up. I wondered from where they could have come. A village elder told me that, earlier the valley was used by fighter aircraft for firing practice. Intrigued, I looked at some old Jeppesen charts and sure enough a *Danger Area* was depicted over this area.

To re-build the sunburnt soil, 1200 truckloads of farmyard manure was used. We started by growing mostly legumes and sowing green fertilizer that was ploughed back into the soil. I planted *Amla, Kathal* (jackfruit), mango, lime, and grapefruit trees. My friend Vayasji, a Vedic scholar insisted I plant, what he referred to as the "Holy Trinity" (Brahma, Vishnu, and Mahesh) which as per him were represented by the *Bargat (Banyan), Pipal, and Neem* trees. Which were traditionally believed to be oxygen-generators. They produce oxygen at night unlike other trees that produce carbon dioxide. These were the only trees that supposedly, *Rishis* and holy men seeking enlightenment meditated under for continuous days and nights. The tree usually associated. With Lord Shiva is the *Bel* tree so as a measure of abundant caution I also planted the *Bel tree.*

Within two years, we found an ecosystem taking shape. First came the butterflies, then the bees and birds. The farm was taking shape. I soon bought a tractor with all required implements, hired a manager and 6 farm labor.

Being a new, enthusiastic farmer, I started getting seeds from all over the world: flower seeds from England and Australia, tulips, gladioli and narcissi bulbs from Holland, pine and silver oak tree from Kasauli, coconuts from Kerala, papaya from Bangalore and banana from Saharanpur. It was a fool's errand. The soil and climate was not suitable for most. Only the silver oaks did well. As did the papaya and banana. The coconuts and pines bombed. Only one coconut and pine survived: they live together as strange bedfellows, but the coconut refuses to bear fruit. The biggest disappointment were the tulips: they flowered very briefly in mid-February, but never lasted more than a few days.

I suspected this was largely due to the strong winds that blew across our farm. From September to May, the prevailing winds were North-Westerly. To the west of the farm the valley narrowed like a throat and the Venturi effect increased the wind speed: its effect was more pronounced due to the height of the land compared to the surroundings.

I had to plant and then transplant a number of trees to our northern border so that the shade did not fall on the fields being cultivated, and on our western borders to act as wind breakers.

All this time I was actively involved with the airline and could devote only the weekends to the farm. We had the firm (that had reconstructed Latur in the mid-nineties after a devastating earthquake) build us a Porta-cabin at the farm; it was a one-room suite with an attached bathroom and kitchen. We used this when we spent weekends at the farm.

Gradually, the villagers started referring to the farm as 'Captain Farm' and 'Lumba Farm'. I hated both names and decided that we will name the farm 'Laksh Farms' after my mother. I was told my father called her "Laksh", short for Lakshmi, which was her name. We also built a temple on the bank of the lake under a Banyan tree in her memory. Everything that I had become and achieved was because of her sacrifice, and the farm could only be bought because of the inheritance she left me.

It was after we built the temple and sanctified it and changed the name to Laksh that the farm really started blooming. It seemed that my mother's soul was pleased and we had her blessing given to us by Nature.

My wife never liked the idea of using chemical fertilizers and pesticides and insisted on natural farming practices. She procured worms from a friend who was a progressive farmer in Ludhiana, Punjab and we started 'Vermi' composting.

Cow dung was the raw material required which we procured from neighboring dairy farms. Someone suggested that we keep cows rather than spend so much money buying cow dung. Ila decided to set up a dairy and insisted that we should get only Haryana Desi cows instead of the more popular hybrid cows. Mainly because of A2 milk they produced. These breeds were hardier than hybrid cows and used to grazing. Only the milch cows were kept at the farm. The rest were sent out to graze on herbs and grass on the nearby Aravalli range. Besides the desi cows required little or no vet visits.

Her decision to only keep desi cows was the fallout of an episode that took place in early 1990 when we hosted an exchange school child from France.

My son's school, The Sri Ram School in Vasant Vihar, had a student exchange program with a school in Toulouse, France. Which sent students to live and attend school in India. The students were hosted by Sri Ram parents. We were requested to host a special child, Xavier. He was to live with us for about a month and attend school with my son. School was hardly a ten minute walk from our home.

Xavier arrived, along with him came an insulated box full of a dozen injection ampules packed in dry ice. The ampules needed to be kept refrigerated. He also had a box of different colored medicines to be give morning, noon, evening and night. There were highlighted instruction from his parents.

It now dawned on us that Master Xavier had an acute and fatal allergy to milk and milk products. In case he inadvertently consumed any milk product he could go into shock. The antidote was to be injected within 20 minutes of an incident, and if not, it could be fatal. Out went all milk and milk products from the house to be replaced with Soya and Almond milk.

Xavier, my son and the other kids in the Airline Colony got along well. Their favorite games were cricket and basketball which Xavier learnt to play passably well. He was also picking up Hindi words, mostly expletives: they are the ones most people first learn in a foreign language. His favorite was *'Chutia'*.

On one long weekend, we had gone to visit my mother, at her home in Rampur. The house was on a 2 acre plot in the town. My mother loved cows and used to sell cow milk from a herd of 8 to 10 cows she kept. They were milked and fed under her supervision. On our second day in Rampur in the evening, I could not see Xavier. My kids were playing with each other. Looking for him, I ended up in the dairy. There he was, sitting on a *'Murha'* (a stool) with my mother. She was speaking in Punjabi and he in French. They seem to be communicating. Just then, to my horror I saw him bend down and drink a squirt of milk direct from the cow's udder. I yelled for ILA to come quick to carry him home to administer the antidote.

My mother was alarmed and confused. I told her of his fatal allergy to milk. She laughing said, "What allergy? He's been drinking milk straight from the cow since yesterday. He likes it". We were taken aback: Xavier seemed fine. He understood our panic and told us, "India milk good, I like *beaucoup*, French milk bad, make me '*Mal*'".

Thereafter, we could not keep him away from cold coffee, *lassi*, and milk. He stopped having all the dozens of pills every day too. Back in Delhi, he continued having milk with little or no adverse effects. He also started putting on weight.

We were intrigued to find out how come he was allergic to milk at home, but not in India. This is when we learnt the difference was due to the cows. In addition to the fact that the European milk was fortified with various vitamins and had additives for longer shelf life. The essential difference was that the milk produced by the Indian indigenous cow differed in chemical composition from the milk produced by the European cows. This is when we learnt about A2 milk.

European cow breeds with no horns and flat backs produce milk with A1 proteins, while Indian indigenous cows, with their humped back and long horns produce milk with A2 proteins.

I am avoiding a complex scientific explanation: those who desire more information should Google it, but in short, the basic protein in milk is Casein: the structure of this protein differs between A1and A2 milk, the latter being nearest to mother's milk. A1 milk causes lactose intolerance and tummy upsets for some, while A2 milk is better tolerated. Indian cows produce much lesser milk than European or hybrid cows but it costs nearly 3 times more than packaged milk.

In the late 60s, the government started 'Operation Flood'. They imported different European breeds to be crossbred with Indian breeds. Milk production rose greatly across the country and was marketed by Milk cooperatives. The downside was that in the next 30 to 40 years pure indigenous breeds were hard to come by. While we were importing European cows, Australia and Brazil were importing pure Indian breeds.

Australia imported the '*Brahmi*' bull for their dairy and meat industry, Brazil the famous '*Gir* cow' from Gujarat. In recent years, India has started importing back, pure indigenous cow breeds.

By the year 2000, things took an adverse turn for the worse around Mangar. The Government leased out the whole ridge, between the valley and the Gurgaon-Faridabad Road, for quarrying. The ridge was raped for rock mining to support the construction boom. The whole area was like a war zone: dynamite blasts could be heard 24 hours a day. The ridge was pock marked with quarry craters. Once the miners hit rock bottom, they also reached the water table below which was red silica sand locally known as *'Badarpur'*.

To extract the *Badarpur,* ground water was pumped out. At any time, there would be over a hundred pumps extracting water and hundreds of trucks (dumpers) ferrying Badarpur and rocks to crusher zones. The Aravali was being devastated, but the powerful were raking in big money.

The Haryana Government was greedy for revenue it earned from this mining. It was about then that 'The Pioneer' of Chandigarh did a front page in-depth article on the fast depletion of ground water around Delhi due to mining in the Aravalli.

The Supreme Court had a 'green bench' and the country an environment crusader, a senior lawyer, MC Mehta, who petitioned the court in a public interest litigation. The Court banned mining within 5 km of the Delhi Border. This did not deter the greedy contractors or the government. They started mining beyond the 5 km distance which brought them all around the farm. We were devastated.

Fortunately, the Supreme Court banned mining on the total Aravalli range that runs right across through Rajasthan into Gujarat. The Haryana Government then built 'check dams' on the main water paths that channeled the rain run-off into the valley and tried to convince the Court that they were recharging the Aravalli and mining should be permitted once again. The court did not agree.

Unfortunately, while the court banned mining, it did not ban the stone crushers. Strangely, in the Statutes, the term 'mining' included the raw material crushing. Since, the crushers remained operational, illegal mining continued happily as it does till this day and will as long as the crushers are nearby to process the raw material.

As recently as Feb 2021, the Haryana Government has again petitioned the Supreme Court to restart mining in the Aravali for economic reasons. The petition is pending before the Supreme Court and is being opposed by the public spearheaded by the *'Aravali Bachao Andolan'*.

The state desperately needs to generate money to sustain the state's economy that is shrinking. This was not only Haryana's problem but the country's too, after the national economy was shattered, millions unemployed and thousands of businesses shut due to the Covid-19 pandemic.

The Dhauj Jheel has been dry for over ten years and the ground water level has dipped from 10 ft' to 80 ft'. The lakebed is now home to an adventure camp, The Agaman Farm, which has constructed a large double story structure on the lakebed.

Once I had committed to start IndiGo, Ila took over the farm. She learnt from the villagers their traditional practices and realized these were basic common sense and low-cost methods of doing everything. We realized that traditional houses built were well ventilated. Their high roofs, mud and cow-dung plastered walls rendered the inside cool in summer and warm in winter unlike city homes that became ovens in the summer and freezers in the winter.

To build our home, we decided to only go for traditional architecture, using traditional material and thereby halving the total cost. About this time The Haryana Tourism Department invited us to participate in their Farm Tourism program.

We initially built two airy, comfortable, medium sized rooms with attached bathrooms and heating and cooling equipment installed for winter and summer. These were gradually increased to 8 rooms, spread around the farm in the mango and *amla* orchards, and under trees around the farm.

On her many trips to the farm, Ila saw children and women breaking stone. She decided that she had to do something to help the women earn a living and get the children back to school. She discussed the issue with me and I totally supported her.

We registered two charitable societies. The Laksh Foundation and Laksh Foundation Education Society. Under the former we started the women's self-help initiative, and the latter we open a small school to coax the children back to school. The first thing we did was build a toilet for the girls and boys and taught them the basics of personal hygiene, most importantly washing their hands after every toilet visit. We provided the initial seed money for both the initiatives and then went around with a begging bowl soliciting donations from friends, family and corporates.

Friends were generous; most corporates tight-fisted. Rahul Bhatia supported our charities in kind, with enough construction material to build a small school on the farm.

Ila's public relations and networking skills are largely responsible to bring in the required funds to run the two charities. An old friend, Abha Adams, who had earlier been a Director of the Sri Ram Schools and was then an education consultant advised us that instead of opening a school, we should support the local government school by providing tutorial support to the children. This was where the children got their identity and other certificates and also a subsidy for attending school.

We took her advice. A team from Warwick University was in touch with Abha looking for a charity that they could support. Warwick was already working in rural Africa and was now looking at India; Abha suggested us to Warwick. They liked the concept and the Warwick-Laksh program was born with the first batch of 3 volunteer girls who came for 4 weeks. It slowly expanded to 12 volunteers for 12 weeks.

By June 2010, I had finished my cooling period with IndiGo. We moved bag and baggage into make-shift accommodation at the farm with the intent to start the construction of our home. The work on which could only start after the Commonwealth Games, but which we could complete in a record 8 months.

We were finally home.

By now the farm was booming. I was told that it had great energy due to the *'Vastu'* of the land. It was aligned East-West. I had a water body created in the Northeast for geese and by-and-large, the Northeast was unobstructed. So was the South-East. There were hills-to the North, and the West was higher than the East. Everyone who visited remarked how much at peace they felt when they were at the farm and how they got to sleep better. A large variety of birds have made Laksh their home. We also have visiting honeybees.

Laksh is ideally located within an hour from Delhi, Gurgaon and Noida. The nearest weekend getaway from these cities. Ila and I enjoy the farm-days and farm-night stays that was set up. Our food is all organic. The air is clean, the sky blue and at night one can see the stars.

The farm-days and nights became popular especially with the expat crowd that appreciated the privacy, nature and simple home-cooked food made by '*Rajjo*', Laksh's brand ambassador. Our Indian kitchen, '*Rajjo ka Chula*', is very popular. The food is all traditional, often cooked on 'chulas' or open fires, and Rajjo is spare with her masalas. One gets to smell and taste the food, feel the silence and enjoy the inactivity.

In early 2011, I was approached to restart the defunct MDLR Airlines It was owned by Shri Gopal Kanda, a politician who was then Home Minister of Haryana. I reluctantly agreed to meet him. MDLR was shut down by the ministry a year or two before for violation of safety criteria and lack of funds. Mr. Kanda assured me that he had an investor who would invest ₹500 crore initially and an equal amount later.

He gave me written assurance on all my requirements most importantly, that he would not try to micro-manage the airline. He even agreed to change its name.

I quickly put together a start-up team of proven professionals. We started restructuring the old airline under a new avatar, Air Sapphire. Earlier, the airline had operated the four engine BAE 146. They were all grounded and tied up in complex litigation with the Lessors.

I suggested that the airline look at old or leased A320s, but Kanda wanted new ones. I quickly got in touch with Kiran Rao in Airbus and briefed him on a tentative order of 20 aircraft with an option for another 10 a couple of years later.

Kiran was scheduled to go to Singapore for a couple of days and agreed to rearrange his schedule with a stopover at Delhi. We met with Kiran and the Airbus team at the Leela Palace Hotel in Chanakyapuri and arrived at a tentative price. Kanda was happy.

Kiran took me aside and told me in confidence that Airbus would sign subject to the airline furnishing a $2 million bank guarantee. Airbus had burnt its fingers with Vijay Malaya's A320 and A380 orders. This I considered reasonable.

Back in office, I briefed Kanda of this prerequisite requirement, prior to a final order. He issued a press release that he was restarting MDLR as Air Sapphire and the airline was in final stages of ordering 20 A320 aircraft.

A maelstrom ensued. I was inundated by calls from pilots and engineers from IndiGo waiting to sign on. Aditya Ghosh called to request not to hire IndiGo pilots. I assured him it was early days still and nothing was finalized. I also gently suggested to him to start looking after his pilots and make IndiGo the employer of choice for pilots.

It soon came to pass that the investor had skipped the country as the Enforcement Directorate had issued him a *Notice* for whatever reasons they issue notices. It must have been serious since the promoter had flown the coop. Kanda was left high and dry. I soon found out that he did not have the money for new aircraft and neither did he have enough to furnish a bank guarantee.

This was a bummer. I quickly took my team into confidence and told them about the changed situation. They were disappointed. I had a frank word with Kanda, ensured that everyone was paid their salary, accepted their resignations, and shut the MDLR door.

There was a moral responsibility to get all those who had resigned their erstwhile jobs to join me, re-employed. This I was able to do quickly – a combination of God's grace and plentiful goodwill that I had fostered in the aviation industry.

By 2012, I was running out of funds, and ended up selling two acres of land to 'Isky' Lalji, a cousin of Saleem Zaheer: I got a tidy sum that would see me through for a long time. Both Ashim Mitra and Indira Sharma, who were now married, decided to offload their acre each. Now we had money to put in a swimming pool among the trees, away from the main house and guest rooms. Swimming on a summer moonlit night gives the illusion that one is out in the wilderness. One guest described it like being in the 'Masai Mara'.

Laksh Farms had become a four-in-one entity: organic farming, Laksh NGO, Laksh Dairy and Laksh Farm Stay and it was time to let go and hand over responsibilities. My daughter Pallavi relocated back to the farm from Bombay where she was a script writer and the television industry was badly hurt by the pandemic. She had little or no work and it was pointless for her living in Bombay. She joined her mother and took on responsibilities in Laksh Foundation. Ila took over the responsibility for the diary and the education society: she loves cows like my mother did. My son, Shiv, took over responsibility for the Farm

Stay and I for the farm. We shook hands on a non-interference agreement, but to support each other when needed. This arrangement has worked smoothly and has paved the way for domestic harmony. It has also got my children involved with the farm which will one day be their inheritance.

In early 2013, I was contacted by Capt. Adrian Jenkin's of Air Asia Bhd. They had partnered with the Tata group of companies to start Air Asia India. The Government, in an about turn was now permitting up to 40% equity in an Indian airline by a foreign airline!

In the mid-1990s, the government, at the behest of Jet Airways, had banned foreign airline equity in an Indian airline. This scuttled the Tata-Singapore Joint Venture to start an airline in India, post-repeal of the Air Corporation's Act.

Jet Airways was now in a desperate need for investment after its disastrous takeover of Air Sahara. Subroto Roy, the promoter of Air Sahara, had gone laughing to the bank and Naresh Goyal had ended up scrounging for investment. Etihad's CEO James Hogan was willing to invest.

Not exactly by coincidence, but all of a sudden, foreign equity in Indian airlines was now made permissible. Besides the Etihad injection of funds into Jet Airways, the Tatas also set up a joint venture with Singapore Airline to start a full service carrier, Vistara.

Air Asia wanted me as Director of Flight Operations (DFO) for their India venture. I sounded out Kiran asking him for a lowdown on Tony Fernandes, the promoter of Air Asia. Tony was operating LCCs in Malaysia, Thailand, Indonesia and Japan under the Air Asia banner.

He gave me the thumbs up and ended up recommending me to Tony by an email which I quote:

"Tony

I had a call from an old friend of mine called Capt. Shakti Lumba. He was contacted by Adrian to consider working with you to set up Air Asia India. Capt. Lumba is the best guy you can get. He set up India's first low cost airline, Alliance Air and he helped create Indigo.

He has all the contacts with pilots, DGCA and others. He knows what to do and more importantly what not to do.

He would be a great asset. Adrian did the right thing to contact him. Kiran"

I informed Adrian that I wished to visit Kuala Lumpur (KL) to study the Air Asia Operation first-hand. He arranged a visit. I spent five days in KL observing Air Asia's key departments and was impressed.

While talking with their Flight Operations bosses, I got to know that they had already prepared an Operations Manual and pilot employment contract for the India venture. I studied both.

By then, I had a fair grasp of Air Asia's operation: it was very professional, in some areas IndiGo could learn a few things from them on Low Cost Operations, especially fuel monitoring. I however, had strong reservations on their management structure and control of operations.

Although each Air Asia Airline was independent, they however came under a 'Super Group' that exercised effective control of all their airlines operations and engineering functions. Their HR policies were harmonized for all the airlines. In effect, in Air Asia India, I would just be a puppet of Adrian, the Super Director of Operations. I knew this would not work, given my independent nature.

In a meeting with Bo Lingam, Air Asia's COO, and a team of Senior Managers, I plainly told them that their proposal to start in 6 months was a pipe dream, that the DGCA would throw their Operation Manual into the dustbin. Not that it was not a well-written manual but because it was not in compliance with DGCA's Civil Aviation Regulations, both in content and format. Also, the pilot contracts would have no takers: the salary was too low compared to the Indian market's pilot wage.

They would have to provide duty transportation to both pilots and cabin crew, in the company's interest and in compliance with Indian laws for providing female employees escorted transport home at night. I respectfully declined their job offer and wished them well.

Mr. Mittu Chandilya, from Singapore, had been selected as CEO of Air Asia India by Tony Fernandes. Bo Lingam requested I join as a consultant- cum-advisor. This I declined. I informed him I could consider a COO position in their India venture. This he regretted as Air Asia had only one COO and he was the one.

I returned home, parting as friends. Adrian requested me to suggest someone to take the position of Director Flight Operations (DFO). I suggested Capt. Ashim Mitra: I knew Ashim since 1996, when I employed him in Alliance Air as a co-pilot on the B737, brought him into IndiGo, where he had risen to be one of the three Directors in Flight

Operations.

Ashim has very good people skills, is a good pilot and a fine Instructor. Ashim and Adrian hit it off. When Ashim went to inform Aditya Ghosh, the President of IndiGo that he would be leaving for Air Asia, Aditya matched Air Asia's offer and made Ashim the Vice President Flight Operations. Good move. I would have done the same.

The question of "effective control" hung like a Damocles Sword over the Air Asia -Tata joint venture. Everyone denied it; no one asked the Air Asia Leadership team.

After Mittu Chandilya exited Air Asia India he sent an iCloud message to my phone. 'Capt. Lumba, the biggest mistake Air Asia made was not grab you with both hands'. I wished him well.

I was happy to be back at Laksh, which for me was a safe haven like *TARA* was for Scarlett O'Hara in the novel 'Gone in the Wind'. I enjoyed being 'The Portly Country Squire".

The Tatas had very little expertise of aviation, which they had exited after the demise of the legendary JRD Tata. So naturally even in their JV with Singapore Airlines they let SIA wear the pants in the house.

Incidentally, the Tata Group had bid for Air India which the government was keen to disinvest. Finally, in October 2021 their bid was successful. They had bought back Air India after it was *stolen* by the Government.

Now they have a huge challenge ahead. It is now a Shakespearean Hamlet moment... *now that the deed was done, what would they do with the dagger.*

The Tata group has tremendous expertise in running very large companies, be it hotels, steel, motor vehicles, internet technology and even salt. They have deep pockets and patience and a very ethical work culture and management philosophy. Hopefully they will source Aviation management talent for Air India and their other two Airlines. However, successful Airlines have been run by people that have come from other Industries and professions.

In Feb. 2014, I was contacted by a former employee of IndiGo, Debottom Mookerjee, who had left as a co-pilot on the A320, relocated to Dubai in the UAE, and was now the President and CEO of Nashwan

Investments. His partner was an Iranian and they wanted to start an airline operation into and out of Iran.

It was a strange proposal since Iran was under both US and UN sanctions. I wondered how it was possible. To see for myself, I was invited to Dubai.

A week later I was there, and met with Debottom who filled me in. He was in final negotiations to buy an airline AOC. With this, they proposed a start an airline based in Dubai. Using the sanctions waiver clauses, they could operate in and out of Iran, with certain conditions, such as the Operations Control of the airline could not be with Iran, the airline main base could not be in Iran and no spares, aircraft or equipment could be based at any Iranian airport.

Under those conditions, it was doable. I contacted old, reliable Kiran Rao and inquired if he could arrange not older than 10 years old A320s, and we would require at least 5 of them, and another 3 Airbus 330s.

I briefed him on the proposed operations and how it would be sanctions compliant. This was exciting. There were a whole host of Indian pilots flying in Emirates, Etihad, Air Arabia and Gulf Air. Most were either ex-IndiGo or Indian Airlines, and they could be relied on.

I returned to India and was back in Dubai a fortnight later for a longer stay. Meanwhile, I had spread the word around of our intended start up and was looking forward to meet any of my former colleagues who may be interested. I got into Dubai on a Friday morning: Lo and behold, over 2 dozen pilots dropped in. The A330 pilots were excited but the A320 ones more so, as they were looking to upgrade onto the A330. Most were willing to sign up on short notice.

In the meanwhile, I got in touch with a British MRO (Maintenance, Repair Organization) company based in UAE and had preliminary discussion on line and major maintenance and the services of an engineer for each flight as a part of the crew on an exclusive all-inclusive power-by-the-hour agreement.

Within a week, most loose ends were tied up. The A320 was to operate from Dubai to Tehran on to 3 other cities and be back to Dubai at night. Three aircraft could provide connectivity across Iran. One A330 would start from Dubai to Tehran and then out to India, back via Tehran to Dubai. The other two would connect Tehran to cities in Europe.

Most of the pieces of the puzzle were in place, except the AOC and permission from the Iranian Govt. On a letter of comfort from the airline selling its AOC, an application was moved to DGCA, Iran. The DCGA Iran approved it expeditiously but it hit a brick wall with the Government of Iran. They insisted that Operations Control would have to remain within Iran. It was unacceptable to them to permit Operations Control outside Iran. This was a total deal breaker. If Operations Control was with Iran then the operation would be subject to sanctions. That was the end of Air Nashwan. The only airline that died before being born. Besides me, there were a large number of disappointed people.

In 2014 also the Civil Aviation Ministry brought out a policy document on their proposal to commence a Regional Connectivity Scheme (RCS). I thought it was a brilliant idea as it would provide air connectivity to tier 2 and 3 cities that had small airfields and airports which were being bypassed in the present scheme of things.

In my misplaced enthusiasm I wrote an email to Rahul Bhatia and explained the potential that this scheme held for IndiGo. I suggested he start a small airline, 'Une Petite IndiGo' with suitable 40 seater turboprop aircraft, much in line like the Alliance Air and Indian Airlines set up which was a proven model. Unfortunately, not only did Rahul not acknowledge my mail, he totally ignored it; so I let it slide.

In March 2017, Rahul Bhatia surprised me with a message asking if I was free to meet Mr. Rakesh Gangwal the next day at the Oberoi Gurgaon. I confirmed that I would meet him. I liked Rakesh and loved talking to him. I had a lot of respect for him but was not in awe of him. He knew that too, because I was the only one who stood up to him and argued my case during the time I was with IndiGo.

Rakesh met me cordially and cut to the chase. He told me that during his last visit he had flown from Jaipur to Udaipur on a SpiceJet Bombardier Q400 and that the flight was full. He saw a business opportunity here.

He straightaway decided that IndiGo should get a small turboprop fleet. He desired that I take on this project and that he was in talks with ATR for their ATR-600. My first question was whether Rahul and Aditya were on board for this decision which he confirmed.

I drew up a concept paper largely on the Alliance Air model. It was a model that worked: I saw the ATR operation as an independent operation that was only in the business of flying airplanes.

An airline operation has three modules. Input, Carriage, and Output. Input is marketing, ticket sales and all airport land and air side activity. The Output is the safe delivery of everything carried after a flight. This is a Commercial responsibility. The Carriage is the physical carrying of passenger and freight from origin to destination safely and efficiently. This is a Flight Operation responsibility. Maintenance is responsible to ensure that all equipment required for the three modes is kept serviceable. This is an Engineering responsibility.

I decided that it would be best to out-source maintenance, input and output to IndiGo. Maintenance on a power-by-the-hour basis and input/output on a per flight basis. This would provide an additional revenue stream to IndiGo. The ATR group would be responsible for direct operating cost and salaries of pilots, cabin attendants and catering. Ticket sales would be their revenue stream.

I bounced this off Rakesh: he was in agreement. By the first week of May he informed that it was decided to start with an order of 40 to 50 aircraft to be delivered over two years with the first arriving in December 2017. The ATR Company was willing to commit to supplying pilots for the first two years, at a cost.

I was of the firm opinion that although the pilot provisioning provided a level of comfort, the cost of doing business this way would be too high. An expat pilot crew set would cost us $50,000 per month. I had to produce my own pilots quickly to bring the cost down.

There were only two main ATR Operators in the country, Jet Airways and Alliance Air. My plan was to first acquire a pilot production capability by hiring type-rated instructors and examiners, and then start recruiting pilots. General Duty pilots being released from the Air Force and pilots from charter operators could kick-start the supply chain.

I had another belief that somebody *UP THERE* liked Rahul Bhatia: whenever he required pilots, one or another airline got into trouble.

During the start-up of IndiGo, it was Air Sahara, followed by Air Deccan, then Kingfisher Airlines.

Now Jet Airways was floundering. So, my logical target was Jet Airways. I moved quickly to poach instructors and examiners from Jet and got commitments from 3 Examiners who were confident of bringing in with them ten sets of pilots. The price had to be right. Rakesh had agreed that fixing pilot salary was my call and not that of HR.

By 10th May 2017, everything was in place, excluding my two-year contract and team appointment. I was informed by Rakesh to come to the 'I Fly' building on 12th morning. It was a Friday. The ATR team was there and I was introduced to them.

Shortly thereafter, Rakesh addressed the middle and senior management of IndiGo in the 'I Fly' auditorium; *Steve Jobs style.*

He officially informed everyone that the company would be buying the ATR-600 and the first flight was planned for Dec. 2017, in seven months. Then came the bomb shell: He had chosen Capt. Shakti Lumba as the Head of the ATR project. He further stated that the ATR project was important for IndiGo going ahead and all departments needed to cooperate with me; the ATR was not to be treated as a stepchild. There was mixed reaction to my appointment. Most were happy but a few sulked.

I took aside the flight operations team and requested Capt. Ashim Mitra, if I could meet with his team the next day in office, he agreed. We met on Saturday and I was brought up to date on all the background work done till then. It happened to be the birthday of one of the senior officers. A cake was cut, a takeaway lunch was arranged; someone posted the cake cutting on Facebook. A journalist from *Mint* picked it up and using titbits from his contacts, came out with a headline that I was now the Head of IndiGo's ATR project.

I had not even signed a contract which was to be signed on Monday at 10am with the Head of HR. Monday morning, I was in office by 9:30 am. Administration had arranged a cubicle with a laptop and printer. Vice President HR, Sukhjit Pasricha was a no-show. So was IndiGo's PR man, Vikram Chona. He was supposed to take me to the Civil Aviation Ministry and the DGCA and introduce me.

So I twiddled my thumbs and by 10:30 am I got a call to come and see Rahul Bhatia urgently. I walked across where he and Aditya Ghosh were waiting.

Without much ado I was informed that both MOCA and DGCA had reacted adversely to the Mint article and had categorically objected to my appointment and had stated in no uncertain terms that if I was involved with the ATR project then IndiGo should not expect any cooperation from either of them.

Apparently, I had on number of occasions, tweeted and referred to MOCA as the Moron of Civil Aviation and the DGCA as the Duffer General of Civil Aviation, when they deserved it. Which was often.

IndiGo would not have been able to survive without the cooperation from either of the two authorities. They withdrew their offer of appointment.

That must have been the shortest top management Aviation employment in history and would surely merit a mention in the Guinness book of records. Only Three days: Hired on a Friday, fired on the Monday.

To save face, IndiGo put out a bullshit press release that I had rejected the offer to head the ATR project due to health reasons.

I was as healthy as an ox.

I decided to have nothing to do with either Aditya Ghosh or Rahul Bhatia after that. This was the second time I had been stabbed in the back.

I had Laksh Farms, waiting for me with open arms ready to heal. I had a good life surrounded by family and friends. To all the workers and villagers I was *'Bauji'*, the elder that everyone respected and held in affection. My word was in violate.

All of Maslow's Hierarchy of Needs were satisfied.

Things are seldom what they seem

Skimmed milk masquerades as cream

Black sheep dwell in every fold

All that glitters is not gold

– Gilbert & Sullivan

16. THE LAST WORD

Just before this book was published we received exciting news from the Department of Tourism, State government of Haryana. Laksh farms had been chosen to be awarded a Certificate of Appreciation for outstanding contribution and promotion of Farm Tourism in the State of Haryana.

This is like the icing on the cake. My family and I were thrilled with the recognition for all the hard work and passion we all have put into Laksh Farms. My son Shiv has been handling the farm stay and farm day visits. He has reinvented himself as a Master Chef. Proud of him and his contribution to Laksh Farms, my 3rd Start-up, which now is getting the recognition it deserves.

ABOUT THE AUTHOR

About Capt. Shakti Lumba

Capt. Shakti Lumba is an alumnus of St. Joseph's College, Nainital, and St Stephen's College, Delhi. He started flying in 1969 and finally hung up his wings in 2010.

Capt. Lumba's fascinating journey in aviation as a pilot, union leader and airline executive with Indian Airlines parallels the evolution of modern Indian aviation from 1970 to 2010. Not merely did he have a ringside view of the seminal moments of that period, more often he was one of the major protagonists within that very ring. By sharing his journey as a pilot, richly peppered with incidents, vignettes and behind-the-scene developments, he chronicles the story of contemporary Indian aviation.

His aviation memoirs take one through the by-lanes of Indian Civil Aviation in all its glory. The creation of Alliance Air, an airline within an airline, is possibly India's first low cost carrier. He successfully handled the operational start-up of IndiGo, one of India's premier and most successful low-cost airlines, before landing safely at Laksh Farms, a place termed as a piece of heaven on earth.

The book is a vivid recollection of his experiences as he cruised through making memories and history together.

About Capt. Priyanka Arora

A software engineer by qualification and a commercial pilot by passion, Capt. Priyanka Arora is a potent combination of a dreamer and dream chaser. The belief that life should be lived laterally makes her a Jane of all trades and a master of some.

A voracious fiction reader, Priyanka has been blogging for over two decades. Her flights of fancy have been fueled by the parables of her adventurous life.

Her debut novel, *Simple Plane Love*, was inspired by the stories gathered from being a part of the aviation industry for over a decade, both in the cabin and the cockpit.

Co-authoring this book has been one of her favorite experiences; one that can make a bestseller of itself.

When not writing, she is found speaking her mind on Twitter as @captain_speakin or clicking neck-twisting selfies for @ipriyanka.arora on Instagram.

She is the co-founder of India's premier Sufi music festival, The Sufi Route, and the co-creator of Project Nirmaan, a youth outreach program designed for the amelioration of life in the UT of J&K.

Priyanka lives in Goa with her dog, Her Puppyness Lil Miss Hibiki.

Manufactured by Amazon.ca
Acheson, AB